THIRD REVISED
AND EXPANDED EDITION

THROUGH
CHINESE EYES

TRADITION, REVOLUTION,
AND TRANSFORMATION

EDWARD VERNOFF
AND
PETER J. SEYBOLT

D1446206

A CITE BOOK
New York
Copyright © 2007 by Edward Vernoff. Copyright © 1974, 1981, 1983, 1988
by Leon E. Clark and Peter J. Seybolt.
Third Revised Edition

Published by the Center for International Training and Education (CITE),
a program of the Council on International and Public Affairs
777 United Nations Plaza, Suite 3C, New York, New York 10017
Telephone/fax: 800-316-APEX (2739)
E-mail: cipany@igc.org
Web Page: www.cipa-apex.org

CITE Books are distributed by The Apex Press, an imprint of the Council on
International and Public Affairs.

Library of Congress Cataloging-in-Publication Data

Vernoff, Edward.
 Through Chinese eyes : tradition, revolution, and transformation /
Edward Vernoff and Peter J. Seybolt. -- 3rd rev. ed.
     p. cm.
 Includes bibliographical references and index.
 ISBN 0-938960-51-2 (pbk) -- ISBN 0-938960-52-0 (hardcover)
 1. China--History--1949- I. Seybolt, Peter J. II. Title.

 DS777.55S4525 2007
 951--dc22
                                        2007005508

Cover and Interior Design by Mary Ellen McCourt
Printed in the United States of America

About the Authors

Edward Vernoff is a Professor of History at Bard High School Early College in New York City. He has a Master of International Affairs degree from Columbia University and Master of Arts and Ph.D. degrees in Education from New York University. He taught at Shanghai Teachers University during the 1993-1994 academic year. He is co-author of *The Penguin International Dictionary of Contemporary Biography* and co-editor of *The Left Academy.*

Peter J. Seybolt is a Professor of History Emeritus of Asian Studies at the University of Vermont. He has a Master of Arts in Teaching degree and a Ph.D. in History and East Asian Languages (Chinese and Japanese) from Harvard University. His publications include *Throwing the Emperor from His Horse, Portrait of a Village Leader in China, Revolutionary Education in China, Language Reform in China,* and *The Rustication of Urban Youth in China* as well as numerous journal articles, reviews, and translations from Chinese. He is also the creator of an educational game on the history and culture of China, "Feilong: The China Game."

Contents

List of Boxes	*viii*
Preface	*ix*
Acknowledgments	*xi*

Part I
Revolution: A Nation Stands Up

Introduction	3
Linxian County: A Recollection of the Past	7
Stone Wall Village Turns Over: Part I	11
Stone Wall Village Turns Over: Part II	17

Part II
The Conservative Tradition

Introduction	25
The Confucian Heritage	27
The Traditional Family Ethic	31
Religion in Traditional China	37
Lessons for Women	41
The Status of Women	45
The Leakage System	53

Part III
The Seeds of Revolution

Introduction	61
The Legacy of the Distant Past	63
The Legacy of the Nineteenth and Twentieth Centuries	67

Part IV
The Era of Mao Zedong

Introduction   75

The Peasant as Revolutionary   77

"It's Terrible" or "It's Fine"   79

The Long March   83

Maoist Ethics: The "Three Constantly
    Read Articles"   89

The People's Democratic Dictatorship   95

Leadership and Democracy   99

"A Sticky Problem"   105

Meng Hsiang-ying Stands Up   113

The Status of Women: New Laws   119

The Paupers' Co-op   121

The Iron Man of Daqing   131

Barefoot Doctors   137

The Red Guards   143

A Tough Guy   149

Maoism as Religion   155

The Disillusionment of Youth   159

The Results of the Cultural Revolution   167

The Official Legacy of Mao   173

Part V
The Era of Reform

Introduction   177

The Call for Change   179

Manifestations of Discontent   183

The Tiananmen Crisis   195

The Intensification of Reform   203

Wealth and Consumerism   207

Problems of the City and the Countryside   215

The Private Economy   223

Cultural Life   233

Confusionism: Images of Western Influence
    and Cultural Confusion   241

Education   255

Youth   261

Women   269

New Morality and Its Psychological Effects   273

Crime and Corruption   279

Environmental Issues   287

Human Rights   297

Health   303

Population   309

Religion   315

Part VI

China and the World

Introduction   323

"Never the Twain Shall Meet"   325

The Village and the Outside World   329

China and the United States   333

Current Chinese Views of World Politics   339

Epilogue   351

Chronology   353

Sources   355

List of Boxes

Confucian Inequalities 30

Footbinding—Henan Province 46

Mao's Warning to His Comrades 93

The Spirit of the Great Leap Forward 128

A Red Guard Remembers 146

Revolutionary Aphorisms in Praise of Mao Zedong 158

Tiananmen Protest Song 197

The Disease of "Bourgeois Liberalization" 200

The Language of Consumerism 210

A Migrant's Lament 218

Rural Problems 220

The New "Three Irons" 229

Popular Rhymes 230

Impressions of a Veteran Cadre Touring Special
Economic Zones 232

"The Imperialists Are Back" 234

Old Opera Landmark Bows Out on Low Note 236

Basic Budget for a Primary School Child in Shanghai 256

Visions of Sugarplums and Big Cars 264

Male/Female Income Gap 270

Psychological Problems on Campus 274

Standing on One's Own Feet 275

The Virus of Corruption 284

Cars and Pollution 295

The Decline of Health Services 306

Preface

This edition of *Through Chinese Eyes* is a revised, updated, and expanded version of a volume that originally appeared in 1974 and was slightly revised in 1981. The original revision was published just as China was changing course economically and was beginning to emerge from the self-imposed isolation of the Maoist period and the era of the Cultural Revolution. None of the readings, therefore, reflected any of the enormous changes that have taken place over the last two decades.

This new edition is about twice the size of the original version. Approximately half of the material in this new edition relates to the changes in Chinese society since the 1980s. Most of the articles that appeared in the original volumes have been retained in this revision. However, some new material has been added to the chapters on pre-1981 China, including sections on the Taiping Rebellion, the May Fourth Movement, and the Great Leap Forward. As in the earlier editions, almost all of the material was written by Chinese authors and was originally published in China. Some of the articles were produced by Chinese scholars and writers who are now residing in the West. Articles by non-Chinese writers contain extensive quotes by Chinese citizens, including officials, editors, and scholars.

This volume is divided into six parts. Part I, *Revolution: A Nation Stands Up*, recounts the conditions in rural China in the 1940s and the Communist transformation of a village during the civil war. Part II, *The Conservative Tradition*, presents aspects of Confucianism which dominated Chinese society for over two millennia. Part III, *The Seeds of Revolution*, discusses examples of the Chinese counter-tradition of equality and rebellion. Part IV, *The Era of Mao Zedong*, presents the story of the Communist Revolution from its beginnings in the 1920s until the death of Mao in 1976. Part V, *The Era of Reform*, describes the changes, engineered primarily by Deng Xiaoping, that have taken place in China during the last two decades. Finally, Part VI, *China and the World*, discusses the role of China on the world stage, with a particular focus on international relations since the 1970s. It includes a section on Chinese relations with the United States.

Editor's Note: Names of prominent people and places appear in the *pinyin* system of transliteration. (*Pinyin* is a way of spelling Chinese in Roman script that was approved by the government of the People's Republic in 1958 and adopted as the official phonetic system in 1979.) However, in sources published before the mid-1970s, using other systems, the original version is maintained followed by the *pinyin* in parentheses.

*Dedicated to the
memory of Matthew Hall
(1984-2003)*

Acknowledgments

Through Chinese Eyes has been continuously published since 1974 and we are grateful to Ward Morehouse, President of the Council on International and Public Affairs, which publishes the "Eyes" series, for keeping this book alive and available to schools and the general public for three decades. Cynthia Seybolt played a major role in the production of the first edition. Her critical advice and expert editing contributed significantly to the final form of the manuscript. We are also indebted to the late Dr. Leon E. Clark who initiated the "Eyes" project and deserves a large part of the credit for the success the books have had. The structure and content of the first edition of *Through Chinese Eyes* bear the imprint of his wise counsel and insightful editing. Dr. Helene Dunkelblau played an important role in the production of the revised edition. We also benefited from the suggestions and advice of Professor Frank Tang, Professor A. Tom Grunfeld, and Dr. Yi Yi Wu. Finally, we would like to thank the late Claire Malcolm Lintilhac for her gentle advice, and for sharing her rich insights derived from having lived for 50 years in China.

PART I

REVOLUTION: A NATION STANDS UP

Introduction

. . .once China's destiny is in the hands of the Chinese people, China, like the rising sun in the east, will illuminate every corner of the land with a brilliant flame, swiftly clean up the mire left by the reactionary government, heal the wounds of war, and build a new, powerful people's republic worthy of the name.

Mao Zedong, June 1949*

We have a common feeling that our work will be recorded in the history of mankind, and that it will clearly demonstrate that the Chinese, who comprise one quarter of humanity, have begun to stand up. . . .

Henceforth our nation will enter the large family of peace-loving and freedom-loving nations of the world. . . . Our nation will never again be an insulted nation. We have stood up.

Mao Zedong, September 1949**

MAO ZEDONG, CHAIRMAN of the Communist Party of China, uttered these words in 1949, shortly before the Communists established a new government called the People's Republic of China. Mao's words reveal a sense of destiny, an awareness that the Chinese revolution then taking place would have a profound impact not only on China but on the whole world.

Today we are only beginning to realize how prophetic his words were.

What did Mao Zedong mean when he said "China has stood up"? Stood up to whom? Why was China down? To appreciate the significance of this phrase we must have some knowledge of China's past.

---

* Mao Tse-tung, *Selected Works of Mao Tse-tung*, Vol. IV, Peking: Foreign Languages Press, 1961, p. 8.

** Stuart Schram, *The Political Thought of Mao Tse-tung*, New York: Praeger, 1969, p. 167.

3

For over two thousand years, until the late 1800s, the Chinese considered themselves the only truly civilized people on earth. They felt they needed nothing from the outside world and had nothing to learn from it.

Their sense of superiority was not empty self-delusion. Chinese poets and painters were at the height of their creative genius a thousand years ago, when Europe was in the "Dark Ages" and the Western Hemisphere was, as yet, unknown to Europeans. The compass, gunpowder, and movable-type printing were all invented in China long before they were known in Europe.

These inventions, which played so great a part in the development of the modern West, changed almost nothing in China. In traditional China, harmony and stability were valued. Conflict and change were avoided. The idea of progress was unknown.

Secure in their sense of superiority and their self-sufficiency, the Chinese were blind to the changes taking place elsewhere in the world. Then, in 1840, the British defeated the Chinese in a war and imposed treaties on them that gave foreigners special rights in China and put them above Chinese law. A once superior people became inferior, discriminated against in their own country. China's system of government, which for two thousand years had provided a unity and stability unknown elsewhere in the world, rapidly disintegrated in the face of Western demands. The last Chinese emperor abdicated in 1911. Four decades of chaos followed. All attempts to build a new nation and to free China from foreign domination failed until 1949, when Mao Zedong and the Chinese Communist Party provided the leadership and inspiration that enabled China to "stand up."

For Mao and the Communists, standing up meant far more than casting off the weight of foreign oppression. It also meant casting off tradition, which for centuries had burdened the peasant with an almost intolerable load. China stood up because the Chinese peasant stood up. Peasant revolution brought the Communists to power.

There is much to admire in traditional China. The appeal of Chinese art, literature, and philosophy is timeless and very broad. But let us not confuse the gems of a civilization with the daily life of the majority of the people. Until recently, most Chinese could not read, much less afford to own the exquisite jade ornaments or beautiful glazed porcelain ("china") that we associate with Chinese culture. For them life was a continual struggle for survival. The old ruling class, for all its accomplishments, had purchased the pleasures and refinements of high culture with the sweat of laboring people. Taxes, rents, and interest on loans provided the rich with their treasures and kept the worker and peasant on the threshold of starvation.

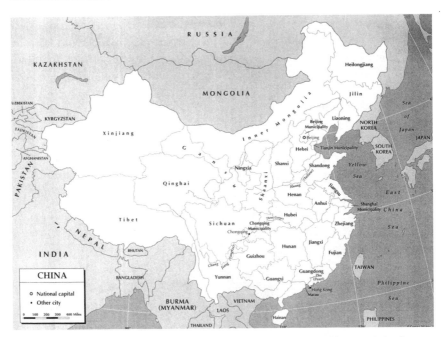

(From *Current History*, Vol. 101, No. 656, September 2002, reprinted by permission.)

Finally, the pressures for change introduced by the West combined with long-standing grievances of the laboring poor to form an explosive mixture. "Maoism" was the spark that changed age-old peasant rebelliousness to revolution.

After Mao's death, and the political defeat of his followers in the late 1970s, China changed course. By reversing Mao's economic and social policies, reintroducing elements of capitalism, and opening China to foreign investments, Communist leaders Deng Xiaoping and Jiang Zemin created a revolution within the revolution and dramatically transformed the country. Their policies, which they called "socialism with Chinese characteristics," have resulted in unprecedented economic growth and a more open society, but have also led to growing social and economic inequalities, disruptive mass migrations from rural areas to the cities, rising rates of unemployment and crime, rampant consumerism, increasing Western cultural influence, and pervasive corruption.

Although the Communist Party still controls China, the course of the Chinese revolution has been radically altered. What was the nature of this revolution and how has it changed over time? What did it originally mean to the Chinese people and what does it mean to them today? How has it changed their lives? This book will attempt to answer these questions and will raise others. As you study the Chinese experience, you should keep in mind that approximately one of every five people in the world is Chinese. China is the most populous nation on earth and one of the largest geographically. What happens in China will inevitably influence the rest of the world in one way or another.

Linxian County:
A Recollection of the Past

Editor's Introduction: To begin our exploration of the conditions that provoked the Chinese revolution, let us look at life in rural China through the eyes of a Chinese who lived there in the 1930s. His account is one of a collection of stories recalling the bitterness of the past. After the establishment of the People's Republic in 1949, the Communists encouraged the publication of such stories to show young people in China how things have changed and to remind them that continued progress requires the same hard work and constant struggle that eliminated the misery once commonplace for much of the populace.

Not all landlords in China were as bad as Yang Chen-kang, the villain in the story, but there is no question that the landlord system fostered inequality of wealth and much suffering. The Communists define a landlord family as one that owned land but did no work. It lived by renting land to peasants, who often had to give the landlord as much as half of what they produced.

The Communists estimate that families of landlords and "rich peasants" (farmers who worked the land but had a surplus to rent out) were about 8 percent of the rural population before 1949, and that they owned 80 percent of the land. The other 92 percent of the population were classed as "middle peasants" (those who could support themselves without renting land but had no excess land to rent out), "poor peasants" (those who owned land but not enough to support themselves and who had to rent land from others), and hired laborers, who owned no land at all. The story that follows is told by a former poor peasant. [1]

I WAS BORN in . . . Lin-hsien (Linxian) [County], Honan (Henan) Province. As soon as I was able, I began to follow my mother to the fields.

Starving peasants in the 1930s. (Photo courtesy Jean Elliott Johnson)

She went in front digging up the earth. I came behind breaking up the clods. Every day, by noon, my mother sat on the ground, so tired that she did not even want to eat. She only drank water in huge gulps. Usually, I massaged her back, waist, and legs. Once I asked her, "Why doesn't my father show up to help us till the land?" Immediately her eyelids reddened, and I never dared ask that question again.

Every time it rained there were leaks in our thatched roof. We were kept busy rolling up our mats and trying to prevent our pillows from getting wet, but nothing kept dry. In the confusion, my grandmother usually started complaining about my father. . . .

"I've told your husband a hundred times that he should find some time to repair the roof, but he won't listen! He is a farmhand employed on a regular basis, but be is not a slave of the Yangs. His father said as he was dying, 'Never hire out to the Yangs. Never fill the rice bowl of that house.' Ha! But he won't listen! Has he forgotten how his father died? The Yang house killed him with overwork and anger. And he went to his grave with nothing.

"Little Chin-pao, whenever you and your younger brother argue, remember what your grandfather said. Don't go to the Yang house. Don't fill the rice bowl of that house," said my grandmother, hugging my brother and me.

"Of the twenty or thirty families in this village, which one doesn't till the Yangs' land? If we don't till, what will we eat?" my mother asked.

"Does the rice of the Yang house taste so good? Sooner or later, bad things will happen!" my grandmother warned.

After it was all said, my grandmother began to weep, my mother began to weep, and my younger brother, Yin-ao, and I also began to weep. And that rain was still falling through our thatched roof.

Later, I was told that my ancestors had passed down two *mou* of land. [A *mou* is about one-sixth of an acre.] After the birth of my father and his two brothers, Grandfather could not support his family with the meager income from the crop on this small plot. Although he should never have done it, he leased several *mou* of land from the big landlord Yang Chen-kang. He worked hard, the suffering increased, and the back taxes accumulated into a large debt. Yang Chen-kang had the nickname of "Black Snake," and this venomous viper coiled around our family. He wanted to recover the debt by seizing our two *mou* of land. My grandfather could never give up that land, so he had to work for Yang Chen-kang and pay back his debt with his wages. He toiled for more than twenty years, but he was unable to clear the debt. When my grandfather died, we still had that two *mou* of land, which was still insufficient to feed us. Like my grandfather, my father leased a plot of land from Yang Chen-kang. The same things happened again. My father incurred a debt and had to work for Yang Chen-kang and repay his debt with his wages. And so we slaved for the Yang house from one generation to the next.

After the birth of my second younger brother, Ch'üan-pao, which meant another mouth to feed, my mother worried all the more. One night my father returned from work and stood by the *k'ang* and stared at me and my two brothers. He said: "One generation after another! Will they too have to lease land, run up debts, and forever be trampled under the feet of others?" My mother thought he looked strange and asked about it. But he would not say anything. At that time, my father often got together with some of his poor friends. Often he did not come back until midnight. We did not know what he was up to. As soon as someone called him from the yard, he hurried off. This added much to my mother's worries. She feared something would happen. . . .

Early on the morning of December 20, someone knocked at the door and cried: "Oh no, Chin-pao's father has been murdered!" Immediately, my mother pulled me and carried my younger brothers to the riverbank. Oh god! My father's body was there. . . .

Yang Chen-kang had said that he wanted to arrest the culprit, but in fact the culprit was Yang Chen-kang himself. My father and his friends had aroused his suspicion. He was fearful lest the poor people in the village unite against him. He decided to "show his strength by making the first move." In order to kill one to warn a hundred, he ordered one of his lackeys to murder my father. He also planned to seize our two *mou* of land.

When Grandmother heard this story, she grew both angry and vengeful. Her heart was overflowing with the death of her husband and her son, but she could not even tell the world. She lay on the *k'ang* mortally sick. She died a few days later.

My brothers and I helped Mother till our land. We worked from before dawn till after dusk. We were cultivating two plots of land: one was our own two *mou* of land; the other was the four *mou* of land that my father had leased from Yang Chen-kang. . . .

Who would have imagined that God himself would have his eyes closed to us? It did not rain for more than three months, and the wheat sprouts were becoming yellow and wasted. My mother's hopes for paying off our debt were crushed, and she fell sick from worry.

After the autumn harvest, Yang Chen-kang seized our two *mou* of land and took two large earthen vessels and a large wash basin away from us, which in no way diminished our debt. Yang Chen-kang also sent someone to fetch me back so that I could work for him as a shepherd and thereby work off our debt with my wages. My mother was infuriated and she swore at the man: "Black-hearted black snake! You taxed us for using a few *mou* of your land. You tortured my father-in-law to death. You murdered my husband. You seized our land. Now, you're going to lay your hands on my son!" She recalled my grandfather's words: Never make a living by filling the rice bowl of the Yang house. But if she did not send me, they would have no mercy. So, Mother finally sent me off to him with her tears. . . .

Stone Wall Village Turns Over

PART I

Editor's Introduction: Changes in Linxian County did not come about overnight. They were the result of years of struggle and new forms of organization. The peasant family in the preceding story would be unable to conceive of the life that is characteristic of Linxian today. What happened? Part of the answer to that question can be found in events that took place in a farming village not far from Linxian County.

The year is 1947. The Japanese have recently been defeated in World War II by the Chinese and their allies after eight years of fighting on Chinese soil. But war continues in China. Now it is a civil war between the Communists, led by Mao Zedong, and the Nationalists (or Guomindang), led by Chiang Kai-shek, President of the Republic of China before the Communists gained control.

Stone Wall Village, where the story takes place, is in the Communist-held area of China. The Communists are promoting a campaign to redistribute land from the rich to the poor and to overthrow the old ruling class in the countryside. Stone Wall Village, like Linxian, is in a very poor part of the country. In that respect it is not typical of all of China, but the events that took place there were similar to those that were to alter radically social relationships throughout China.

As you read Part I of "Stone Wall Village Turns Over," think of the problems facing those who were promoting land reform. [2]

THE LAND IN this region is rocky, bare of forest, and grudging in its fertility, so that the hard-pressed farmers have been forced to build terraces and cultivate the hill slopes nearly to the top of every peak. . . .

The common farmers, always hungry and always in debt, had a verse about their bitter lot, which ran like this:

Harvest every year; but yearly-nothing.

Borrow money yearly; yearly still in debt.

Broken huts, small basins, crooked pots;

Half an acre of land; five graves.

Politically, Stone Wall Village was in the hands of its village chief, a landlord named Wang Chang-ying. Although his personal characteristics are not germane to this story, it may be mentioned in passing that Landlord Wang was fifty years old, that he wore a small goatee and smoked a long-handled water pipe. In fair weather, it was said that he promenaded on the streets and beat any child who was unfortunate enough to bump into him. At the sight of him, many of the village poor would immediately run indoors.

Wang's possessions included sixty-five acres (no one else owned more than three) of irrigated land, the riverside mill, a large store of grain, one wife, one son, one daughter, one daughter-in-law, and a vengeful nature. . . .

Such was the condition of Stone Wall Village when the Chinese Revolution suddenly descended on it. There had been vague stories of this revolution in the village; there had been murmurings about the [Communist] 8th Route Army, about a thing called democracy, and about villages where there were no landlords and everyone had an equal amount of land. But the people had listened to these rumors with only half an ear; they were poor and fated to be poor; they did not want to fight anybody, they only wanted to be left alone.

Landlord Wang had also heard these rumors; he did not take them seriously either. But as a precaution, he used to tell the people: "Flesh cut from others won't stick to your own body." The people, however, did not need this warning: they had no intention of moving against Landlord Wang.

Nevertheless, the Revolution came to Stone Wall Village.

It did not come like a flash of swift lightning; for a revolution like everything else moves slowly in China. Nor did it announce itself like a clap of thunder, with the beat of drums, the sound of rifle fire, or hot slogans shouted on the country air.

To be more exact, five men brought the Revolution to Stone Wall Village. They were not soldiers, nor were they Communist Party members. One had been a schoolteacher, another a student, a third a waiter, a fourth a shop assistant, and the fifth a farmer. They were all members of the Ho-hsien County Salvation Association, and their job was to "overturn" Stone Wall Village.

"Overturn" is a term of the Chinese Revolution that came into being after the surrender of the Japanese. In Communist terminology, it means to turn over the social, political, and economic life of every village, to overturn feudalism and establish democracy, to overturn superstition and establish reason. The first step of the overturning movement is to "struggle" against the landlords and divide the land.

To do this sounds easy. You have the guns and the power, and you just tell the landlord to give a share of his land to the people. But it is never that easy. In Stone Wall Village, there was no army, there was no militia. The 8th Route Army was far to the south. Even the guerrillas had gone elsewhere. Landlord Wang was the power, and the people were afraid of him.

The leader of the Ho-hsien Salvation team was a thirty-one-year-old cadre [official], the son of a bankrupt rich farmer, named Chou Yu-chuan. When Chou and his fellow workers arrived in Stone Wall Village, they post-ed proclamations . . . announcing that every village had the right to elect its own officials and that land rents and rates of interest should be reduced. Then they called a meeting to explain these proclamations, but the people listened only half-heartedly, kept their mouths tightly shut, and went home without speaking further to the cadres.

For several days, the cadres went individually among the people, asking them about local conditions and their own lives, but no one would talk. Whenever a cadre approached a group of people, they would break apart and move away. One or two men cornered alone admitted they were afraid of the landlord.

Under these conditions, the cadres could not carry on their work, so they decided to seek out one of the poorer men in the village and talk to him alone and in secret.

At this time, Chou and another cadre were living in a cave next door to one occupied by a tenant farmer named Ma Chiutze. Ma had bought his cave before the Japanese war with six dollars earned by his wife spin-ning thread. Now his wife was sick, and Ma often came to the cadres' cave and slept on the same *k'ang* with them. During the night, the three men always talked.

Ever since the Ch'ing (Qing) dynasty [1644-1911], Ma revealed, his family had been poor tenants, renting land and never having any of their own. Every year, he raised eight *piculs* [one *picul* equals 133 pounds] of mil-let, and every year he had to give four of these *piculs* to Landlord Wang. He could afford no medicine for his wife, who he feared was dying. Two years before, his father had died, and he had not been able to buy the old man a coffin but had to wrap him in straw. Now he was thirty-five and he was still

Chiang K'ai-shek in 1931, when, as leader of the Nationalist (Guomindang) Army and government, he tried to destroy the Communist movement. He was finally defeated by the Communists in 1949. (From the collection of Edward C. Carter, at the University of Vermont.)

poor and it looked as if he would always be poor. "I guess I have a bad brain," he would say in summing up the reasons for his poverty.

Then the cadres would ask: "Are you poor because you have a bad brain or because your father left you no property?"

"I guess that's the reason; my father left me no property."

"Really, is that the reason?" asked the cadres. "Let us make an account. You pay four *piculs* of grain every year to the landlord. Your family has rented land for sixty years. That's 240 *piculs* of grain. If you had not given this to the landlord, you would be rich. The reason you are poor, then, is because you have been exploited by the landlord."

They would talk like this for hours, and Ma would finally acknowledge that he was exploited by the landlord. . . .

Ma agreed that the landlords had to be overthrown before there could be any happiness for the poor, but he was only half convinced of his own statements. There was yet a long distance between words and action, and the weight of two thousand years of tradition lay very heavily on Ma, as on most Chinese peasants.

For fifteen days, the cadres talked with Ma. In this period, they had twenty-three formal talks with him besides the numerous evening talks. They conversed with other farmers in the village, but Ma was the most "active" element. From this it can be seen it is not easy to stir a Chinese peasant.

Stone Wall Village
Turns Over

PART II

Editor's Introduction: The cadres who came to Stone Wall Village found that it is not easy to rouse a Chinese peasant to revolt. But slowly, together with their first convert, Ma, they convinced other poor peasants to join in the struggle against landlord Wang. As a warning to the would-be "overturners," the landlord had one of them, a man named Original Fortune Lee, murdered; thus the landlord drew the first blood.

As the account of events in Stone Wall Village continues, this incident has just taken place.

AFTER THE MURDER of Original Fortune Lee, the people went about in terror and shut up again like clams. Even those who had attended the second meeting now said: "We haven't begun to struggle with the landlord, but one of us is gone already."

The cadres were very much surprised by the murder. They thought they had been too careless and had not placed enough belief in the peasants' fears. They also thought a hand grenade might be thrown at any time into their meeting cave. Their biggest fear, however, was that the peasants would give up the overturning movement altogether. Therefore, they decided to hold a memorial meeting in honor of Original Fortune Lee and by this meeting to mobilize the people. . . .

One hundred people of Stone Wall Village attended this meeting, but Landlord Wang did not come. . . . The memorial meeting lasted four hours. After it was over, another meeting was called to decide how to continue "overturning." Only six farmers came to this meeting. No one said directly that he was afraid to attend, but they weakly gave the excuse: "I have a little work to do."

The six men, however, decided that because of the murder they would have to "settle" with Landlord Wang immediately.

At the end of five days, thirty farmers mobilized by the other six gathered in the cave for another meeting. Until nearly midnight, they told stories of how they had suffered at the landlord's hands.

Suddenly, someone said: "Maybe Wang will run away."

"Let's get him tonight," said several farmers at once.

After some discussion, they all trooped out of the cave and started a march on Landlord Wang's home. Among the thirty men, there was one rifle and three hand grenades.

The marching farmers separated into two groups. One climbed on top of the cliffs and worked along the cave roofs until they were over the courtyard. The others marched directly to the gate, knocked loudly, and commanded the landlord to open up.

Wang's wife answered the door and announced that her husband was not at home. Refusing to believe her, the peasants made a search and discovered a secret passage behind a cupboard. Descending through an underground tunnel, they found Wang cowering in a subterranean cave. They took him away and locked him up overnight. . . .

[The next] day, a mass meeting was called in a great square field south of the town, not far from the river. About eighty people came to complain against Wang, while the rest of the village watched—among them Wang's wife and daughter.

In the course of the morning and afternoon, the crowd accused the landlord of many crimes, including betraying resistance members to the Japanese, robbing them of grain, forcing them into labor gangs. At last, he was asked if he admitted the accusations.

"All these things I have done," he said, "but really it was not myself who did it, but the Japanese."

He could not have chosen worse words. Over the fields now sounded an angry roar, as of the sea, and the crowd broke into a wild fury. Everybody shouted at once, proclaiming against the landlord's words. Even the nonparticipating bystanders warmed to something akin to anger.

Then, above the tumult of the crowd, came a voice louder than the rest, shouting: "Hang him up!"

The chairman of the meeting and the cadres were disregarded. For all that the crowd noticed, they did not exist.

The crowd boiled around Wang, and somewhere a rope went swishing over a tree. Willing hands slung one end of the rope around Wang's waist.

Other eager hands gave the rope a jerk. Wang rose suddenly and came to a halt in mid-air about three feet above the earth. And there he hung, his head down, his stomach horizontal and his legs stretched out—a perfect illustration of what the Chinese call a "duck's swimming form."

About his floating body, the crowd foamed, anger wrinkling their foreheads and curses filling their mouths. Some bent down and spit in the landlord's eyes, and others howled into his ears.

As he rose from the ground, the landlord felt a terror that mounted higher as his position became more uncomfortable. Finally, he could bear it no longer and shouted: "Put me down. I know my wrongs. I admit everything."

The spite of the crowd, however, was not so easily assuaged, and they only answered the landlord's pleas with shouts: "Pull him up! He's too low! Higher! Higher!"

After a while, the anger of the people abated and cooler heads counseled. "If we let him die now, we won't be able to settle accounts with him." Then they allowed him to come down for a rest.

At this point, the wife of Original Fortune Lee came up close to Wang and said in a plaintive voice: "Somebody killed my husband. Was it you?"

Wang's face, which had grown red from hanging in the air, slowly was drained of all color. "No, I did not do it," he said.

"Tell the truth," said the crowd. "You can admit everything to us and nothing will happen. But if you don't tell us the truth, we will hang you up again."

"No, it was not me."

These words were hardly out of his mouth before someone jerked on the rope and the landlord flew into the air again. This time the crowd let him hang for a long while. Unable to bear the pain, Wang finally said: "Let me down. I'll speak."

Then, between sobs and sighs, he told how he and his son had seized Original Fortune Lee as he was walking home from the meeting, tied his hands together, held his head under water until he was dead, and then had thrown him in the river, thinking he would float away.

A cry of rage went up as Wang finished speaking.

"You've already killed three of our men in the war," said Liu Kwang. "That could be excused. But now your own life can never repay us for the crimes you've done.". . .

A shout went up from the crowd as Landlord Wang was led to the field. Three guards marched him, pale and shaking, to a willow tree, where he was bound up. With his back against the tree, the landlord looked once at the crowd but quickly bent his head toward the ground again.

A peasant strikes back. (From *Chinese Literature*, No. 3, Peking: Foreign Languages Press, 1972.)

A slight shiver of apprehension went through the audience. They could not believe their enemy was helpless here before them. He was the lamb led to slaughter, but they could not quite believe they were going to kill him.

Ma Chiu-tze stepped before the crowd and called for attention.

"Now the time has come for our revenge," he announced in a trembling voice. "In what way shall we take revenge on this sinful landlord? We shall kill him."

As he said this, he turned around and slapped Wang sharply across the face.

The crack of palm against cheek rang like a pistol shot on the morning air. A low animal moan broke from the crowd, and it leaped into action.

The landlord looked up as he heard the crowd rushing on him. Those nearest saw his lips move and heard him say: "Two words, two words, please."

The man closest shouted: "Don't let him speak!" and in the same breath swung his hoe, tearing the clothes from the bound man's chest and ripping open the lower portion of his body.

The landlord gave one chilling shriek and then bowed his head in resignation. The crowd was on him like beasts. Their faces had turned yellow and their eyes rolled. A big farmer swung his pig knife and plunged it directly into the landlord's heart. His body quivered—even the tree shook—then slumped, but still the farmer drew his knife in and out, again and again and yet once again.

Landlord Wang was quickly dead, but the rage of the crowd would not abate.

The field rang with the shouts of maddened people.

"It is not enough to kill him."

"We must put him in the open air."

"We must not allow him to be buried for three days."

But such convulsive passions do not last long. They burn themselves out. Slowly, the anger of the crowd cooled. The body of the landlord might rot in the open air, and it were better that his wife and daughter be allowed to get him.

That evening, as the sun was going down behind the mountain, the landlord's wife and daughter brought a mule cart slowly across the field to where their husband and father lay. They wept no tears but silently lifted the mutilated body into the cart and drove away.

Few saw them come and few saw them go. And no one said a word. For there was nothing left to say. The struggle against the landlord was ended.

Stone Wall Village had turned over.

PART II
THE CONSERVATIVE TRADITION

Introduction

What eventually was turned over in Linxian county was not merely an oppressive landlord, but a way of life. For 2,000 years China was dominated by Confucianism, a conservative, patriarchal and hierarchical system of beliefs which strongly influenced social, cultural, political and economic relations. It supported a society controlled by the elite gentry class, which has been called "the longest-lived ruling class in world history."* It served as the basis of a political system which provided for stability and unity over a vast geographical area for centuries. It also fostered great advances in science and technology as well as in areas of art, literature and philosophy.

However, Confucianism treated women as inferior to men, rejected concepts of equality and individualism, honored age over youth, and supported an authoritarian system of government led by the emperor and his officials. The Communists, led by Mao, strove to overturn this conservative system and replace it with a new social and political order that reflected the interests of the peasants and workers, the overwhelming majority of the Chinese people.

The articles in this chapter describe the basic elements of the Confucian system.

---

* Maurice Meisner, *The Deng Xiaoping Era*, New York: Hill and Wang, 1996, p. 25.

The Confucian Heritage

Editor's Introduction: For much of the 2,000 years prior to the Communist revolution, the teaching of Confucius prevailed in China. Indeed, if we could use only one word to describe traditional China, that word would be "Confucian."

Confucianism was a way of life, a philosophy of government, a system of ordering society. Like communism, it pervaded all aspects of human activity. It was not a religion as we usually think of religion. Confucius believed in gods, but he was mainly interested in perfecting life on earth, which he felt could be fostered by the rule of an educated elite.

What is Confucianism? To answer that question adequately would take years of study. But some understanding of Confucian values can be gained by reading a few fragments of the conversations between Confucius and his disciples, recorded more than 2,500 years ago and compiled in a book called the *Analects.*[3]

Regard for the past:
Confucius said: I am a transmitter and not a creator. I believe in and have a passion for the ancients."

Education:
Confucius said: "By nature men are pretty much alike; it is learning and practice that set them apart."

Confucius said: "Those who are born wise are the highest type of people; those who become wise through learning come next; those who learn by overcoming dullness come after that. Those who are dull but still won't learn are the lowest type of people."

Humanity:
Confucius said: "Behave when away from home as though you were in the presence of an important guest. Deal with the common people as though

A Confucian official.

you were officiating at an important sacrifice. Do not do to others what you would not want others to do to you. Then there will be no dissatisfaction either in the state or at home."

Confucius said: "To be able to practice five virtues everywhere in the world constitutes humanity. [The five are] courtesy, generosity, good faith, diligence, and kindness. He who is courteous is not humiliated; he who is generous wins the multitude; he who is of good faith is trusted by the people; he who is diligent attains his objective; and he who is kind can get service from the people."

Filial piety [respect for parents]:

Confucius said: "Nowadays a filial son is just a man who keeps his parents in food. But even dogs or horses are given food. If there is no feeling of reverence, wherein lies the difference?"

Religion:

. . . about the worship of ghosts and spirits Confucius said: "We don't know yet how to serve men, how can we know about serving the spirits?" "What about death?" was the next question. Confucius said: "We don't know yet about life, how can we know about death?"

. . . about wisdom Confucius said: "Devote yourself to the proper demands of the people, respect the ghosts and spirits but keep them at a distance—this may be called wisdom."

*The gentleman:**

Confucius said: "The gentleman is always calm and at ease; the inferior man is always worried and full of distress."

Confucius said: "The gentleman understands what is right; the inferior man understands what is profitable."

Confucius said: "The gentleman makes demands on himself; the inferior man makes demands on others."

Government by personal virtue:

Confucius said: "Lead the people by laws and regulate them by penalties, and the people will try to keep out of jail, but will have no sense of shame. Lead the people by virtue and restrain them by the rules of decorum, and the people will have a sense of shame, and moreover will become good."

Confucius said: "The essentials are sufficient food, sufficient troops, and the confidence of the people." Tzu Kung [a disciple] said: "Suppose you were forced to give up one of these three, which would you let go first?" Confucius said: "The troops." Tzu Kung asked again: "If you were forced to

---

* The characters for "gentleman" have also been translated as "superior man" or "virtuous man."

give up one of the two remaining, which would you let go?" Confucius said: "Food. For from of old, death has been the lot of all men, but a people without faith cannot survive."

CONFUCIAN INEQUALITIES

Schoolboys learn[ed] about the inequalities of the imperial order in a beginner's reader that reports an imaginary dialogue between Confucius and Hsiang T'ou. Hsiang T'ou ("Fragrant Head") is a sweet and virtuous lad as well-known as George Washington in our schoolbooks. The boy is questioned by Confucius one day while the Master is out rambling the countryside with his disciples in a carriage.

"I wish to have you go with me, and fully equalize the empire; what do you think of that?"

The lad replied, "The empire cannot be equalized. Here are high hills, there lakes and rivers. Either there are princes and nobles, or there are slaves and servants. If the hills be leveled, the birds and beasts will have no resort; if the rivers and lakes be filled up, the fishes and turtles will have nowhere to go. Do away with kings and nobles, and the common people will have much dispute about right and wrong. Obliterate slaves and servants, and who will there be to serve the prince? If the empire be so vast and unsettled, how can it be equalized?"

Needless to say the Master expresses delight with this answer. Nature itself provides a model for the power gap between peasants and elites.

Source: Leon E. Stover, *The Cultural Ecology of Chinese Civilization*, New York: New American Library, 1974, p. 235.

The Traditional
Family Ethic

Editor's Introduction: For thousands of years the family was the basic social unit in China. Honor and obedience to one's parents and older relatives was the cardinal virtue. The collective family was the principal unit for welfare and social security. The government did little or nothing to provide health insurance or old age pensions. That was left to families. It was an unforgivable breach of ethics to neglect one's parents in their retirement.

To strengthen the family unit, the Chinese often formed clans composed of several generations and many branches of the male line of a family. Large clans included hundreds of members. A certain amount of land would be owned communally and used to support an ancestral temple, a school, a welfare fund, commercial operations, and so on. Clan rules defined proper behavior for all members. To violate those rules and be expelled from the clan was the worst thing that could happen to one of its members, for an expelled person would become isolated and trusted by no one.

Aside from its obligation to obey the laws of the land, the family owed little allegiance to anyone. Rich families felt but slight obligation to aid the poor, and indeed felt justified in pressing their economic and political advantages over them.

The collective ethic of the Communists was an attempt to expand the unit of social concern from the family to the whole society. The implications of that change are suggested in the following selection written in 1935 by Lin Yu-tang, a man in love with traditional Chinese culture but also capable of seeing its weaknesses. [4]

THE CHINESE ARE ... family-minded, not social-minded, and the family mind is only a form of magnified selfishness. It is curious that the word

Photo courtesy Jean Elliott Johnson.

"society" does not exist as an idea in Chinese thought. . . ."Public spirit" is a new term, so is "civic consciousness," and so is "social service." There are no such commodities in China. . . .

To a Chinese, social work always looks like meddling with other people's business. A man enthusiastic for social reform or in fact for any kind of public work always looks a little bit ridiculous. We discount his sincerity. We cannot understand him. What does he mean by going out of his way to do all this work? Is he courting publicity? Why is he not loyal to his family, and why does he not get official promotion and help his family first? We decide he is young, or else he is a deviation from the normal human type.

There were always such deviations from type . . . but they were invariably of the bandit or vagabond class, unmarried . . . willing to jump into the water to save an unknown drowning child. (Married men in China do not do that.) Or else they were married men who died penniless and made their wives and children suffer. . . .

The best modern educated Chinese still cannot understand why Western women should organize a "Society for the Prevention of Cruelty to Animals." Why bother about the dogs, why do they not stay at home and nurse their babies? We decide that these women have no children and therefore have nothing better to do, which is probably often true. The conflict is between the family mind and the social mind. If one scratches deep enough, one always finds the family mind at work.

For the family system is the root of Chinese society, from which all Chinese social characteristics derive. . . . It touches us even in very personal ways. It takes the right of contracting marriage from our hands and gives it to our parents; it makes us marry, not wives, but "daughters-in-law," and it makes our wives give birth, not to children, but to "grandchildren." It multiplies the obligations of the bride a hundredfold. It makes it rude for a young couple to close the door of their room in the family house in the daytime, and makes privacy an unknown word in China. . . .

The Doctrine of Social Status, as Confucianism has been popularly called, is the social philosophy behind the family system. It is the doctrine that makes for social order in China. It is the principle of social structure and social control at the same time. . . .

In theory at least, Confucius did not mean family consciousness to degenerate into a form of magnified selfishness at the cost of social integrity. . . . He meant the moral training in the family as the basis for general moral training, and he planned that from the general moral training a society should emerge which would live happily and harmoniously together. Only in this sense can one understand the tremendous emphasis placed on "filial piety" [respect for parents], which is regarded as the "first of all virtues." ...

Confucius said:

The reason why the gentleman teaches filial piety is not because it is to be seen in the home and everyday life. He teaches filial piety in order that man may respect all those who are fathers in the world. He teaches brotherliness in the younger brother, in order that man may respect all those who are elder brothers in the world. He teaches the duty of the subject, in order that man may respect all who are rulers in the world.

Several generations under one roof—a traditional Chinese ideal. (From Robert Goldston, *The Rise of Red China*, Indianapolis: Bobbs Merrill, 1967.)

Again, Confucius said:

Those who love their parents dare not show hatred to others. Those who respect their parents dare not show rudeness to others....

Every family in China is really a communistic unit, with the principle of "do what you can and take what you need" guiding its functions. Mutual helpfulness is developed to a very high degree, encouraged by a sense of moral obligation and family honor. Sometimes a brother will cross the sea thousands of miles away to redeem the honor of a bankrupt brother. A well-placed and comparatively successful man generally contributes the greater, if not the entire, share of the expenses of the whole household, and it is common practice, worthy of no special merit, for a man to send his nephews to school. A successful man, if he is an official, always gives the best jobs to his relatives, and if there are not ready jobs, he can create sinecure ones. Thus sinecurism and nepotism developed, which, coupled with economic pressure, became an irresistible force, undermining . . . any political reform movement. The force is so great that repeated efforts at reform, with the best of intentions, have proved unsuccessful.

To look at it kindly, nepotism is no worse than favoritism of other sorts. An official does not place only his nephews in the office, but he also has to place the nephews of other high officials..., who write him letters of recommendation. Where is he going to place them except in sinecure posts and "advisorships"? ...

It is quite natural that charity should begin at home. For the family system must be taken as the Chinese traditional system of insurance against unemployment. Every family takes care of its own unemployed, and . . . its next best work is to find employment for them. It is better than charity because it teaches in the less lucky members a sense of independence, and the members so helped in turn help other members of the family. Besides, the minister who robs the nation to feed the family, either for the present or for the next three or four generations, by amassing half a million to ten million or more dollars, is only trying to glorify his ancestors and be a "good" man of the family. . . .

Certain social characteristics arise from the family system, apart from nepotism and official corruption. They may be summed up as the lack of social discipline. It defeats any form of social organization, as it defeats the civil-service system through nepotism. It makes a man "sweep the snow in front of his door, and not bother about the frost on his neighbor's roof." This is not so bad. What is worse is that it makes a man throw his refuse outside his neighbor's door. . . .

Religion in
Traditional China

Editor's Introduction: To understand religion in the Chinese context, we must put aside for the moment our Western notions about religion. We must begin with an awareness that the Chinese were not Christians or Jews. Hard as the Christian missionaries tried before the Communists came to power, they never converted more than half of 1 percent of the population to Christianity. Nor were all Chinese Buddhists, as so many Westerners tend to believe. Buddhism had its day in China as the major religion of the country, but the great age of Buddhism ended by about 900 A.D. In the last Chinese dynasty (1644-1911), Buddhism was actually outlawed but was unofficially tolerated as long as it did not interfere with affairs of state.

The following selection, written by Francis Hsu, a Chinese anthropologist who taught in the United States, describes the place of Buddhism and other religious beliefs in traditional Chinese society. [5]

IT IS COMPLETELY inaccurate to describe the Chinese . . . as Buddhists, Taoists, Confucianists, or ancestor-worshippers in the same sense that we classify Americans as Jews, Protestants, or Catholics. . . . [A] Chinese may go to a Buddhist monastery to pray for a male heir, but he may proceed from there to a Taoist shrine where he beseeches a god to cure him of malaria. Ask any number of Chinese what their religion is and the answer of the majority will be that they have no particular religion, or that, since all religions benefit man in one way or another, they are all equally good. Most Chinese temples . . . are dedicated to the worship of many gods, and few family shrines are a sanctuary for only a single deity. There are many Chinese temples built expressly to house together Confucius, Buddha, and Lao Tze, the founder of Taoism. In prayer meetings staged by several southwestern

Hired mourners in a traditional funeral procession. Photo by Peter J. Seybolt.

Chinese communities during World War II, I saw included at many an altar the images of not only the numerous Chinese deities but also of Jesus Christ and Mohammed. . . . For the Chinese way in religion is to be more and more inclusive so that my god, your god, his god, and all gods, whether you or I know anything about them or not, must be equally honored or at least not be the objects of either my contempt or of yours. . . .

In every Chinese village we find a variety of temples all dedicated to the worship of many different gods. A typical village temple usually houses the Goddess of Mercy, who answers all kinds of prayers; the God of Wealth, who is indispensable to all businessmen; the Dragon God, who brings rain in times of drought; and the Earth God . . ., who is the local emissary of the other world. The inventory of gods in city temples is much larger. There are temples housing the God of Literature; Confucius and his seventy-two famous disciples; the God of Agriculture; the God of Medicine; the Goddess of Measles, Eyes, and other ailments or bodily parts; Ch'eng Huang, or God of the District, flanked by courts of the ten judges . . . and the gods who are said to be founders and patron deities of various crafts. . . . No one knows how many gods there are in China. There seems to be no limit to them, and most of them are unrelated to each other. . . .

I do not know of a single city or town in mainland China before 1949, or in Taiwan today, that is without diviners or geomancy readers, physiognomists, phrenologists, mediums, and all kinds of fortunetellers. For a fee, these persons offer to foretell the length of a person's life and his business prospects, or to determine the marriageability of a boy and girl, or to decide on the ritual suitability of a new house site or graveyard. They will often undertake to arrange a meeting or communication with the gods or with one's ancestors. There is literally no question they do not attempt to answer and almost no matter relating to the gods that they refuse to interpret. It is safe to say that no individual of prominence in traditional China failed to have his fate told, not once, but many times, by different professional fortunetellers. . . .

After death, the soul of every Chinese is subject, according to its deserts, to reward, punishment, or both. The courts of the ten judges, each of which successively reviews the merits, and demerits of every newly departed soul, are well known among the Chinese for the tortures they may inflict. A soul may be sawed in half, restored, and then boiled in oil, next ground to a mush, then slowly drowned in a river of blood, after which its eyes are poked out and its tongue cut off, and so on *ad nauseam*, After all of these exasperating experiences, the soul may yet be banished to more suffering in one or all of the numerous hells. Some Chinese sources indicate that there are eighteen hells, one situated on top of the other, while other sources insist that there are many more.

A meritorious person's soul is treated very differently. Immediately after its departure from the body, it is met at the threshold of the world of spirits by a special reception party, playing music and bearing food that has been dispatched by one of the judges. The newcomer progresses from court to court, residing in guesthouses at each stopping place. On these occasions he is entertained lavishly for long periods of time and has various honors conferred on him. He may then be offered an appointment as a local god upon earth or as a higher official in the court of the Supreme Ruler. If especially deserving, he may ultimately be entitled to a place of eternal happiness in the Western Paradise. . . .

ANCESTOR WORSHIP

I know of no Chinese, save the relatively few Christians and Mohammedans, who do not adhere to [the cult of ancestor worship.] It is literally the universal religion of China. . . .

Ancestor worship is an active ingredient in every aspect of Chinese society, from the family to the government, from local business to the national economy.

The Chinese have at least three basic assumptions about ancestor worship. First, all living persons owe their fortunes or misfortunes to their ancestors. A man may be a beggar because of his laziness, and this fact may be well known to everyone in the community; but had his ancestors accumulated enough good deeds while they were alive, they probably never would have had such a lazy descendant. A great official may attain prominence by excellence of scholarship and strength of character, and everyone who knows him may testify to these virtues. But his very achievement is evidence of his ancestors' high moral worth. . . .

The second assumption of ancestor worship is that all departed ancestors, like other gods and spirits, have needs that are not different from those of the living. To prevent one's ancestors from degenerating into spiritual vagabonds, it is the duty of every man to provide for his departed ancestors just as faithfully as he provides for his parents while they are alive. Accordingly, the dead, to the limit of the male descendant's financial ability, must be offered food and life-sized paper models of clothing, furniture, sedan chairs, horses, donkeys, cows, and servants, so that the departed may set up house in the other world. . . .

This concept explains why a Chinese man or woman who dies without male heirs is an object of public pity. For that person is doomed to an existence as spirit tramps, depending entirely upon handouts from charitable families or consuming the leftovers of better situated spirits. . . .

The third assumption is that the departed ancestors continue, as in life, to assist their relatives in this world, just as their living descendants can also lend a hand to them. That is, a person's present lot may be improved by the spiritual efforts of departed ancestors, and the spiritual welfare or misery of a departed ancestor may likewise be enhanced or mitigated by the worldly actions of living descendants. . . .

[In short, the] Chinese maintain a positive and close relationship with their departed ancestors just as they do with their living kinsmen, while their attitude toward the other gods is neutral and distant, reflecting their attitudes toward the emperor and his officials. . . .

Lessons for Women

Editor's Introduction: Ban Zhao (Pan Chao), who is sometimes called the most renowned woman scholar in China, wrote the famous "Lessons for Women" for her daughters in the first century A.D. They were based on customs and values handed down through the centuries, and for nearly two thousand years they continued to be the standard of proper conduct for every young lady. As you read them, try to imagine what a similar essay called "Rules for Men" might prescribe. [6]

HUMILITY

ON THE THIRD day after the birth of a girl, the ancients observed three customs: (1) to place the baby below the bed; (2) to give her a potsherd with which to play; and (3) to announce her birth to her ancestors by an offering. Now, to lay the baby below the bed plainly indicated that she is lowly and weak and should regard it as her primary duty to humble herself before others. To give her potsherds with which to play signified that she should practice labor and consider it her primary duty to be industrious. To announce her birth before her ancestors clearly meant that she ought to esteem as her primary duty the continuation of the observance of worship in the home.

These three ancient customs epitomize a woman's ordinary way of life and the teachings of the traditional ceremonial rites and regulations. Let a woman modestly yield to others; let her respect others; let her put others first, herself last. Should she do something good, let her not mention it; should she do something bad, let her not deny it. Let her bear disgrace; let her even endure when others speak or do evil to her. Always let her seem to tremble and to fear. Then she may be said to humble herself before others.

Let a woman retire late to bed, but rise early to duties; let her not dread tasks by day or by night. Let her not refuse to perform domestic duties whether easy or difficult. That which must be done, let her finish completely, tidily, and systematically. Then she may be said to be industrious.

41

Chinese women, photographed in the nineteenth century. (From C. W. Browne and N. H. Dole, *The New American and the Far East*, Boston, 1907.)

Let a woman be correct in manner and upright in character in order to serve her husband. Let her live in purity and quietness [of spirit] and attend to her own affairs. Let her love not gossip and silly laughter. Let her cleanse and purify and arrange in order the wine and the food for the offerings to the ancestors. Then she may be said to continue ancestral worship.

No woman who observes these three [fundamentals of life] has ever had a bad reputation or has fallen into disgrace. If a woman fails to observe them, how can her name be honored; how can she but bring disgrace upon herself?

HUSBAND AND WIFE

If a husband does not control his wife, then the rules of conduct manifesting his authority are abandoned and broken. If a wife does not serve her husband, then the proper relationship [between men and women] and the natural order of things are neglected and destroyed.

RESPECT AND CAUTION

If husband and wife have the habit of staying together, never leaving one another, and following each other around within the limited space of their own rooms, then they will lust after and take liberties with one another. From such action improper language will arise between the two. This kind of discussion may lead to licentiousness. Out of licentiousness will be born a heart of disrespect to the husband. Such a result comes from not knowing that one should stay in one's proper place. . . .

WOMANLY QUALIFICATIONS

A woman [ought to] have four qualifications: (1) womanly virtue; (2) womanly words; (3) womanly bearing; and (4) womanly work. . . .

To guard carefully her chastity; to control her behavior; in every motion to exhibit modesty; and to model each act on the best usage—this is womanly virtue.

To choose her words with care; to avoid vulgar language; to speak at appropriate times; and not to weary others [with much conversation] may be called the characteristics of womanly words.

To wash and scrub filth away; to keep clothes and ornaments fresh and clean; to wash the head and bathe the body regularly, and to keep the person free from disgraceful filth may be called the characteristics of womanly bearing.

With wholehearted devotion to sew and to weave; to love not gossip and silly laughter; in cleanliness and order [to prepare] the wine and food for serving guests may be called the characteristics of womanly work.

These four qualifications characterize the greatest virtue of a woman. No woman can afford to be without them. In fact they are very easy to possess if a woman only treasure them in her heart. The ancients had a saying: "Is love far off? If I desire love, then love is at hand!" So can it be said of these qualifications.

WHOLEHEARTED DEVOTION

Now in the "Rites"* is written the principle that a husband may marry again, but there is no Canon that authorizes a woman to be married the second time. Therefore it is said of husbands as of Heaven, that as certainly as people cannot run away from Heaven, so surely a wife cannot leave [a husband's home]. . . .

The ancient book "A Pattern for Women" says: "To obtain the love of one man is the crown of a woman's life; to lose the love of one man is to miss the aim in woman's life."

IMPLICIT OBEDIENCE

Whenever the mother-in-law says, "Do not do that," and if what she says is right, unquestionably the daughter-in-law obeys. Whenever the

---

* *The Book of Rites*, one of the ancient texts comprising the Confucian classics, sets out rules for the conduct of everyday life.

mother-in-law says, "Do that," even if what she says is wrong, still the daughter-in-law submits unfailingly to the command.

Let a woman not act contrary to the wishes and the opinions of parents-in-law about right and wrong; let her not dispute with them what is straight and what is crooked... .

The Status of Women

Editor's Introduction: The "Lessons for Women" clearly indicate the inferior status of women in traditional China, but they do not tell the whole story. The following selections describe some of the other disadvantages of being born female.

FOOTBINDING:

The clearest indication of female subservience in traditional China was the bizarre custom of footbinding. It began in about the tenth century A.D. and continued for a thousand years, until the middle of the twentieth century. There are many theories about the original reasons for footbinding, but no one seems to know how it began. Whatever the origin, small feet became an obsession with Chinese men.

Well-bound feet were about three inches long and they made women walk with an unusual swaying motion. The stigma attached to large feet was such that most women (except in a very few areas of China) had their feet bound. Grandmother Ning, who was born in 1867, was a working woman who had been a beggar for part of her life. She described the binding of her feet in an interview that was originally published in 1945. [7]

THEY DID NOT begin to bind my feet until I was seven because I loved so much to run and play. Then I became very ill and they had to take the bindings off my feet again... .

When I was nine they started to bind my feet again and they had to draw the bindings tighter than usual. My feet hurt so much that for two years I had to crawl on my hands and knees. Sometimes at night they hurt so much I could not sleep. I stuck my feet under my mother and she lay on them so they hurt less and I could sleep. But by the time I was eleven my feet did not hurt and by the time I was thirteen they were finished. The toes were turned under so that I could see them on the inner and under side of the foot. They had

Left: A woman in the nineteenth century displaying bound feet unwrapped.

Above: A comparison of a bound foot and a normal foot.

come up around. Two fingers could be inserted in the cleft between the front of the foot and the heel. My feet were very small indeed.

A girl's beauty and desirability were counted more by the size of her feet than by the beauty of her face. Matchmakers were not asked "Is she beautiful?" but "How small are her feet?" A plain face is given by heaven but poorly bound feet are a sign of laziness.

My feet were very small indeed. Not like they are now. When I worked so hard and was on my feet all day I slept with the bandages off because my feet ached, and so they spread.

FOOTBINDING—HENAN PROVINCE

Both of my sisters had bound feet, as did most of the women around here, some until the late 1940s.

There was an old saying: "big feet, loss of face." I remember the ribbons binding my sisters' feet. My sisters mostly stayed at home. If they went out on the street, the village people would laugh at them and look down on them for being out. Because women with bound feet could do no farm work, those in the poorest families didn't bind their daughters' feet. The first concern was survival. But, I would say that about 80 percent of the women here had bound feet even though Houhoa was a very poor village. It was difficult for my sisters to walk. It took my older sister over an hour to walk three li to Taiping Village, where her second husband's family lived. It is a twenty minute walk for me. My older sister died of a large tumor when she was forty-six or forty-seven years old.

Testimony of Wang Fucheng. (From Peter J. Seybolt, *Throwing the Emperor from His Horse*, Boulder, CO: Westview Press, 1996, p. 21.)

SLAVERY

Female slavery was an institution that was maintained for centuries in traditional China. Poor families often sold their daughters to the rich. Not infrequently slave girls became concubines (second, third or fourth wives) to wealthy men. The following autobiographical account by a young woman, Chang Siao-hung, was first published in 1933. [8]

"MY NAME IS Chang Siao-hung. I was born in 1902 of a very rich and well-known family of Hong Kong. All the wealth of the large joint family of which I am a member was earned by my grandfather, who began life as the servant of a British enterpriser. . . .

"My grandmother was a very cunning and capable woman of the old school, and despite the wealth of the family she was never satisfied unless more money was pouring through her fingers into the family coffers. After my grandfather died, shortly before the overthrow of the Manchu [Qing] Dynasty, my grandmother became almost supreme authority in our home... .

"One of my earliest memories was of the slave trade in which my grand-mother took a part. For, as I said, she was a woman never satisfied unless money was pouring through her fingers. The slaves in whom she dealt were always girls, courteously called *mui tsai*—which literally means domestic drudge—and there are Chinese and British apologists who try to dignify their lot by calling them 'adopted daughters.'

"This phrase is one of the many whited sepulchers of China. The *mui tsai* are slaves, bought and sold for money, and their owners have the power of life and death over them; they can be resold whenever or wherever it pleases the fancy of their owners; they may be sent as workers into the factories to earn money for their owners; they may be used as prostitutes—they may be sold to rich and degenerate men as concubines. These girls are the daughters of peasants of South China provinces, peasants so poor that they cannot afford the luxury of maintaining their daughters until they can be married into other families.

"There are few homes even of moderate means in South China and Hong Kong that do not have one or more girl slaves who do all the heavy drudgery of the household. The beautiful girls are usually sold for high prices as concubines of rich men. Still others are sold as prostitutes into the sing-song houses or to the 'flower boats'—that is, the brothels—of Canton, Macao, Hong Kong, or all the cities of the South Seas. Beautiful Cantonese concubines or prostitutes are also much sought after by the rich of Shanghai and other North China cities.

"Our own home rested upon the labor of such girl slaves, for all of our servants were *mui tsai*. More still. Into our home were brought girls to be sold to the rich men of our class. My grandmother did the selling. As a tiny child I recall standing by my grandmother's side when men came to look at these girls. Sometimes it was a fat official from Canton, or a rich merchant, or the sensuous and lazy son of merchants or officials of Canton or Hong Kong. They came looking for concubines. Less often it was a man or woman seeking household slaves. When such men called in their long, flowing silk gowns, they would be served tea, and my grandmother would express concern about the health and prosperity of their honorable families.

"Then, when the purpose of their visit was finally discussed, the girls would be brought in, nicely dressed for the occasion, their faces beautifully powdered and painted. But the buyers were very cunning businessmen and could not be cheated, and often they would compel the girl to lift her long, broad trousers or her gown that they might see the color of the skin on her legs. Now and then a man would take a cloth, wet it, and rub the powder off a girl's face to make certain the skin was fair beneath. And there were times when he would feel her body here and there.

"When satisfied, the man would go close to the girl, grin sensuously into her face, and ask: 'Would you like to be my concubine?' The girl, her head bowed to her chest, would answer 'Yes.' And big tears would roll from her eyes, leaving long traces on her sad face. Then she would withdraw and the purchaser would bargain with my grandmother; but before paying the full price he would often insist upon proof that his commodity was a virgin. If after the first night he found she was not, he would return her and demand his money back.

"Some men have chosen to say the taking of a concubine is a 'love mating,' and that although the first wife is the conventional way of maintaining the family and providing for the worship of ancestors, the concubine system provides for the element of love. But I ask—love for whom? The concubine is a slave, bought and sold, and she can be resold if it please the fancy of her master or if he becomes poor and needs money. Or she may be presented by her influential owner to one of his subordinates. Love! This purchase of helpless poor women by rich men is what the ruling class of my country call love. But even for the men who buy these women it is nothing but physical lust.

"Do you think I speak of the dark ages, of the past, or even of a quarter of a century ago when I was a child—of customs dead and gone? No, I speak of the present. For women and girls are sold into slavery in North, South, East, and West China today; and as my country has sunk into deeper poverty and deeper subjection, so has the buying and selling of slaves sunk deeper roots. The highest officials and militarists in the various governments, whether Nanking, Canton, or Peking, have their purchased concubines, and Chiang Kai-shek, whom the foreigners so admire and support, 'put away' four 'wives' in order to marry a woman on whose connections he expected to build his personal and political fortunes.

"I was the daughter of a wealthy family, blessed with every comfort that money could buy. My mother loved me dearly, protected me, planned for my future happiness. But even as a little child I used to wonder what would have happened to me had I been born the daughter of a peasant or some other poor man, as were the girls in our kitchen and those who passed through the lady-like hands of my grandmother. Even as a little child I could never forget the tears of girls as they said 'yes' to some rich man as they were being sold, and in my childhood fantasies I thought of myself as the general of a powerful army going forth to fight and free all the slave girls.

ARRANGED MARRIAGE

Arranged marriages were very common in traditional China. Girls were often betrothed when they were children and had no choice but to marry the men their parents had chosen for them. Tremendous pressure was exerted on the girls to follow through with the marriage, even if they strongly objected. The alternatives were running away from home and family, or suicide. In the early twentieth century many girls began to rebel and to stand up to their parents. Several wrote memoirs of their defiant refusal to accept their arranged marriage. The following account was written by Hsieh Ping-ying who was promised in marriage to the son of one of her father's friends when she was only three years old. She eventually fled her home, joined a revolutionary women's army, and returned home after it was demobilized (1927) to break her engagement. This heated discussion between Ping-ying, her mother and her father, took place after she declared that she would not marry the man that her parents had chosen for her. [9]

'WHAT! NOT MARRY him? You want to break off the engagement?' My father looked very angry. 'Yes, certainly, father,' I replied calmly and firmly. My mother could not keep silent any longer and began to scold me by saying: 'Beast, beast! . . . Marry you must, and I will see to it myself. . . .' I knew it would be no good to continue the discussion with my mother, and I retired to my bedroom to write a long letter, about five thousand words, giving my father all the reasons for my proposal to break off the marriage. I handed the letter to my father the next morning, and I was surprised to see that after he had read it he was not moved in the least, but began to upbraid me even more severely than before:

'As you say in your letter, the reasons for breaking off this engagement are chiefly these two: first there is no love between you, and second, your ideas are different. Let me answer you very frankly. First, love can only be created between husband and wife after their marriage. To have love before they are married is ridiculous. As you have not yet married Kwang, how can you expect to have love for him? The second point is his ideas. Now that term can only be applied to revolutionary people, and has nothing to do with man and wife. Your marriage into the Shiao family is not a revolutionary affair, but is to fulfill your duty as a woman. The best you can do is to follow our ancient teaching, so that you can have a family in which "when the husband sings, the wife shall join in," to present descendants to the family and look after the cooking and all other domestic affairs of the house, and then you will become a good wife and a kind mother. Since this is not a revolutionary affair, what do you care about ideas? . . . Ideas? Why should women have such dangerous things?'

'Please stop arguing with her,' my mother shouted to my father. 'This beast cannot be considered as a human being! Don't you realize that "father and mother are greater than heaven"? How dare she oppose our wishes? I sent you to school hoping you would learn propriety, righteousness, temperance and purity, but who would have thought that education would turn you into a beast without respect for your father and mother! Your marriage had been arranged by your father and mother when you were still at my breast. If you dare to oppose your marriage arrangements, it is as good as daring to oppose your father and mother. That would be a very shameful act indeed, and it would ruin our reputation and bring your ancestors into disgrace. I would rather die than allow you to do this. . . . Do you know that "a marriage may be arranged thousands of miles apart by a single piece of immortals' red thread?" Man and wife were arranged actually before their present existence. How dare you oppose the will of the immortals?. . .

'Aren't you ashamed of yourself, you, an unmarried girl, to talk about selecting a husband! The Shiao family is a very respectable one . . . they know the rules of propriety. . . . Now in return you want to commit this outrageous act against them. What face shall I have to see them again? You should remember the old proverb: "A good horse will not turn back to eat the grass behind him, and a good girl will never marry a second husband."'

Before my mother had finished my Father put in:

'She would never read anything like that now. What girls of her type react to nowadays are love stories in which girls commit suicide simply because they are not allowed to marry a young man of their own choice. Also stories in newspapers about girls breaking away from their homes because of their differences with their parents. Since they are influenced by these novels and newspaper stories, it is quite natural that we should have a girl who is dead set against her parents and the rules of propriety!'

'This is ridiculous! How can one set oneself against the rules of propriety?' my mother shouted in anger. 'They were established by our Sage, and for many thousands of years they have been governing our lives. How dare a mere girl like our daughter act against them? How can it be possible that with all pagodas and monuments erected in honour of chaste women of all ages, they cannot be a reminder to the girls of our generation? When we learn that a girl of twelve could determine to remain a widow when her future husband died, can it be possible that the modern girl would think of marrying twenty-four husbands in a year and still be without a husband when New Year's Day comes?'

I said nothing because I had now decided that to argue any further would be entirely useless. The only way was that I should be resolute in my struggle and never stop until the engagement was broken off.

The Leakage System

Editor's Introduction: The Confucian emphasis on humanity and self-perfection no doubt had an influence on China's rulers and helped to perpetuate the Confucian ethos for so many centuries. Those entrusted with government were supposed to be humane and unselfish, to devote themselves to a lifelong study of moral principles, and to set an example by their own conduct. Their main function as government officials was to maintain the peace and well-being of society.

There were no castes in traditional China. The ruling class was not born to a position of authority like the European or Japanese aristocracy. The highest positions in government were open to any man (women were excluded). Any male with the leisure and the money to pay a tutor could study the Confucian books and could take a series of civil service examinations that would qualify him for government service and high honors. Education, then, was the key to success in Confucian China, and, in theory, everyone had an equal chance.

In fact, however, there was little equality of opportunity. Few people of humble background could afford the many years of study required to learn the very difficult Chinese classical written language (it has been greatly simplified today) and virtually memorize the dozen or so basic Confucian books.

Furthermore, once a person had passed the exams and was awarded a degree, he was elevated to a position infinitely higher than that of the common people. He was guaranteed wealth, power, and status. Confucian society erected a rigid barrier between "gentlemen" and "small men." The gentlemen were "mental workers" who governed the small men and were supported by them. They disdained any sort of physical labor. The long gowns they wore and their long fingernails, which sometimes reached six inches, were symbols of their non-laboring status. It was in an effort to destroy this tradition and the attitudes of superiority and disdain for working people it produces that Mao Zedong insisted that all students, intellectuals, and government officials engage in physical labor together with working people.

In Confucian China, it was not just custom but also law that kept class distinctions clear. One's social rank determined the kind of clothes he could wear, the size of his house, and the kind of food he could eat. Criminal laws were not applied equally to the great and the small. In a lawsuit between people of the two classes, it was assumed that the gentleman, with his extensive moral training, was the innocent party. If he was found guilty, his sentence for most crimes would be lighter than that for a man of lower status found guilty of the same crimes. In short, Confucianism did everything possible to maintain class distinctions, to keep everyone in his place. Only in this way, Confucius taught, could peace and harmony be maintained.

Confucius said: "The gentleman cherishes virtue; the inferior man cherishes possessions." This was the ideal, and there were gentlemen—officials who sacrificed their own well being and material comfort for the good of the people. But a far more common situation is revealed by the expression, "Become an official and get rich." In the next selection, Chiang Monlin, former Chancellor of Beijing University, writing in 1947, describes how some officials under the traditional system acquired a fortune. [10]

FROM THE GOVERNMENT offices through which public revenues passed, the government required only certain fixed amounts to be forwarded to the national treasury. The officials in charge of the revenues could, by various means and all sorts of excuses and plausible reasons, attach a variety of fees to the regular taxes, In this way, for every tael of silver that flowed into the government treasury, at least the same amount or even more would be diverted to "leakage" funds. In the later years of the imperial regime, more wine leaked into private cups than remained in the public barrel. The government, finding itself parched as a fish in a dry pond, pressed hard for more money—whence still more "leakage" for public servants and heavier burdens for the people. . . .

But as to the "leakage" system and how it worked. China was then divided into some twenty-two provinces, comprising about two thousand *hsien* [counties]. The chief executive of the *hsien* was the magistrate, who took charge of all financial matters and concurrently filled the role of administrator of justice in his district. His salary—not more than a few *taels* a month—was nominal. All expenses incurred by the holder of the office had to be paid out of "leakage" funds. When higher officials of the imperial gov-

An official at home with his family and servants,

ernment passed through his district, he had to entertain them and secure for them all the "necessities" required for their travel. To the entourage of any higher official he had to offer "presents," usually in the form of money.

On the banks of the Yao-kiang River, just outside the city wall of my native Yu-yao, stood a welcome pavilion at which the magistrate welcomed passing officials of higher rank. One sunny afternoon some forty years ago, I noticed crowds gathering at a distance from the pavilion. I joined them and watched the landing of the Imperial Examiner and his entourage, on their way to Ning-po to hold civil examinations in that prefecture. On the previous day, the magistrate had "caught," or requisitioned, many houseboats from the people, and the one set aside for the Imperial Examiner was loaded with sealed cases, their contents known only to those who had prepared them.

I watched the party change boats. The Imperial Examiner stepped into the most prominent; the sails were set and the little flotilla with the officials and "leakage" gifts on board floated downriver with the ebbing tide to the seaport city of Ning-po. Under that inspiration, I said to myself that from now on I must study hard, so that some day I myself might be an Imperial Examiner blessed with such mysterious gifts as lay hidden in those cases.

Regular "gifts" had to be presented to the secretaries of the civil governor of the province. Failing that, a magistrate could not expect them to speak kind words for him to the governor and would find them faultfinding in his official relations with the governor's office. Added together, the amount required for plain sailing in his career was by no means small. Human nature also made him not unmindful of the necessity to provide for a rainy day. And he had his family and followers to support.

Candidates for magistracy who had pull were covetous of the districts with large revenues. I remember that in the *hsien* in which we lived during my school days, no magistrate had ever held office for more than a year. The regular term of office was three years, in which a magistrate could realize approximately a hundred thousand dollars. In those times, this sum was considered very great. So the governor appointed acting magistrates, whose term was usually one year. In this way there would be more chances for expectant magistrates to share the profit.

When a magistrate retired from office after the expiration of his term and paid an official call on the governor, he was usually asked by his superior whether his district had been a good one, meaning how much he had got out of the "leakage" funds. His friends and relatives also asked him the same question by way of starting a conversation.

The higher the rank of the official through whose hands the government revenues passed, the more "leakage" flowed into his private coffer. The *tao-tai* of Shanghai was known to reap a profit of some 100,000 *taels* a year. Governors and viceroys of rich provinces and the powerful princes and grand ministers in Peking (Beijing) usually enjoyed large yearly incomes. . . .

The poisonous sap penetrated even to the households of the well-to-do. The cook would poke "holes" in his vegetable and meat baskets in order to make them "leak." Servants got something from the purchases they made for the household—especially in Peking the shops always added a certain percentage to the price for the servants who made the purchase. . . .

The practice of "leakage" permeated the entire system of *likin* [a tax on commerce]. And *likin,* like a gigantic octopus with tentacles reaching to every communication line in the country, sucked the blood out of the trade and commerce of the nation.

It worked this way. Anyone who knew how to "squeeze" the people would bid—say two hundred thousand dollars a year—to government agents for the right to run the *likin* at a certain station or a number of stations established at points on the highway where merchandise passed from one city to another. The person who won the bid would become *likin* commissioner at that station or group of stations and had the right to assess duties on the goods passing through. If he could realize a sum of three hundred thousand dollars within the year, he would turn over two hundred thousand to the government and keep the remainder for himself and his partners. So he would make most goods dutiable in order to swell his private fortune.

Once I saw a boat loaded with watermelons passing under the bridge at a station. It was stopped by a long bamboo hook from shore and several inspectors jumped down and began to thrust iron rods into the melons. The owner begged them to desist and promised to pay any amount they demanded. The "duties" were paid; the poor farmer sailed on.

> *Editor's Postscript:* The "leakage" system of acquiring money was normal and legal in China. Indeed, as the article suggests, it was the only way underpaid officials and others providing services could live. But although custom regulated the amount of "leakage" that was acceptable, and the government removed officials who were especially voracious, the whole system was open to abuse by its very nature, and Confucian morality often exerted little restraint on outright greed. This seems to have been particularly true in the late nineteenth century, when Western power forced a breakdown of Confucian institutions. Customary leakage degenerated into widespread corruption, and this continued into the twentieth century, providing fertile soil for the growth of the Communist movement.

PART III
THE SEEDS OF REVOLUTION

Introduction

The Confucian values of stability, conservatism and social hierarchy dominated China for two millennia. However, a counter-tradition emphasizing freedom, love, equality and revolution has also existed throughout Chinese history. While weakened and overshadowed by the forces upholding the status quo, this counter-tradition was never completely destroyed by them and it inspired philosophical, literary and political movements down through the centuries, including the Communist revolutionary movement of the twentieth century.

The Legacy of
the Distant Past

Editor's Introduction: Perhaps the earliest example of a Chinese expression of social equality appears in the *Liji* or *Book of Rites*, the collection of essays compiled during the Han dynasty but written at an earlier time. A section called *Liyun* or *Evolution of Rites*, traditionally attributed to Confucius, describes an ideal society, *datong*, or the age of *Great Harmony* or *Grand Unity*, which supposedly existed in China prior to the era of Confucius. [11]

WHEN THE GREAT WAY was practiced, the world was shared by all alike. The worthy and the able were promoted to office and men practiced good faith and lived in affection. Therefore they did not regard as parents only their own parents, or as sons only their own sons. The aged found a fitting close to their lives, the robust their proper employment; the young were provided with an upbringing and the widow and widower, the orphaned and the sick, with proper care. Men had their tasks and women their hearths. They hated to see goods lying about in waste, yet they did not hoard them for themselves; they disliked the thought that their energies were not fully used, yet they used them not for private ends. Therefore all evil plotting was prevented and thieves and rebels did not arise, so that people could leave their outer gates unbolted. This was the age of Grand Unity.

A similar vision of society was described by Mozi, the philosopher who was born several years after Confucius' death and who became one of his most influential critics. Mozi believed that to improve society people must obey the will of heaven by practicing universal love. Rejecting partiality, the idea of love based on one's relationship to others, he claimed that only through practicing universal love, the love for all people, "One would regard others as one's self." He wrote that: [12]

PARTIALITY IS TO be replaced by universality, But how is partiality to be replaced by universality? Now, when everyone regards the states of others as he regards his own, who would attack the other's state? One would regard others as one's self. When everyone regards the cities of others as he regards his own, who would seize the others' cities? One would regard others as one's self. When everyone regards the houses of others as he regards his own, who would disturb the others' houses? One would regard others as one's self. Now when the states and cities do not attack and seize each other, and when the clans and individuals do not disturb and harm one another—is this a calamity or a benefit to the world? Of course it is a benefit.

When we come to inquire about the cause of all these benefits, whence have they arisen? Is it out of men's hating and injuring others? We must reply that it is not so. We should say that it is out of men's loving and benefiting others. If we should classify one by one all those who love others and benefit others, should we find them to be partial or universal in their love? Of course we should say they are universal. Now, since universal love is the cause of the major benefits in the world, therefore Mo Tsu (Mozi) proclaims that universal love is right... .

> Mozi believed in the unity of thought and action and was widely admired for his energetic proselytizing, his simple lifestyle, and his advocacy of peace among the Chinese states.
>
> The ancient philosophy of Daoism, with its emphasis on personal freedom, spontaneity, spirituality, mysticism and nature, represented, in many ways, an alternative to Confucianism. Although many of the writings of Laozi one of the founders of Daoism, are vague and ambiguous and have been viewed as a philosophy of retreat and isolation from the real world, some of his writings relate to social and political matters. These selections support minimal governmental interference in the lives of the people and show how apparent weakness and humility can become all-powerful forces. [13]

WHY ARE THE people starving?
Because the rulers eat up the money in taxes.
Therefore the people are starving.

Why are the people rebellious?
Because the rulers interfere too much.
Therefore they are rebellious.
(chapter seventy-five)

The hard and strong will fall.
The soft and weak will overcome.
(chapter seventy-six)

Under heaven nothing is more soft and yielding than water.
Yet for attacking the solid and strong, nothing is better;
It has no equal.
The weak can overcome the strong;
The supple can overcome the stiff.
Under heaven everyone knows this,
Yet no one puts it into practice.
(chapter seventy-eight)

> These ideas have, in turn, influenced Chinese society down through the centuries.
>
> Many of the anti-Confucian ideas noted above were incorporated in the great medieval Chinese epics which dealt with peasant rebellions. These novels, notably *The Three Kingdoms* and *Outlaws of the Marsh*, are among the most widely-known works of Chinese literature and were an inspiration to Chinese revolutionaries during the nineteenth and twentieth centuries. The following is an excerpt from *The Three Kingdoms*: [14]

THE REBELS WERE known as the Yellow Scarves. Their leader was Chang Chüeh, a man who had failed the official examinations and retired to the hills to gather healing herbs. There he had met an ancient mystic, emerald-eyed and young of face, leaning on a staff of goosefoot wood. The mystic led Chang Chüeh into a cavern and handed him three sacred texts.

"These are called the *Essential Arts for the Age of Equality*," the old man had said. "Now that you have them, propagate their teachings as Heaven's messenger to promote universal salvation. Use them for any other purpose and retribution will follow." With that, the old man transformed himself into a breath of crystal air and vanished.

Chang Chüeh had attacked the text. He learned to summon the winds and invoke the rain and came to be called Dao-Master for the Age of Equality. When pestilence spread through the land, he traveled far and wide curing the afflicted with charms and potions. He styled himself Great Worthy and Good Doctor, and his followers, numbering over five hundred, bound up their heads with yellow scarves. They were as mobile as the clouds, and all could write the charms and recite the spells.

As his following grew, Chang Chüeh set up thirty-six commands under his chieftains and began to prepare an insurrection against the Han. He and his two brothers assumed patriarchal titles and told their people: "The Han's fated end is near. A mighty sage emerges. Let one and all, in obedience to Heaven, in true allegiance, strive for the Age of Equality."

> Thus, concepts of equality, universality and insurrection, as well as elements of Daoism, were all combined in one of the most popular books ever written in China.

The Legacy of the Nineteenth and Twentieth Centuries

Editor's Introduction: The Opium War opened a new chapter in the history of China. Many view it as the beginning of modern Chinese history. The defeat of China by the British not only meant that the country was opened up, for the first time, to European exploitation, but that Chinese economic and social relationships began to change. In addition, in the years after the war the strength of the anti-Confucianist counter-tradition began to grow and movements demanding radical change sprung up throughout China. The Communist Revolution of 1949 was the ultimate step of a century-long process.

As a result of the Treaty of Nanking (1842) that ended the Opium War, the British took control of Hong Kong, received an indemnity of 21 million silver dollars, gained access to five Chinese ports for trade, controlled Chinese tariffs, and gained the right of extraterritoriality.* In addition, apart from the treaty, they expanded their importation of opium to China. The following selection is from a 1976 booklet compiled by historians at Fudan University, in Shanghai, and Shanghai Teachers' University. [15]

CHINA'S DEFEAT IN the Opium War and the conclusion of the Treaty of Nanking had enormous consequences, as from then on China had lost its independence and significant changes occurred within its society. Under the increasingly violent impact of foreign capitalism, China's self-sufficient natural economy gradually disintegrated, while large numbers of peasants and handicraftsmen were bankrupted. To the contradiction between feudalism and the masses of people, the principal contradiction in Chinese society, was

---

* Extraterritoriality meant that British citizens accused of a crime in China would be tried under British, not Chinese, law. Special European courts were established in the treaty ports for those cases.

now added the contradiction between foreign capitalism and the Chinese nation. Step by step China became a semi-colonial and semi-feudal society. As the contradiction between imperialism and the Chinese nation and that between feudalism and the masses of people sharpened, class relationships and class struggle in Chinese society underwent an unprecedented change....

After the war, the Ching [Qing] government squeezed the people in every possible way in order to pay the cost of the war expenses and the indemnities, the two items totaling 70 million silver dollars. Public administration became more corrupt than ever as extra levies and extortion by officials at every level multiplied. The despotic gentry and landlords worked closely with the authorities to shift their own burden on to the peasants. Under merciless political oppression and heavy economic exploitation, the masses of people finally rose in revolt. In the *Tung Hua Lu (Annals of the Ching [Qing] Dynasty)* alone, more than 100 uprisings are mentioned. They were staged by the Han, Hui, Miao, Tibetan, Yi, Yao, Chuang and other nationalities between 1841 and 1849, and extended over almost the whole country. Many secret organizations, such as the Nien, the Fu, and the Tien Ti Hui (Heaven and Earth Society), became active among the people. All this foreshadowed the great revolutionary upheaval which was to shake the land of China.

> That upheaval was the Taiping Rebellion, or, as it is known in China, the Taiping Revolution.
>
> The Taipings were not merely rebels who wanted to change the government. They wanted to "turn over" Confucianism and the social, political and economic systems that supported it. Preaching equality, communal property and a form of Christianity, the Taipings started out as a small band of revolutionaries in Southern China in 1850. Over the next few years they organized a powerful and disciplined army, gained millions of followers, and won control over much of southern and central China. Although eventually weakened and then destroyed (1864) by their own disunity and corruption as well as by the military opposition of the British and the French (who supported the Chinese government), the Taipings carried out a revolutionary program for over a decade. Their socialist and utopian vision inspired Communist revolutionaries in the twentieth century, many of whom had roots in areas of China that had once been dominated by the Taipings and grew up learning of their exploits.
>
> The following is an excerpt from "The Land System of the Heavenly Dynasty," an official Taiping document written in 1853, that proposed an economic and governmental system for the areas the Taipings controlled. [16]

THE DIVISION OF land must be according to the number of individuals, whether male or female; calculating upon the number of individuals in a household, if they be numerous, then the amount of land will be larger, and if few, smaller; and it shall be a mixture of the nine classes. If there are six persons in a family, then for three there shall be good land and for three poorer land, and of good and poor each shall have half. All the fields in the empire are to be cultivated by all the people alike. If the land is deficient in one place, then the people must be removed to another, and if the land is deficient in another, then the people must be removed to this place. All the fields throughout the empire, whether of abundant or deficient harvest, shall be taken as a whole: if this place is deficient, then the harvest of that abundant place must be removed to relieve it, and if that place is deficient, then the harvest of this abundant place must be removed in order to relieve the deficient place; thus, all the people in the empire may together enjoy the abundant happiness of the Heavenly Father, Supreme Lord and Great God. There being fields, let all cultivate them; there being food, let all eat; there being clothes, let all be dressed; there being money, let all use it, so that nowhere does inequality exist, and no man is not well fed and clothed.

All men and women, every individual of sixteen years and upwards, shall receive land, twice as much as those of fifteen years of age and under. . . .

At the time of harvest, every sergeant shall direct the corporals to see to it that of the twenty-five families under his charge each individual has a sufficient supply of food, and aside from the new grain each may receive, the remainder must be deposited in the public granary. Of wheat, pulse, hemp, flax, cloth, silk, fowls, dogs, etc., and money, the same is true; for the whole empire is the universal family of our Heavenly Father, the Supreme Lord and Great God. When all the people in the empire will not take anything as their own but submit all things to the Supreme Lord, then the Lord will make use of them, and in the universal family of the empire, every place will be equal and every individual well fed and clothed. This is the intent of our Heavenly Father, the Supreme Lord and Great God, in specially commanding the true Sovereign of Taiping to save the world. . . .

This one rule is applicable throughout the empire. In the use of all things let there be economy, to provide against war and famine. As for marriages in the empire, wealth should not be a consideration.

> The struggle to transform China continued, in muted form, throughout the nineteenth century, although it was not until the twentieth century that a mass movement for change was reconstituted.
>
> The event that sparked the revived revolutionary movement in China was the decision of the participants at the Versailles Peace

Conference (1919), who drafted the peace treaty at the end of World War I, to transfer to Japan land in Shandong province held by Germany before the war. China had declared war on Germany in 1917 and the Chinese people had expected China to regain control of the area after the war. They were enraged at their betrayal by both the great powers at Versailles as well as by their own government, which they learned had secretly agreed to the transfer in 1918. When news of the Versailles decision was made public, students from 13 colleges and universities in Beijing held a mass protest demonstration on May 4, 1919 in Tiananmen Square, denouncing the treaty and the government and demanding political and social reforms. Protests, including strikes and boycotts, spread immediately throughout the country and participants included workers and businessmen as well as students and intellectuals. The demonstrations, soon known as the May Fourth Movement, meshed with and enhanced the New Culture Movement. Begun several years earlier, that movement of intellectuals attacked Confucian values and advocated the adoption of the Western concepts of science and democracy in order to build a strong, free, and independent China.

The May Fourth Movement had a galvanizing effect on Chinese intellectuals, many of whom founded new radical cultural and political organizations. One of these, the Chinese Communist Party, was established in 1921. Hundreds of new journals and newspapers criticized traditional values and spread the ideas of the counter-culture. Chen Duxiu was one of the most important leaders of the Movement. An iconoclastic Beijing intellectual, he had founded the radical magazine *New Youth* (1915) and was widely known for his attacks against Confucian values and his advocacy of Western science and democracy. He subsequently became the first general secretary of the Chinese Communist Party in 1921, but was purged in 1927. The following excerpts from his works represent the spirit of the May Fourth Movement. [17]

CRITICS ACCUSED THIS magazine *[New Youth]* … of intending to destroy Confucianism, the code of rituals, the "national quintessence," chastity of women, traditional ethics (loyalty, filial piety, and chastity), traditional arts (the Chinese opera), traditional religion (ghosts and gods), and ancient literature, as well as old fashioned politics (privilege and government by men alone).

All of these charges are conceded. But we plead not guilty. We have committed the alleged crimes only because we supported the two gentlemen, Mr.

Democracy and Mr. Science. In order to advocate Mr. Democracy, we are obliged to oppose Confucianism, the codes of rituals, chastity of women, traditional ethics, and old-fashioned politics; in order to advocate Mr. Science, we have to oppose traditional arts and traditional religion; and in order to advocate both Mr. Democracy and Mr. Science, we are compelled to oppose the cult of the "national quintessence" and ancient literature. Let us then ponder dispassionately: has this magazine committed any crimes other than advocating Mr. Democracy and Mr. Science? If not, please do not solely reprove this magazine: the only way for you to be heroic and solve the problem fundamentally is to oppose the two gentlemen, Mr. Democracy and Mr. Science.

*   *   *

THE CHINESE COMPLIMENT OTHERS by saying, "He acts like an old man although still young." Englishmen and Americans encourage one another by saying, "Keep young while growing old." Such is one respect in which the different ways of thought of the East and West are manifested. Youth is like early spring, like the rising sun, like trees and grass in bud, like a newly sharpened blade. It is the most valuable period of life. The function of youth in society is the same as that of a fresh and vital cell in a human body. In the processes of metabolism, the old and the rotten are incessantly eliminated to be replaced by the fresh and the living. . . . If metabolism functions properly in a human body, the person will be healthy; if the old and rotten cells accumulate and fill the body, the person will die. If metabolism functions properly in a society, it will flourish; if old and rotten elements fill the society, then it will cease to exist. . . .

1. Be independent, not servile
All men are equal. Each has his right to be independent, but absolutely no right to enslave others nor any obligation to make himself servile. By slavery we mean that in ancient times the ignorant and weak lost their right of freedom, which was savagely usurped by tyrants. Since the rise of the theories of the rights of man and of equality, no red-blooded person can endure the name of slave. . . .

Emancipation means freeing oneself from the bondage of slavery and achieving a completely independent and free personality. I have hands and feet, and I can earn my own living. I have a mouth and a tongue, and I can voice my own likes and dislikes. I have a mind, and I can determine my own beliefs. I will absolutely not let others do these things on my behalf, nor should I assume an overlordship and enslave others. For once the inde-

pendent personality is recognized, all matters of conduct, all rights and privi-
leges, and all belief should be left to the natural ability of each person; there
is definitely no reason why one should blindly follow others. On the other
hand, loyalty, filial piety, chastity and righteousness are a slavish morality. . . .

2. *Be progressive, not conservative*

"Without progress there will be retrogression" is an old Chinese saying.
Considering the fundamental laws of the universe, all things or phenomena
are daily progressing in evolution, and the maintenance of the status quo is
definitely out of the question; only the limitation of man's ordinary view has
rendered possible the differentiation between the two states of things.

. . . All our traditional ethics, law, scholarship, rites and customs are sur-
vivals of feudalism. When compared with the achievement of the white race,
there is a difference of a thousand years in thought, although we live in the
same period. Revering only the history of the twenty-four dynasties and
making no plans for progress and improvement, our people will be turned
out of this twentieth-century world, and be lodged in the dark ditches fit
only for slaves, cattle and horses. . . . The progress of the world is like that
of a fleet horse, galloping and galloping onward. Whatever cannot skillfully
change itself and progress along with the world will find itself eliminated by
natural selection because of failure to adapt to the environment. Then what
can be said to defend conservatism!

*   *   *

DESTROY! DESTROY THE IDOLS! Destroy the idols of hypocrisy! My
beliefs are based on true and reasonable standards. The religious, political,
and moral beliefs transmitted from ancient times are vain, deceptive, and
unreasonable. They are all idols and must be destroyed! If we do not destroy
them, universal truth and our own heartfelt beliefs will never be united.

> *Editor's Postscript:* By the 1920s rural China was still dominated by a
> gentry class and Confucian values. However both were coming under
> increasing attack. The government was weak, the country was divid-
> ed as regional warlords exerted great power, and, after 1927, civil war
> raged between Nationalist and Communist forces. In the 1930s
> China was invaded by Japan. It was amidst these chaotic circum-
> stances that the Communist Party under Mao Zedong became a
> national force and began to "turn over" China.

PART IV
THE ERA OF MAO ZEDONG

Introduction

From the Long March in the 1930s through the turmoil of the 1970s, Mao Zedong was the dominant figure in the Chinese Communist Party. As early as the mid-1920s he tried, unsuccessfully, to reorient the Party towards the peasantry and away from its proletarian roots. His views, though, ultimately prevailed and after he assumed Party leadership in 1935 he led a movement, the foremost goal of which was the liberation of the Chinese from both domestic oppression and foreign exploitation.

When the Communists finally triumphed and established the Peoples' Republic of China in October 1949, they faced an immense task. Agricultural production had been disrupted not only by warfare but also by the struggle to redistribute the land which had been the cornerstone of Communist policy during their rise to power. The urban economy had stagnated under conditions of insecurity and mismanagement. Money had become worthless as policies of the previous Nationalist government under Chiang K'ai-shek led to uncontrolled inflation.

Poverty, ignorance and disease were endemic. Sanitation had broken down and disease was rampant. Malnutrition affected more than half the population. Opium addiction and venereal disease, a legacy of foreign imperialism, were major problems. Illegal secret societies and criminal rackets flourished during the years of political degeneration. The task of reconstruction was complicated for the Communists by the fact that in two decades of struggle with the Nationalists they had never controlled a major city. Suddenly, they had to manage the largest society on earth.

Their early successes were remarkable. By the end of 1952 they had thrown unwanted foreigners out of China for the first time in a century, stopped civil strife, carried out land reform and increased agricultural production to previously unattained levels, ended inflation, reactivated industry and commerce, initiated highly successful campaigns to wipe out epidemic diseases, brought criminal elements under control, and virtually eliminated prostitution, venereal disease and opium addiction. All this was accomplished through a combination of force, persuasion, and the willing cooperation of millions who welcomed the restoration of peace, productivity and national autonomy.

This does not mean the Communists had solved all of China's problems. China specialists often disagree about the effectiveness of various economic measures, or the justice of social reforms, or the ethics of the political system, and so on. And in China itself there had been an intense, sometimes violent, struggle to determine what the future course should be.

In this complex struggle involving many issues, two main groups emerged. One side favored class conflict and the other side class harmony. Mao Zedong, the leader of the first group, believed that China must engage in a continual struggle against the elite classes if it ever hoped to achieve the Communist goal of an egalitarian society. He especially called for constant vigilance and mass criticism of those in authority who were not directly serving the interests of the masses. Moreover, he advocated class discrimination in favor of the peasants and workers rather than the elites who run the country. Only through constant class struggle, Mao felt, could Marx's vision of a classless society be realized.

On the other side were those who favored class harmony, following the lead of Liu Shaoqi and Deng Xiaoping. The supporters of this line criticized Mao's emphasis on class struggle because, they said, it creates chaos, uncertainty and anxiety, making it difficult if not impossible, for the leaders to lead. Also, they pointed out, it discriminates unjustly against the children of the old ruling classes and against the intellectuals who traditionally served as China's ruling elite. This faction argued that mental workers are also workers, and that all citizens can contribute more effectively to socialism in China if they are free of the constant pressure of class struggle, provided of course that they follow Party guidelines.

Mao launched the Cultural Revolution in 1966 (see page 143 and page 167) to advance his increasingly revolutionary vision of society. After his death his ideological opponents, led by Deng Xiaoping, took power and, again, remolded China. However, for almost 30 years Mao's philosophy prevailed. Mao's leadership not only produced a Communist victory but it also led to a social, economic and political revolution that changed, for several decades, almost every aspect of Chinese life: ideology and religion; the status of women and the family; land ownership; and the role of peasants and workers in politics.

The Peasant as Revolutionary

Editor's Introduction: More than any other leader, Mao Zedong was responsible for shifting the focus of the Chinese Communist Party from the urban workers to the rural peasantry. From the mid-1920s Mao was convinced that the peasants were the most revolutionary force in China and that the Communist Party must concentrate its efforts in the countryside. His views were solidified after spending a month in rural Hunan Province in early 1927 and witnessing the extent of peasant radicalism. The following is an excerpt from his "Report on an Investigation of the Peasant Movement in Hunan" which he presented to the Communist Party in March 1927. Although his analysis represented a minority position at the time, it became the dominant position of the Communists when he became leader of the Party in 1935. [18]

DURING MY RECENT visit to Hunan I made a first-hand investigation of conditions in the five counties of Hsiangtan, Hsianghsiang, Hengshan, Liling, and Changsha. In the thirty-two days from January 4 to February 5, I called together fact-finding conferences in villages and county towns which were attended by experienced peasants and by comrades working in the peasant movement, and I listened attentively to their reports and collected a great deal of material. Many of the hows and whys of the peasant movement were the exact opposite of what the gentry in Hankow and Changsha are saying. I saw and heard of many strange things of which I had hitherto been unaware. I believe the same is true of many other places, too. All talk directed against the peasant movement must be speedily set right. All the wrong measures taken by the revolutionary authorities concerning the peasant movement must be speedily changed. Only thus can the future of the revolution be benefited. For the present upsurge of the peasant movement is a colossal event.

In a very short time, in China's Central, Southern, and Northern provinces, several hundred million peasants will rise like a mighty storm, like a hurricane, a force so swift and violent that no power, however great, will be able to hold it back. They will smash all the trammels that bind them and rush forward along the road to liberation. They will sweep all the imperialists, warlords, corrupt officials, local tyrants, and evil gentry into their graves. Every revolutionary party and every revolutionary comrade will be put to the test, to be accepted or rejected as they decide. There are three alternatives. To march at their head and lead them? To trail behind them, gesticulating and criticizing? Or to stand in their way and oppose them? Every Chinese is free to choose, but events will force you to make the choice quickly.

GET ORGANIZED!

The development of the peasant movement in Hunan may be divided roughly into two periods with respect to the counties in the province's central and southern parts where the movement has already made much headway. The first, from January to September of last year, was one of organization. In this period, January to June was a time of underground activity, and July to September, when the revolutionary army was driving out Chao Heng-ti, one of open activity. During this period, the membership of the peasant associations did not exceed 300,000 to 400,000, the masses directly under their leadership numbered little more than a million, there was as yet hardly any struggle in the rural areas, and consequently there was very little criticism of the associations in other circles. Since its members served as guides, scouts, and carriers of the Northern Expeditionary Army, even some of the officers had a good word to say for the peasant associations. The second period, from last October to January of this year, was one of revolutionary action. The membership of the associations jumped to two million and the masses directly under their leadership increased to ten million. Since the peasants generally enter only one name for the whole family on joining a peasant association, a membership of two million means a mass following of about ten million. Almost half the peasants in Hunan are now organized.

"It's Terrible" or
"It's Fine"

Editor's Introduction: The "turnover" of a village such as Stone Wall Village (see page 11), was often accompanied by violence against landlords or officials. Were the rage and violence of the peasants of Stone Wall Village necessary? Were they just? The answer depends on one's conception of necessity and justice. "Necessary" for what? "Just" by what standards?

People and nations through the ages have tried to justify violence. The bloodiest wars in history have been fought in the name of justice, freedom, religion, even love.

The revolutionary must weigh the violence of overturning the old society against the violence of keeping it. In traditional China, for centuries there was at least one famine a year, on the average, in some part of the country. A famine in northwest China from 1928 to 1930 killed an estimated three to six million people. In 1943 alone, a famine in one province, Henan, killed three million. While some people were dying, others were hoarding grain. While some peasants sold their land and even their children for the price of a meal, unscrupulous landlords took advantage of the low prices to get rich.

The Communists and their supporters would argue that they were able to alleviate many social problems only because there was a violent revolution. Mao Zedong, the leader of that revolution, worked for years to overturn the landlord system. He wrote "It's Terrible" or "It's Fine" in 1927, in the very early stages of the land revolution addressing the phenomenon of revolutionary violence. [19]

THE PEASANTS' REVOLT disturbed the gentry's sweet dreams. When the news from the countryside reached the cities, it caused immediate uproar among the gentry. Soon after my arrival in Changsha, I met all sorts of peo-

Mao Zedong talking to peasants in the 1930s.

ple and picked up a good deal of gossip. From the middle social strata upwards to the . . . right-wingers, there was not a single person who did not sum up the whole business in the phrase "It's terrible!" Under the impact of the views of the "It's terrible!" school then flooding the city, even quite revolutionary-minded people became downhearted as they pictured the events in the countryside in their mind's eye; and they were unable to deny the word "terrible." Even quite progressive people said, "Though terrible, it is inevitable in a revolution." In short, nobody could altogether deny the word "terrible."

But . . . the fact is that the great peasant masses have risen to fulfill their historic mission, and that the forces of rural democracy have risen to overthrow the forces of rural feudalism. . . . This is a marvelous feat never before achieved, not . . . in thousands of years. It's fine. It is not "terrible" at all. It is anything but "terrible." "It's terrible!" is obviously a theory for combating the rise of the peasants in the interests of the landlords; it is obviously a theory of the landlord class for preserving the old order of feudalism and obstructing the establishment of the new order of democracy, it is obviously a counterrevolutionary theory. No revolutionary comrade should echo this nonsense.

If your revolutionary viewpoint is firmly established and if you have been to the villages and looked around, you will undoubtedly feel thrilled as never before. Countless thousands of the enslaved—the peasants—are striking down the enemies who battened on their flesh. What the peasants are doing is absolutely right; what they are doing is fine! "It's fine!" is the theory of the peasants and of all other revolutionaries.

Every revolutionary comrade should know that the national revolution requires a great change in the countryside. The Revolution of 1911 [which overthrew the 2000-year-old imperial system and attempted to establish a republic] did not bring about this change; hence its failure. This change is now taking place, and it is an important factor for the completion of the revolution. Every revolutionary comrade must support it, or he will be taking the stand of counterrevolution.

THE QUESTION OF "GOING TOO FAR"

Then there is another section of people who say, "Yes, peasant associations are necessary, but they are going rather too far." This is the opinion of the middle-of-the-roaders. But what is the actual situation?

True, the peasants are in a sense "unruly" in the countryside. Supreme in authority, the peasant association allows the landlord no say and sweeps away his prestige. This amounts to striking the landlord down to the dust and keeping him there. The peasants threaten, "We will put you in the other register!"* They fine the local tyrants and evil gentry, they demand contributions from them, and they smash their sedan-chairs. People swarm into the houses of local tyrants and evil gentry who are against the peasant association, slaughter their pigs, and consume their grain. They even loll for a minute or two on the ivory-inlaid beds belonging to the young ladies in these households. . . . At the slightest provocation, they make arrests, crown the arrested with tall paper hats, and parade them through the villages, saying, "You dirty landlords, now you know who we are!" Doing whatever they like and turning everything upside down, they have created a kind of terror in the countryside. This is what some people call "going too far," or "exceeding the proper limits in righting a wrong," or "really too much."

Such talk may seem plausible, but in fact it is wrong, First, the local tyrants, evil gentry, and lawless landlords have themselves driven the peasants to this. For ages they have used their power to tyrannize the peasants and trample them underfoot; that is why the peasants have reacted so strongly. The most violent revolts and the most serious disorders have invariably

---

* To be regarded as a recalcitrant.

occurred in places where the local tyrants, evil gentry, and lawless landlords perpetrated the worst outrages.

The peasants are clear-sighted. Who is bad and who is not, who is the worst and who is not quite so vicious, who deserves severe punishment and who deserves to be let off lightly—the peasants keep clear accounts, and very seldom has the punishment exceeded the crime.

Second, a revolution is not a dinner party, or writing an essay, or painting a picture, or doing embroidery; it cannot be so refined, so leisurely and gentle, so temperate, kind, courteous, restrained, and magnanimous. A revolution is an insurrection, an act of violence by which one class overthrows another. A rural revolution is a revolution by which the peasantry overthrows the power of the feudal landlord class. Without using the greatest force, the peasants cannot possibly overthrow the deep-rooted authority of the landlords, which has lasted for thousands of years. The rural areas need a mighty revolutionary upsurge, for it alone can rouse the people in their millions to become a powerful force.

The Long March

Editor's Introduction: Twenty-two years elapsed between the time Mao wrote "'It's Terrible' or 'It's Fine'" and the Communist conquest of China in 1949. Conditions were right for the Communist movement, but the road to power was not without its twists, turns, and detours.

The Communist Party of China was founded in 1921. It grew slowly in the 1920s, but it did not develop large-scale mass support until the early 1930s, when Mao Zedong and General Zhu De (Chu Te) established a base in a rural area in south-central China and began to redistribute land.

The Nationalist government, which supported the landlords, turned all its might against the Communists and, after five "extermination campaigns," managed to drive them from their base area in 1934. Those Communists, often estimated to number 80,000 to 100,000, who escaped the Nationalist attack embarked on a 6,000-mile trek, which is now called "the Long March."

The Long March was the turning point in the Chinese Communist movement. Against enormous odds, the Communists marched and fought their way to a safe area in northwest China. In 368 days, an army of tens of thousands with all its equipment covered an average of almost twenty-four miles per day when on the move. They crossed eighteen mountain ranges, five of them perennially snow-capped, and sixty-two rivers. All the while, they fought an average of a skirmish a day and spent fifteen whole days fighting major battles.

In every area they passed through, they publicized their movement in mass meetings and theatrical performances. More important, they redistributed the land and other property of the landlords to the poor peasants, leaving in their wake thousands of armed peasants and cadres to train guerrilla forces.

The Communists emerged from the Long March with heavy losses, but confident that they had passed the severest of tests and that nothing could prevent their ultimate victory. Today the Long March is celebrated in song and story as the great epic of the Communists' rise to power. It represents a triumph of human will and endurance in overcoming the most difficult obstacles.

Numerous accounts of the March have been collected and widely publicized in China. In the one that follows, a Communist regimental commander who participated in the action recalls the crucial battle for the Lu-ting Bridge, which crosses the swift Ta-tu River. Had the Communists not captured the bridge, they almost surely would have been trapped and destroyed by Chiang K'ai-shek's troops. As the narrative begins, the Communist troops on one side of the Ta-tu River are racing some of Chiang K'ai-shek's troops (the enemy in the story) on the other. Each army is trying to reach the Lu-ting Bridge first. [20]

SUDDENLY A FEW flickering lights appeared on the opposite side of the river. The next moment, they grew into a long string of torches. The enemy troops were making a forced march by torchlight! I immediately conferred with our regimental commander, our chief of staff, and our Party secretary. We decided that we, too, would carry torches. Should the enemy signal across the river and ask us to identify ourselves, we would pretend we were the three enemy battalions we had already defeated. We directed our bugler to be prepared to sound the calls used by the enemy. Since the enemy troops were all [from the province of Szechuan (Sichuan)], we picked some Szechuan (Sichuan) men from our own ranks and from the prisoners to shout back replies to any questions.

We bought reeds from the folks in the hamlet, made torches, and issued one to each man, with instructions that they were not to be wasted.

Our aim was to cover at least three miles per hour. I had a leg wound that was causing me some inconvenience, and the comrades, especially the regimental commander, urged me to continue on horseback. But I decided it was my duty as an officer to set an example. Instead of riding, I issued a challenge, "We will all march together, comrades. Let's see who walks the fastest. Let's see who gets to the Lu-ting Bridge first!"

Taking up the challenge, the men held their torches high and pressed forward.

Torchlight crimsoned the waters of the Ta-tu. Our lights and those of the enemy writhed along the riverbanks like two fiery dragons.

The sharp notes of an enemy bugle rang out, followed by the cry, "Which unit are you?" Our bugler blew the necessary call, and our Szechuan (Sichuan) men shouted a reply. The enemy was fooled. They never suspected that the gallant Red Army they hoped to wipe out was marching parallel with them.

They stayed with us for almost ten miles. Around midnight, the rain grew heavier, and the torches on the opposite bank disappeared. We guessed they had found the going too hard and encamped. The news spread quickly through the regiment, causing many comments among the men: "This is our chance! March on! Faster!" In single file, we pushed on for all we were worth.

The rain pelted down mercilessly and the mountain gullies turned into rushing torrents. The twisting path became as slippery as oil, so that our walking staffs were of little use. We could not march; we slipped and slithered, scrambled and crawled along. And when we came to an even stretch, the weary men would doze off as they walked. A soldier would come to a halt and the comrade behind would push him and yell, "Keep going! Keep going!" The man would awaken and hurry to catch up. Finally the men took off their puttees [leg wrappings] and tied themselves together in a long chain.

In this way we kept up the forced march all night and reached our destination on time. In twenty-four hours, in addition to fighting and repairing wrecked bridges, we had covered eighty miles. This was truly an exploit of winged feet.

We first captured the west bank and the western approaches to the Lu-ting Bridge. Having occupied several buildings and a Catholic church, our men prepared for the coming battle. Regimental Commander Wang and I went out with the battalion and company officers to study the situation. We were taken aback by the difficulties to be overcome. The river's reddish waters cascaded down the mountain gorges of the upper reaches and pounded against ugly boulders in midstream, tossing white foam high into the air. The roar of the rushing water was deafening. Fording or crossing in boats was out of the question.

We examined the bridge. It was made of iron chains, thirteen in number, each link as thick as a rice bowl. Two chains on each side served as hand-railings; the other nine formed a catwalk. Planks had originally been laid across these, but they had been taken by the enemy, leaving only the black chains hanging in mid-air.

At the head of the bridge, on a stone slab, two lines from a poem were inscribed:

Towering mountains flank the Lu-ting Bridge,
Their summits rise a hundred miles into the clouds.

Storming the Lu-ting Bridge over the Ta-tu River. Oil painting.

The city of Lu-ting lay directly beyond the eastern end of the bridge. It was built half along the shore and half on the mountain slope and was surrounded by a wall over twenty feet high. The west gate of this wall was just past the end of the bridge. The city was garrisoned by two enemy regiments, and strong fortifications had been built along the mountainside. Machine-gun emplacements close to the bridge kept us under continual fire, and mortar shells rained down on us.

The enemy was confident that this position was impregnable. "Let's see you fly across!" they yelled. "We'll give up our arms if you can do it!"

Our soldiers shouted back: "We don't want your arms. We want your bridge!"

Back from our reconnaissance, we first positioned a battalion to cover the path on the other side of the river. That was the only way enemy reinforcements could come. Then we went round our companies to begin the battle rallies. Morale was high. Each company submitted a list of volunteers for an assault party, and each wanted to be given the honor of taking the bridge. . . .

The attack began at four o'clock in the afternoon. The regimental commander and I directed it from the west end of the bridge. The buglers gathered together to sound the charge, and we opened up with every weapon we had. The sound of the bugles, the firing, and the shouts of the men reverberated through the valley.

Then the twenty-two heroes, led by Commander Liao, climbed out cross the swaying chains in the teeth of intense enemy fire. Each man carried a tommy gun, a broadsword, and twelve hand grenades. Behind them came the officers and men of the Third Company, each carrying a heavy plank as well as full battle gear. They fought and laid planks at the same time.

Just as the assault force reached the eastern bridgehead, huge flames sprang into the sky outside the city gate. The enemy was trying to throw a wall of fire across our path. The blaze licked fiercely around the end of the bridge.

The outcome of the attack was hanging by a hair. The assault squad hesitated for a few seconds, then plunged boldly into the flames.

Commander Liao's cap caught fire, but he threw it away and fought on. The others also dashed through the flames and smashed their way into the city. In the street fighting that followed, the enemy brought their full weight to bear against our gallant force. Our men fought until all their ammunition was spent. There was a critical pause as the Third Company came charging to their rescue. Then Regimental Commander Wang and I sped across the bridge with our reinforcements and entered the city.

In two hours, we had destroyed over half of the enemy's two regiments, and the remainder broke ranks and scattered, By dusk we had completely occupied the city of Lu-ting and were in control of the bridge. . . .

General Liu examined every detail of the iron chains as if he were trying to memorize the entire bridge. On the way back, he stopped in the middle and leaned over the side chains to look down on the turbulent waters of the Ta-tu below. Tapping his foot on the boards, he murmured, "We've spent plenty of blood and energy to get you, Lu-ting Bridge, but we've got you!"

The following day, Commander Lin Piao (Biao) marched up with our main force. . . . Then Chairman Mao arrived, and thousands of our troops marched across the Lu-ting Bridge. We had conquered the seething barrier of the Ta-tu River.

Editor's Postscript: The Communists arrived in northwest China after the Long March with fewer than 20,000 men. They occupied an area that was easy to defend but sparsely populated, and noted for its poverty. Fewer than one million people lived in the Communist area in early 1937. But in 1949, only twelve years later, the Communists controlled the whole China mainland. Only Taiwan (Formosa) and a few other islands remained in the hands of Chiang K'ai-shek and the former government of China.

The success of the Communists can be explained by a number of factors. The war with Japan from 1937 to 1945 disrupted the country. And during the war, Chiang K'ai-shek's government became corrupt and inefficient. But the main reason for the Communist victory is summarized in a few words from a study made by the U.S. War Department (now called the Department of Defense) in 1945:

> Practically all impartial observers emphasized that the Chinese Communists comprise the most efficient, politically well-organized, disciplined, and constructive group in China today. This opinion is well supported by facts. It is largely because of their political and military skill, superior organization, and progressive attitude, which has won for them a popular support no other party or group in China can equal, that they have been expanding their influence throughout the past seven years.*

---

* Lyman P. Van Slyke, ed., *The Chinese Communist Movement, A Report of the U.S. War Department, July 1945*, Stanford: Stanford University Press, 1968, pp. 7-8.

Maoist Ethics: The "Three Constantly Read Articles"

Editor's Introduction: The "progressive attitude" attributed to the Communists by the U.S. War Department study in 1945 is illustrated in "The Three Constantly Read Articles," all of which were written by Mao Zedong in the 1930s and 1940s. The Communists were convinced that a genuine and lasting revolution would depend not only on institutional change, such as land reform, but also on a change in the way people think. Like their Confucian predecessors, the Communists were very concerned with thought, for they believed that ideas and action are closely related. "Correct" ideas will lead to "correct" actions and vice versa. In the past, as in the present, there has been a single orthodoxy in China with little tolerance for deviation.

The values expressed by Mao in the "Three Constantly Read Articles" are both a product of, and a departure from, traditional Chinese ethics. The Chinese have always rejected individualism, so valued in the West, considering it synonymous with selfishness. The selfless, collective ethic espoused by Mao is also found in the family ethic of traditional China. Mao simply extended it to a broader social context, but in so doing he signaled a monumental change.

The three short pieces in this chapter were chosen by Mao Zedong from the hundreds of articles he had written as most representative of the values which he hoped would provide the guidelines for the new China. Originally addressed to members of the Communist Party, they later became essential reading for a nation. [21]

SERVE THE PEOPLE
September 8, 1944

IF WE HAVE shortcomings, we are not afraid to have them pointed out and criticized, because we serve the people. Anyone, no matter who, may point out our shortcomings. If he is right, we will correct them. If what he proposes will benefit the people, we will act upon it. . . .

If, in the interests of the people, we persist in doing what is right and correct what is wrong, our ranks will surely thrive.

We hail from all corners of the country and have joined together for a common revolutionary objective. And we need the vast majority of the people with us on the road to this objective. Today, we already lead base areas with a population of 91 million, but this is not enough; to liberate the whole nation more are needed. In times of difficulty we must not lose sight of our achievements, must see the bright future and must pluck up our courage. The Chinese people are suffering; it is our duty to save them and we must exert ourselves in struggle. Wherever there is struggle there is sacrifice, and death is a common occurrence.

But we have the interests of the people and the sufferings of the great majority at heart, and when we die for the people it is a worthy death. Nevertheless, we should do our best to avoid unnecessary sacrifices. Our cadres must show concern for every soldier, and all people in the revolutionary ranks must care for each other, must love and help each other. . . .

IN MEMORY OF NORMAN BETHUNE
December 21, 1939

Comrade Norman Bethune, a member of the Communist Party of Canada, was around fifty when he was sent by the Communist parties of Canada and the United States to China; he made light of traveling thousands of miles to help us in our War of Resistance against Japan. He arrived in Yenan in the spring of last year, went to work in the Wutai Mountains, and to our great sorrow died a martyr at his post.

What kind of spirit is this that makes a foreigner selflessly adopt the cause of the Chinese people's liberation as his own? It is the spirit of internationalism, the spirit of communism, from which every Chinese Communist must learn. . . .

Comrade Bethune's spirit, his utter devotion to others without any thought of self, was shown in his boundless sense of responsibility in his work and his boundless warmheartedness toward all comrades and the people. Every Communist must learn from him. There are not a few people who are irresponsible in their work, preferring the light to the heavy, shoving the heavy loads on to others and choosing the easy ones for themselves. At every turn they think of themselves before others. When they make some small contribution, they swell with pride and brag about it for fear that others will not know. They feel no warmth toward comrades and the people but are cold, indifferent, and apathetic. In fact such people are not Communists, or at least cannot be counted as true Communists. No one who returned from the front failed to express admiration for Bethune whenever his name was mentioned, and none remained unmoved by his spirit. . . . Every Communist must learn this true communist spirit from Comrade Bethune.

Comrade Bethune was a doctor, the art of healing was his profession, and he was constantly perfecting his skill, which stood very high in the 8th Route Army's medical service. His example is an excellent lesson for those people who wish to change their work the moment they see something different, and for those who despise technical work as of no consequence or as promising no future.

Comrade Bethune and I met only once. Afterward he wrote me many letters. But I was busy, and I wrote him only one letter and do not even know if he ever received it. I am deeply grieved over his death. Now we are all commemorating him, which shows how profoundly his spirit inspires everyone. We must all learn the spirit of absolute selflessness from him. With this spirit everyone can be very useful to the people. A man's ability may be great or small, but if he has this spirit, he is already noble-minded and pure, a man of moral integrity and above vulgar interests, a man who is of value to the people.

THE FOOLISH OLD MAN
WHO REMOVED THE MOUNTAINS

June 11, 1945

. . . There is an ancient Chinese fable called "The Foolish Old Man Who Removed the Mountains." It tells of an old man who lived in northern China long, long ago and was known as the Foolish Old Man of North Mountain.

His house faced south, and beyond his doorway stood the two great peaks, Tai-hang and Wang-wu, obstructing the way. With great determination, he led his sons in digging up these mountains hoe in hand. Another graybeard, known as the Wise Old Man, saw them and said derisively, "How silly of you to do this! It is quite impossible for you few to dig up these two huge mountains." The Foolish Old Man replied, "When I die, my sons will carry on; when they die, there will be my grandsons, and then their sons and grandsons, and so on to infinity. High as they are, the mountains cannot

Moving the mountains.

grow any higher and with every bit we dig, they will be that much lower. Why can't we clear them away?"

Having refuted the Wise Old Man's wrong view, he went on digging every day, unshaken in his conviction. God was moved by this, and he sent down two angels, who carried the mountains away on their backs.

Today, two big mountains lie like a dead weight on the Chinese people. One is imperialism, the other is feudalism. The Chinese Communist Party has long made up its mind to dig them up. We must persevere and work unceasingly, and we, too, will touch God's heart. Our God is none other than the masses of the Chinese people. If they stand up and dig together with us, why can't these two mountains be cleared away? . . .

MAO'S WARNING TO HIS COMRADES

Preserve the Style of Plain Living and Hard Struggle
March 5, 1949

Very soon we shall be victorious throughout the country. This victory will breach the eastern front of imperialism and will have great international significance. To win this victory will not require much more time and effort, but to consolidate it will. The bourgeoisie doubts our ability, to construct. The imperialists reckon that eventually we will beg alms from them in order to live. With victory, certain moods may grow within the Party—arrogance, the airs of a self-styled hero, inertia and unwillingness to make progress, love of pleasure and distaste for continued hard living. With victory, the people will be grateful to us and the bourgeoisie will come forward to flatter us. It has been proved that the enemy cannot conquer us by force of arms. However, the flattery of the bourgeoisie may conquer the weak-willed in our ranks. There may be some Communists, who were not conquered by enemies with guns and were worthy of the name of heroes for standing up to these enemies, but who cannot withstand sugar-coated bullets; they will be defeated by sugar-coated bullets. We must guard against such a situation. . . . The comrades must be helped to remain modest, prudent and free from arrogance and rashness in their style of work. The comrades must be helped to preserve the style of plain living and hard struggle. We have the Marxist-Leninist weapon of criticism and self-criticism. We can get rid of a bad style and keep the good.

Source: *Selected Readings from the Works of Mao Tsetung,* Peking: Foreign Language Press, 1971, pp. 362-363.

Studying the "Three Constantly Read Articles."

The People's Democratic Dictatorship

Editor's Introduction: The Communists regard the Confucian system as a dictatorship, meaning that the ruling class was using government power primarily in its own interests. By this definition, Chiang K'ai-shek's government was a dictatorship in support of the landlord class and the new bourgeoisie (the middle class of industrialists and businessmen in the cities). Dictatorship can disappear, the Communists reason, only when there are no classes, when everyone is equal and no one exploits anyone else. To bring this situation about, they say, there must be a "people's dictatorship"—that is, the use of government power in support of the workers and peasants, the great majority of the population, against those who have always oppressed them. Mao Zedong explained the concept in an essay he wrote in 1957, reprinted here. [22]

OURS IS A people's democratic dictatorship, led by the working class and based on the worker-peasant alliance. What is this dictatorship for? Its first function is to suppress ... those exploiters in the country who range themselves against the socialist revolution, to suppress all those who try to wreck our socialist construction; that is to say, to solve the contradictions between ourselves and the enemy within the country.

For instance, to arrest, try, and sentence certain counterrevolutionaries, and for a specified period of time to deprive landlords and bureaucrat-capitalists of their right to vote and freedom of speech—all this comes within the scope of our dictatorship. To maintain law and order and safeguard the interests of the people, it is likewise necessary to exercise dictatorship over robbers, swindlers, murderers, arsonists, hooligans, and other scoundrels who seriously disrupt social order.

Mao Zedong and Zhou Enlai shortly after the establishment of the new Chinese government. (From *Jen-min hua-pao*, 1971, No. 10, p. 30.)

The second function of this dictatorship is to protect our country from subversive activities and possible aggression by the external enemy.... Should that happen, it is the task of this dictatorship to solve the external contradiction between ourselves and the enemy. The aim of this dictatorship is to protect all our people so that they can work in peace and build China into a socialist country with a modern industry, agriculture, science, and culture.

Who is to exercise this dictatorship? Naturally it must be the working class and the entire people led by it. Dictatorship does not apply in the ranks of the people. The people cannot possibly exercise dictatorship over themselves; nor should one section of them oppress another section. Lawbreaking elements among the people will be dealt with according to law, but this is different in principle from using the dictatorship to suppress enemies of the people. What applies among the people is democratic centralism.

Our Constitution lays it down that citizens of the People's Republic of China enjoy freedom of speech, of the press, of assembly, of association, of procession, of demonstration, of religious belief and so on. Our Constitution also provides that organs of state must practice democratic centralism and must rely on the masses; that the personnel of organs of state must serve the people. Our socialist democracy is democracy in the widest sense, such as is not to be found in any capitalist country, Our dictatorship is known as the people's democratic dictatorship. . . .

[Some people feel that there is] too little freedom under our people's democracy and that there was more freedom under Western parliamentary democracy. They ask for the adoption of the two-party system of the West, where one party is in office and the other out of office. But this so-called two-party system is nothing but a means of maintaining the dictatorship of the bourgeoisie; under no circumstances can it safeguard the freedom of the working people.

As a matter of fact, freedom and democracy cannot exist in the abstract; they only exist in the concrete. In a society where there is class struggle, when the exploiting classes are free to exploit the working people, the working people will have no freedom from being exploited; when there is democracy for the bourgeoisie there can be no democracy for the proletariat and other working people. In some capitalist countries the Communist parties are allowed to exist legally but only to the extent that they do not endanger the fundamental interests of the bourgeoisie; beyond that they are not permitted legal existence. Those who demand freedom and democracy in the abstract regard democracy as an end and not a means. . . .

While we stand for freedom with leadership and democracy under centralized guidance, in no sense do we mean that coercive measures should be taken to settle ideological matters and questions involving the distinction between right and wrong among the people. Any attempt to deal with ideological matters or questions involving right and wrong by administrative orders or coercive measures will not only be ineffective but harmful. We cannot abolish religion by administrative orders; nor can we force people not to believe in it. We cannot compel people to give up idealism any more than we can force them to believe in Marxism. In settling matters of an ideological nature or controversial issues among the people, we can only use democratic methods, methods of discussion, of criticism, of persuasion and education, not coercive, high-handed methods. In order to carry on their production and studies effectively and to order their lives properly, the people want their government, the leaders of productive work and of educational and cultural bodies, to issue suitable orders of an obligatory nature. It is common sense that the maintenance of law and order would be impossible without administrative orders. Administrative orders and the method of persuasion and education complement each other in solving contradictions among the people. Administrative orders issued for the maintenance of social order must be accompanied by persuasion and education, for in many cases administrative orders alone will not work. . . .

Leadership and Democracy

THE MODEL OFFICIAL

Editor's Introduction: Under the "people's democratic dictatorship," Chinese workers and peasants participate more in government and in many respects have more voice in determining the course of their lives than ever before. They are encouraged to criticize their government and its officials, especially if the latter are corrupt, inept, or authoritarian. Many cadres have been removed on the basis of mass criticism.

But there are limits to criticism and free speech. The government and the Communist Party do not permit criticism of socialism as a system. And while one can criticize the operation of the Party, no one can question the Party's right to lead. Furthermore, the press and radio are closely monitored by the Party and are vehicles for expressing its point of view.

As Mao stated, the Communists believe that restraints on liberty are necessary if Chinese society is really to change. They remind us that the Confucians were even more restrictive of liberty and democracy, for under them the common people had no voice; the overwhelming majority could not even read, much less express themselves freely in print; and the law forbade anyone but officials even to discuss politics.

The following story, which appeared in the journal *Chinese Literature*, published in Beijing in 1973, illustrates the balance between leadership and mass criticism that the Communists sought to attain in their system of "democratic centralism." [23]

IT WAS A typical autumn day of mellow sunshine with cloud flecks drifting across the far distant sky. Leaves rustled in a blustery wind.

Two bicycles were bowling along the highway. One of the riders, as she wiped the sweat from her face with a white towel and glanced at her watch, began to speed up. "Get a spurt on, Young Chang! There's only ten minutes left," she called out to the other rider.

This young woman, Miao Chun-min, was a former textile worker in her early thirties. She looked brisk, neat, and full of pep as she pedaled along with a knapsack slung over her shoulder.

. . . She had recently been elected to the district Revolutionary Committee as a representative of the masses. Later she became the deputy secretary of the district Party committee. Young Chang, also a former factory worker, was transferred to work in the office of the Party committee during the same period.

The two of them were now heading for Green Pines Gardens to keep an appointment with the people living there.

A few days before, while going over the mail, Young Chang had come across a short message written on a slip of paper. In rather crude characters it read:

> *Please tell Comrade Miao Chun-min that Green Pines Gardens will welcome a visit from her if she can spare the time. Why is it that we haven't been able to get in touch with her recently? We have tried several times.*

This slip of paper had been forwarded by the neighborhood Party committee with a note saying that it had been handed in during a residents' meeting there.

Casually Young Chang had put it away in the file, deciding that some time later he would mention it to Miao. Actually he did not want to bother the deputy secretary with what he considered to be a trifle. Because of the absence of the Party secretary, Miao had been up to her neck in work recently and often stayed up till the small hours. Chang was concerned about her health and, wanting to do what he could to help her, he settled many routine matters himself. . . .

But in spite of her heavy load of work, Deputy Secretary Miao took particular interest in the mail—which was mostly letters from people in the district.

One morning, when looking through a file of letters, she noticed that little slip of paper. Seeing that she paused thoughtfully over it, Young Chang went over to her desk to explain:

"It's just one of those chits people keep handing in. . . ."

"No. It's more than that! It should be taken as a sharp criticism of our work," rejoined Miao. "We so often miss criticism of this sort. We seldom hear it at formal meetings or come across it in reports."

"If everybody in the district wants to talk to the Party secretary, how many more secretaries should we need?" argued Chang.

"It's a good thing if the people want to see us."

"But you're so busy . . . and this is only routine."

"The busier we are the closer we should keep to the people. . . . Since the people want to see us, we ought to visit them and pay careful attention to what they say," Miao told Chang. "Besides, this visit will help us sum up our experience of local work.". . .

[A meeting is then arranged at Green Pines Gardens, which Miao and Young Chang attend.]

The meeting went on for about two hours in a warm, friendly atmosphere.

After taking a sip of tea, Miao Chun-min looked around and said in a ringing voice, "For the last two hours you've said a great deal in praise of our work. That's an encouragement to us to do better in future." She paused to look around again and then went on with a smile. "But Chairman Mao teaches us that all things have two sides. This applies to our work. To be strict with a person is for his own good. You should make strict demands on the district Party committee, the district Revolutionary Committee, and above all on me as deputy Party secretary. I'm hoping to hear from you where I'm wrong and how I can correct my mistakes. A person needs to wash his face every day. . . ."

The people listening nodded and smiled in agreement, liking her attitude. Then suddenly someone spoke up from a far corner of the room, "Well, then, let me fire the first shot. If I'm wide off the mark, you mustn't take offense."

It was Grandma Tung, a retired worker, who spoke. She had been one of the mainstays of the propaganda team Miao worked with. Although over sixty and already gray-haired, she was the picture of health.

"During the past few days I've several times tried to reach you but failed. I was told either that you had 'some important business' on hand or that you were too busy to 'receive ordinary calls.' I wonder whether since you've become a leading comrade you've put on bureaucratic airs and forgotten all about us."

A government official (with shovel) heading for work with other peasants. (From *China Pictorial*, 1970, no. 3, p. 9.)

Miao was surprised because nobody had mentioned Grandma Tung's recent calls and she herself had never said anything about "important business."

The entire room was silent but everyone was looking at Secretary Miao. The atmosphere had become a little tense....[Miao thought to herself]: "The fact that people criticize me openly and to my face shows that they have my interest at heart and want to help me. Since I've come here to listen to what they have to say, I must heartily welcome their criticism and then try to discover the reason for it." So she jotted down what Grandma Tung had said, and looking at her modestly and sincerely said: "Please go on."

Her attitude encouraged Grandma Tung. "I went to your office on some important business," she continued. "We retired workers have started a group among the residents to study Marxist ideology and the correct political line. We've begun by recalling our own bitter experiences in the past and

contrasting them with our good life today. You did say once that if we started any new activity I should let you know. So I wanted to see you so that
you could give us some advice."...

After the old woman had finished, Miao said, "Grandma Tung, I accept
your criticism. There's something wrong with my style of work. I have failed
to go deep among the people to see what new things are cropping up. Your
initiative shows your keen revolutionary spirit. We must learn from you."

These few words like a spring breeze set the entire room astir. People
vied with one another for a chance to speak, some giving their opinions and
others telling about the new spirit that was emerging among the retired
workers and about their political activities. Miao quickly jotted down these
vivid accounts, which were full of life. So the gathering turned into a real
briefing. Miao was extremely pleased. That "the masses have a potentially
inexhaustible enthusiasm for socialism," a truth revealed by our great leader
Chairman Mao, was once more being proved true here in Green Pines
Gardens.

On the way back after the meeting a question kept revolving in Miao's
mind. Why, she wondered, had it become so difficult for an old comrade of
hers like Grandma Tung to reach her now? What was the reason?

"Young Chang, what d'you think of the meeting?" Miao asked, turning
toward Young Chang, who was cycling beside her.

"It was good, very good, I think. . . ." Young Chang's thoughts were in
a turmoil. "It never occurred to me that a short note could involve something so important."

"The note was short but its lesson for us is big," Miao lapsed into deep
thought again. After a while she took another look at her comrade and
re-opened the conversation in a very frank and sincere way: "This incident
has taught me a lot. As one of the leading personnel, any incorrect style of
work or political ideology of mine will affect the work and the staff of the
whole Party committee."

"No, no, you've nothing to reproach yourself with," protested Young
Chang. "I'm the one. . . ." Greatly moved by Miao's attitude, he was at a loss
for words.

It was already sunset. Miao glanced back over her shoulder at Green Pines
Gardens, now only a green blur against the crimson sky, She said to Young
Chang with feeling: "Revolution continually makes higher demands on us.
It's true we were both factory workers and can be said to come from the very
midst of the people, but we must be careful never to isolate ourselves from
them. You know what happens to a pine tree if it is uprooted from the soil."

"A Sticky Problem"

Editor's Introduction: We have seen how the "leakage system" (see page 53) undermined the intentions of Confucianism. The story that follows, "A Sticky Problem," is a witty illustration of how social obligations in China have the same effect on communist ideology. This story is a satirical treatment of a very real problem in China, namely, the tradition of "taking care" of one's relatives and friends even if it means breaking a few rules here and there. The Communists have spoken out against this practice, but deeply rooted customs are hard to dig out. The factory director in the story shows extraordinary determination to follow the rules, risking the loss of friends and job. Is he an exception? It would seem that he is.

The author of this story, Wang Meng, is a well-known contemporary Chinese writer. In 1956 he published a short story describing the bureaucratic way of doing things in a district Party committee. The story caused a sensation and a year later Wang Meng was blacklisted and sent "down to the countryside." At that time writers were not free to criticize life in China. Wang was later banished to remote Xinjiang province and was forbidden from publishing his writings. In 1978 he was allowed to return to Beijing where he resumed his career and enjoyed great popularity. He subsequently served as Minister of Culture (1986-1989). [24]

DING YI STIRS UP A HORNET'S NEST

AT HIS NEW post Ding Yi discovered two big problems. Here, the word "discover" is hardly appropriate, because these two problems were as obvious as lice on a bald head. They made him frown and rack his brains every day. First, there was no proper control of the by-product of paste, gluten, which the workers divided among themselves to sell, give to friends or exchange for other goods. This was scandalous. Secondly, the labor discipline was so lax that the foreman sometimes tripped over people sound asleep during their work shifts. So, after consulting everyone concerned, Ding Yi drew up a set of regulations and a system of rewards and penalties. In fact, these were nothing new, just standard practice.

A month went by. In May, Ding Yi decided to make an example of a contract worker named Gong Ding. For one thing, this young man had stayed away from work for four months without asking for leave. For another, he came bold as brass to the factory to demand gluten, and if given none cursed or beat the man in charge. Furthermore, he turned a deaf ear to reprimands. So Ding Yi asked the Party branch committee, Youth League committee, trade union, personnel office and all the other departments to discuss Gong Ding's case. Though he prodded them three times a day, it took them a month and a half to agree to his proposal that this recalcitrant worker should be dismissed. On June 21, an announcement was put up in the factory: In accordance with regulations, Gong Ding's contract is terminated.

Some people knew that Gong Ding was a distant relative of the first county Party secretary Li and felt it was a mistake to fire him, but they did not like to say so. After all, he was only a distant relative. So, the decision was finally reached and announced.

PSYCHOLOGICAL WARFARE BREAKS OUT

Three hours after the announcement was put up, Ding Yi began to have callers. The first was Old Liu from the county Party committee office. Fifty-seven years old, with an affable expression, he prided himself on his diplomacy and good relations on all sides. Smilingly, he put one hand on Ding Yi's shoulder. "Listen to me, Old Ding," he said. "You've worked hard and run the factory well. But as for Gong Ding's case. . . ." Lowering his voice he explained Gong's relationship to the first county Party secretary. He added, "Of course, this has no bearing on his case. You're right to take disciplinary action. Secretary Li would be grateful to you if he knew. It's you I'm thinking of. You'd better not fire him. He'll still have to stay in China, in our county if he's kicked out. We'll still be responsible for him, and he's bound to ask Secretary Li for help. So, better let him off with a warning." He reasoned so earnestly and patiently that Ding Yi began to waver. Just then, however, Zhou, head of the county industrial bureau, rang up.

"What's come over you?" he bellowed. "Why pick on a relative of the county Party secretary to make an example of? What are people going to think? Hurry up and revoke your decision!"

"No, the decision stands!" replied Ding Yi loudly as he hung up the receiver. His face grim, he turned to Old Liu and said, "Outrageous!"

However, visitors kept coming. At dusk, Old Zhao, chairman of the county revolutionary committee, arrived. Zhao had worked in the county since land reform. He was most influential and strongly entrenched. With a certain reserve he shook hands languidly with Ding Yi, then paced the room while issuing his instructions, not even glancing at Ding.

"We must be prudent, mustn't oversimplify issues. Nowadays people are very sensitive. Gong Ding's dismissal would cause general dismay. In view of this, it's more judicious not to fire him."

He said no more, thinking his directive sufficient. He had paced the room slowly enunciating each word, as if weighing and savouring it. Yes, to him his words were as tasty as spiced beef.

When Ding Yi went home after dark, his wife also poked her nose into his business. Of course, she scolded him out of wifely concern.

"You perishing old fool! Don't you see what you've gone and done? Has messing about with paste all day made you softheaded? You stick to principles? Why aren't you a member of the politburo? Remember the bashing you got in 1966? Your principles not only got you into trouble but me and the children too."

This outburst stemmed from bitter resentment and love. And the tears she shed were more eloquent than words. Ding Yi sighed, and was just about to reason with her when in came another visitor. It was Young Xiao, who had befriended Ding Yi when he was in disgrace. Young Xiao had studied in the Philosophy Department of Beijing University where he was labeled a Rightist. Later he had managed to get a job in the county's electricity company. Recently, after his name was cleared, he had been promoted to be a buyer. He was short, big-nosed and extremely ugly. But the more pressure put on him, the more cheery, quick-witted and engaging he grew. His motto was: If someone slaps your face, turn the other cheek. He reckoned that this tactic succeeded three times out of four.

Young Xiao's arrival filled the house with laughter. The first thing he did after taking a seat was to finish up the dumplings left by Ding Yi and his wife who had lost their appetite. Then he asked after everyone in the family, saying admiringly, "How lucky you are to have so many relatives." Next he told them that he would soon buy and send over the TV set, a real bargain, they had long wanted. Finally he related various funny stories about their county, China and other countries till the whole family was roaring with laughter. . . .

Young Xiao took advantage of this to launch his offensive. "Why, there's a small matter I nearly forgot," he said. "It's about that young rascal Gong. He's a real [bastard]! I'll dress him down next time I see him. But Old Ding, you mustn't go too far. You and I haven't got much footing here. Nor do we have powerful backing or commodities that other people want. We depend

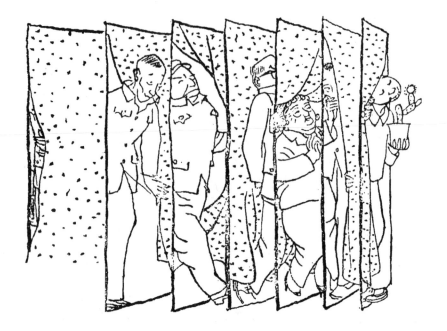

entirely on keeping in with others. Big shots rely on their power, we nobod-
ies on our connections. With power they can get anything they want; by
keeping on good terms with others we can make do. So don't be so
bull-headed. If you haven't learned anything else all these years, you should
have learned how to veer. . . . I know, you needn't explain it to me. The decision has been announced; still, it can be changed. Even the Constitution can
be changed, and Chairman Mao made revisions in his writings. You're only
a small factory director. Think you're more infallible than Chairman Mao
and the Constitution? Go on! Get Gong Ding back. I must make myself
clear. It's not the county secretary who sent me here. I came on my own initiative, having your interests at heart. Of course, Gong Ding did ask me to
come and I told him, 'Don't you worry. Old Ding will do me a little favour
like this.'"

He certainly had the gift of the gab, able to range from the sublime to
the vulgar, to crack jokes or to scoff.

Originally, Ding Yi had not known that Gong Ding was a distant relative of the county's first secretary, and he was not unwilling to reconsider the
case. But all these visitors put him on his guard. If it hadn't been the first secretary's relative, would so many people have come to urge him to "be prudent," "not to oversimplify issues" and to "consider the consequences"? This
question preoccupied him, to the exclusion of other considerations.

In his annoyance he sent Young Xiao packing.

Two days passed. June 23, Sunday, was a hot, long mid-summer day. Mosquitoes had kept Ding awake the previous night, and he had no appetite. At half past four that morning, a visitor arrived by bus. He was Ding Yi's brother-in-law. Tall, bespectacled and bald, he had studied in the Marxist-Leninist Institute in the 1950s and was now teaching in the prefectural Party school. He was the best known theorist in the prefecture and enjoyed great prestige. When listening to his lectures, grassroots cadres kept nodding their heads just like chickens pecking millet from the ground. He was the seventeenth visitor in the past two days. As soon as he set foot in the room, he began to talk from a theoretical point of view.

"Socialist society is a transition period in which there exist the scars of capitalism and pre-capitalism. They are inevitable and independent of man's will. This society is superior but not yet mature or perfect. It's only a transition...."

After this abstract preamble, he continued: "So we say, leaders' power, their likes and dislikes, their impressions, are of vital importance. They cannot be overlooked and very often play the decisive role. We are realists, not utopian socialists like Owen and Fourier."

(Ding Yi thought: Am I a utopian socialist? This label doesn't sound too bad.) "We are not children or pedants. Our socialism is built on the ground under our feet, which, though beautiful, is rather backward and undeveloped." (Ding Yi thought: Have I ever wanted to fly to paradise?) "So when we do any work, we must take all factors into consideration. To use an algebraic formula, there are 'N' factors, not one. The more complicated the world is, the larger the 'N'. . . . So, brother, you were too hasty in handling Gong Ding's case. You didn't use your brain." (Ding Yi thought: A fine brain *you* have, holding forth like this!) "Don't make a gross error, brother, Be statesmanlike. Cancel your decision and invite Gong Ding back."

Ding Yi's wife hastily put in, "That's right, that's right!" A pleased smile appeared on her face. It dawned on Ding Yi that she had asked her theorist brother to talk him round.

While listening, Ding Yi had felt as if his chest was stuffed with hog bristles. His face looked as if he was swallowing a worm. After he had listened attentively for forty minutes, he simply asked, "Did you teach these theories in your Party school?"

Within the twenty-one hours from the arrival of the theorist till 1:45 the next morning, visitors kept coming and going. Some let loose a flood of eloquence, as if they could bring the dying back to life. Some blustered as if they would swallow up the whole world. Some bowed and scraped like swinging willow branches. Some had a well-thought-out plan which they enunciated a word or two at a time, determined not to desist till their goal was reached or, failing that, to hurl Ding Yi over a cliff rather than leave his family in peace. Some brought with them presents ranging from flowers to rancid bean curd. Some promised him a flat with a southern exposure or a brand-new bicycle. Some warned him that he was isolating himself and would come to no good end. Some spoke of the need to protect the Party's prestige—to save the first secretary's face. Some worried about his safety and the fate of his family, some about preserving unity in the country, yet others about human rights, democracy and freedom.

These visitors included Ding Yi's old colleagues, schoolmates, superiors, subordinates, comrades-in-arms, fellow patients in hospital, fellow sufferers, "wine-and-meat" friends and the descendants of his late friends. Some of them were aged people with high prestige, others were promising young ones. Even those who had been in favour of his decision in the factory came over to state that they had changed their minds. Although their motives and manner of speaking differed, they agreed on one point: Gong Ding must not be fired.

Ding Yi had never thought he knew so many people and was known to so many. He could not understand their keen concern for Gong Ding or why his disciplinary action against a contract worker, a hooligan and a distant relative of the county secretary had stirred up such a hornet's nest. He was fast becoming a public enemy! He could neither eat nor rest, nor do any chores. His Sunday was spoilt. He wanted to scream, to smash things, to beat someone up. But instead he gritted his teeth and listened impassively warning himself, "Keep cool and you'll win through!"

Among the visitors was a star whom Ding Yi had admired when young. Forty years ago, she had been the best known actress in the province. And Ding Yi in his teens was infatuated for a spell with this woman thirteen years older than himself, although they did not know each other. He had never told anyone of his romantic dream. It was only in the Cultural Revolution when he was undergoing "labour reform" that he had the luck to meet her, an old lady who had retired and now weighed more than eighty kilograms. Due to his oriental, old fashioned devotion, Ding Yi had always had a special affection for her. To his surprise this "queen" of earlier times also arrived by a donkey cart that day. Sitting on the bed, she prattled through the gaps in her teeth:

"I should have come to see you earlier, Young Ding. Look at me, aren't I an old witch? I don't know why I've aged so suddenly. Why do so many things come to an end before they've really started? It's like the stage: you're still making up when the music for the final curtain sounds. . . ."

Her lamentation over the transience of life made Ding Yi's eyes moist with tears. Of all his visitors that day she seemed to him the only one who had called on him out of pure friendship. But what she went on to say took him aback:

"I hear you're a real martinet. That's no way to run a factory. It turns people against you, doesn't it? Do unto others as you would be done by. Haven't you learned anything from your own experience? You'd better not be too hard on young people."

Still, Ding Yi was grateful to her, recalling his youthful dreams. Among the visitors that day, she was the only one who made no mention of Rose-fragrance Paste Factory, Gong Ding and the county secretary.

SOME STATISTICS

I hope readers will excuse me if now I depart from the normal narrative style to publish some correct but well-nigh unbelievable statistics.

In the 12 days from June 21 to July 2, the visitors who came to plead for Gong Ding totaled 199.5 (the former actress didn't mention his name but had him in mind, so she is counted in as 0.5). 33 people telephoned. 27 wrote letters. 53 or 27% really showed keen concern for Ding Yi and were afraid he would run into trouble. 20 or 10% were sent by Gong Ding; 1 or

0.5% by Secretary Li. 63 or 32% were sent by people approached directly or indirectly by Secretary Li. 8 or 4% were asked by Ding Yi's wife to talk round her "die-hard" husband. 46 or 23% were not sent by anyone and did not know Ding Yi but came on their own initiative to do Secretary Li a service. The remaining 4% came for no clear reasons.

Ding Yi refused all his visitors' requests. His stubbornness enraged 85% of them, who immediately spread word that he was a fool. Ding Yi's petty appointment had gone to his head, they claimed, making him stubborn and unreasonable, and cutting him off from the masses, They asserted that he was fishing for fame and credit, that he had ulterior motives and was taking this chance to vent his spite because the county Party committee had not promoted him to a higher position. Some said he was crazy and had always been reactionary, that he should never have been rehabilitated. Assuming that each of them spoke to at least ten people, 1,700 heard talk of this kind. For a while public opinion was strongly against him. It seemed all were out for his blood. His wife fell ill and her life was only saved by emergency measures. Even the nurse in charge of the oxygen cylinder took the chance to ask Ding Yi to change his mind.

Incidents of this kind happen quickly and end quickly too. They are like the breakfast queues in restaurants, which form as soon as fried cakes and porridge are served and disperse immediately after the food is sold out, no matter how angry those [deprived] of fried cakes are. By August there was no further talk of the case, and by September it had escaped people's minds. Meanwhile, the production in the paste factory had gone up each day. By October, great changes had taken place. When talking together, people stuck up their thumbs saying, "Old Ding Yi really knows a thing or two!"

By December, the fame of the paste factory really had the fragrance of roses. It had become a model for all the small enterprises in the province. The Rose-fragrance Paste it produced was consistently of first-rate quality. Ding Yi went to attend a meeting in the provincial capital at which he was asked to report his experience. He went on to the rostrum, his face flushed, and said, "Communists are made of steel, not paste. . . ."

This caused a general sensation.

He added, "If we don't get down to business, our country's done for!"

He broke off there, choking, and tears ran down his cheeks.

There was a solemn silence for a moment in the auditorium.

Then, thunderous applause!

Meng Hsiang-ying
Stands Up

With the rise of the peasant movement, the women in many
places have now begun to organize rural women's associations;
the opportunity has come for them to lift up their heads ....

—*Mao Zedong, 1927*

Editor's Introduction: We have seen the importance of land reform and
thought reform in revolutionary China. We have also seen how the
Communists have tried to change the traditional Chinese family,
rejecting the old family ethic as the basis of social morality. The
Communists insist that the interests of the family should not take
precedence over the interests of the society at large.

In addition, they have taken steps to alter relationships and
behavior within the family. This is particularly true in regard to the
role of women. The changed status of women in China today is one
of the most remarkable differences between the new and the old
China even though negative discrimination persists.

The next selection begins by describing some of the "old rules"
that regulated the lives of women and goes on to illustrate how the
status of women changed. The story takes place in the 1940s, during
the war with Japan. The heroine, Meng Hsiang-ying, lives in a village
in a Communist-controlled area. Other areas were controlled by the
Japanese and still others by the Chinese Nationalist government of
Chiang K'ai-shek.

There are significant similarities between the movement for land
reform, as described in 'Stone Wall Village Turns Over" (see page 11)
and "The Paupers' Co-op" (see page 121) and the movement for
women's liberation. [25]

THIS IS WILD hill-country: As they used to say in the old days, "the mountains are high and the emperor is far away," which could be brought up to date as "the mountains are high and the government is far away"—it is some fifteen miles to the district government office. For this reason the customs here have not changed much since the last years of the Ch'ing (Qing) dynasty [nineteenth century]. For women the old rule still holds good that as a daughter-in-law you have to put up with beating and abuse, but that once you become a mother-in-law yourself you can beat and curse your daughter-in-law. If you don't, you're failing to put up a good show of being a mother-in-law. The old rule for men in handling their wives is, "A wife you've married is like a horse you've bought—you can ride them or flog them as you like." Any man who does not beat his wife is only proving that he is afraid of her. . . .

One day Meng asked her mother-in-law for some cloth with which to patch her husband's clothes, and the mother-in-law told her to ask the father-in-law for it. According to the old rules she should not have had to ask him for patching cloth, and when Meng argued the point with her mother-in-law, leaving her without a leg to stand on, the mother-in-law started abusing her again. The mother-in-law, realizing that she could not possibly win against Meng, who was in the right and prepared to argue, hurried to the fields to call her son.

"Mei-ni" (this was Meng's husband's name), "come back at once. I can't do anything with that young madam of yours. She wants to eat me alive."

As she could not control the young madam, Mei-ni had to come back and flaunt his authority as young master. The moment he arrived he grabbed a stick and went for Meng—according to the old rules there was no need for him to bother to ask why. But Mei-ni did not have much authority himself, being a lad of only sixteen and a year younger than his wife, and Meng snatched the stick back from him.

This caused real trouble. By the old rules, when a man beat his wife she was expected to take a few blows and then run away, after which somebody else would take the stick from him and that would be the end of the matter. But Meng had not simply refused to be beaten and to run away, she had actually disarmed him, making him feel thoroughly humiliated. In his rage he picked up a sickle and hacked a bloody wound on Meng's forehead, from which the blood kept gushing out even after they had been pulled apart.

The people who broke up the fight seemed to think that Mei-ni had done wrong. Nearly everyone said that if he had to hit her, he should have done so anywhere but on the head. They were only saying that he had hit her in the wrong place. Nobody asked why he had hit her. By the old rules there was no need to ask why a man had hit his wife.

After the fight everyone dispersed as though it were no business of theirs. The only person not to take so casual an attitude was Meng herself. If her head had been cut open when she was completely in the right, and nobody was going to say a fair word for her, then it seemed that there was nothing to stop her husband from hitting her whenever he wanted to. Was this to go on forever? The more she thought about it the more hopeless it seemed. Finally she decided on suicide and swallowed some opium.

As she did not swallow enough she did not die but started retching violently. When her relations discovered this they poured some dirty water, in which combs had been cleaned, down her throat, which made her bring it all up.

"If you like swallowing opium that's fine," her mother-in-law said. "I've got a whole jar of it. I hope you can swallow the lot." Meng would have been glad to, but her mother-in-law did not produce it. . . .

In 1942 a [Communist Party] worker came [to the village]. When he asked them to choose a leader for the Women's National Salvation Association the villagers suggested Meng. "She can talk," they said, "and that means she can keep a firm grip on what is right." But nobody had the courage to discuss the proposal with her mother-in-law. "I'll go myself," said the worker, but he met with some opposition. "She won't do," said Meng's mother-in-law. "She's a failed suicide, she couldn't cope. . . ."

The worker, a young man, lost his patience when all his arguments were met with "she couldn't cope" by Meng's mother-in-law. "If she can't," he shouted, "then you'll have to." To his surprise this did the trick. Meng's mother-in-law had always thought that being a village cadre was dangerous, because sooner or later you were bound to get shot by [Chiang K'ai-shek's] 40th Army. The reason why she did not want Meng to be one was not so much out of love for her as that she was afraid of being in trouble herself as a cadre's relation. This was why, after all her refusals, the worker's suggestion that she should do it herself threw her into a panic. She would get into less trouble by having her daughter-in-law as a cadre than by being one herself. So she became much more amenable: "It's none of my business, none at all. If she can cope, let her."

The worker had won. From then on Meng headed the Women's Association.

(From *Jen-min hua-pao*, 1971, Nos. 7-8.)

As a village cadre she had to go to meetings. Meng would say to her mother-in-law, "Mother, I'm going to a meeting," and off she would go. Mother-in-law was astonished at the idea of a young woman going to a meeting, but she could not stop Meng for fear that the worker would make her take the job on herself. . . .

Meng's mother-in-law had mixed feelings about women taking part in meetings. She would have liked to go along and have a look but decided she had better not; if she did, [Chiang K'ai-shek's] 40th Army would say when they came that she had gone to meetings organized by the "[Communist] 8th Route faction." The next day her curiosity made her go along to find out what a lot of young women together talked about at a meeting. Her investigations shocked her. The women wanted emancipation; they were against being beaten and sworn at by their mothers-in-law and husbands; they were for ending footbinding; they wanted to gather firewood, fetch water, and till the fields; they wanted to do the same work and eat the same food as the men; they wanted to go to winter school.

In her view, this was rebellion. If mothers-in-law and husbands could not beat young wives, who would? Surely someone had to beat them. Meng had feet that she would not allow her mother-in-law to bind small enough, no matter how she was beaten and cursed; surely she did not have the nerve to demand that they be allowed to grow bigger still. Would women who gathered firewood and fetched water still be women? Meng was uncontrollable enough while illiterate, but if she learned to read and write she'd be even more high and mighty. What was the world coming to?

Meng was not particularly bothered by her mother-in-law's worries. With the worker's help her job ran smoothly. She went to a lot of meetings and frequently attended winter school. When a young wife was beaten by her mother-in-law or bullied by her husband, she told Meng, who told the [Communist Party] worker. Then there would be meetings, criticism, and struggle. . . .

No matter what everyone else thought, Meng's mother-in-law was developing a stronger and stronger dislike for her. . . . In her view, a daughter-in-law should be like this: her hair should be combed as straight as a broom handle and her feet should be as small as lotus-leaf cakes; she should make tea, cook, husk millet, mill flour, offer soup and hot water, sweep the floor, and wipe the table clean. From the moment when she started the day by emptying the chamberpots till she set the bedding out at night, she should be at her mother-in-law's beck and call, without wandering off for a single moment. She should hide whenever she saw a stranger, so that outsiders would never know you had a daughter-in-law unless you told them yourself.

This was how she felt daughters-in-law should be, even though she had not always lived up to it in her own youth. She felt that Meng was getting further and further from being a model daughter-in-law. . . . Instead of discussing things with her mother-in-law and keeping some of them from the [Communist] worker, she told him everything. As the mother-in-law made this summary, she thought gloomily, "What am I to do? I can't beat her, I can't swear at her, I can't control her, and I can't sell her. She won't regard herself as a member of the family much longer. Anyone would think the worker her own father." After many sleepless nights she finally thought of a solution: to divide the household.

She asked Niu to be the witness to the division. It was a fair one—if it had not been, Meng would probably not have agreed to it. Meng and her husband took two-thirds of an acre of level land and the same amount of sloping land, but they did not get any grain. "It's all been eaten," her mother-in-law said, "because we harvested so little." After the division the husband went back to his mother's house to eat and sleep, which left Meng free to go her own way by herself.

After the division, in which all the food she got was less than three pounds of turnips, Meng had nothing to eat but the wild plants. As she had no grain at the New Year, she borrowed nearly three pounds of millet, seven of wheat, and one of salt.

As the district government office is some fifteen miles away, they could not oversee work there, and besides, local cadres were very hard to find. The district Women's Association found it most unreasonable that someone as good as Meng was, both at working herself and at organizing others to beat famine, should be driven from home and left to go hungry. Besides, it hindered work throughout the district. They asked higher authority for permission to issue her with some grain to help her out, and kept her there to organize some of the Women's Association work at the district level.

Meng has been a most successful district cadre this year. . . . In the spring she organized the women to hoe ninety-three acres of wheat and dig two acres of level land as well as seven and a half of hillside. In the struggle against locusts that summer, they cut over ten tons of grass for burning to smoke them out. There is no need for me to go into her other achievements—harvesting wheat, loosening the soil, raking with branches, stripping the twigs of the paper-mulberry tree, and gathering wild plants to eat—because it has all been reported in the press.

The Status of Women: New Laws

Editor's Introduction: When the Communists came to power in 1949, one of the first laws the new government passed was the "Marriage Law," which made women legally the equals of men. The provisions of this law leave no room for doubt that past customs and attitudes were no longer acceptable.

THE MARRIAGE LAW

[Promulgated by the Central People's Government on May 1, 1950.]

CHAPTER 1. GENERAL PRINCIPLES

Article 1. The arbitrary and compulsory feudal marriage system, which is based on the superiority of man over woman and which ignores the children's interests, shall be abolished.

The new democratic marriage system, which is based on free choice of partners, on monogamy, on equal rights for both sexes, and on protection of the lawful interests of women and children, shall be put into effect.

Article 2. Bigamy, concubinage, child betrothal, interference with the remarriage of widows, and the exaction of money or gifts in connection with marriage shall be prohibited. . . .

CHAPTER III. RIGHTS AND DUTIES OF HUSBAND AND WIFE

Article 7. Husband and wife are companions living together and shall enjoy equal status in the home.

Article 8. Husband and wife are in duty bound to love, respect, assist, and look after each other, to live in harmony, to engage in production, to care for the children, and to strive jointly for the welfare of the family and for the building up of a new society.

Article 9. Both husband and wife shall have the right to free choice of occupation and free participation in work or in social activities.

Article 10. Both husband and wife shall have equal right in the possession and management of family property.

Article 11. Both husband and wife shall have the right to use his or her own family name.

Article 12. Both husband and wife shall have the right to inherit each other's property.

> *Editor's Postscript:* Women in China are equal to men according to the law, but true equality has not been realized. Women are supposed to receive equal pay for equal work, but often they do not. More boys than girls attend school at the higher levels, and many more men than women occupy positions of responsibility in government, in production, in schools, and so on.
>
> But in no other country was women's liberation promoted so vigorously.

The Paupers' Co-op

Editor's Introduction: Eighty percent of China's people lived in the countryside when the Communists took power. As we have seen, the revolution overthrew the traditional landlord system and redistributed the land to the peasants. Unfortunately, land reform did not solve the economic problems in the rural areas. Farmers were given small, inefficient plots of land to work, and most of them had no recourse but to sell their new land and become tenants again. The alternative was to move to overcrowded cities where jobs were scarce or nonexistent.

    The Communists' solution to this dilemma was to form collective farms. The goal was to create larger, more efficient farms and thus encourage peasants to stay in the rural areas. The following selection, "The Paupers' Co-op," is a fictionalized account of how a farming cooperative got started in one area. It describes the benefits of cooperative effort and the obstacles that must be overcome to attain it.

    As you read "The Pauper's Co-op" bear in mind that stories of this sort—sometimes called "new socialist literature"—were originally written not for foreigners but for the Chinese. The purpose of such stories is to teach a lesson or provide a model of good conduct. [26]

IN A CERTAIN county of Hopei (Hebei) stands a mountain called Ch'ang-yu, and in the valley below lies Ch'ang-yu Village, a village always known for its poverty: poor hills, poor water, poor soil, and poor people, too. . . .

The village had 154 households, but three out of four consisted of poor peasants or hired hands, of whom several dozen had to beg for a living.

Soon after Liberation came land reform, when the poor and lower-middle peasants were given some land of their own. But lack of tools, draft animals, fertilizer, and funds made it impossible to grow good crops or to cope with drought and flood. Some of the former poor peasants and hired hands found themselves having to sell their newly won land.

The few [Communist] Party members in the village cudgelled their brains day and night to think of some way out. One of these, Wang Ku-hsing, was a big, burly man and a good farmer. He foresaw that the 1952 crop failure would make it hard for the villagers to last through the winter; and it would be a disgrace if they had to apply to the state again for relief. . . .

Wang went to see District Party Secretary Tsao. He was back the next morning and told Tu Hung, "Good news!"

"What good news?"

"The district cadres are examining some directives on agricultural cooperation. They want to have another try at setting up a few co-ops. Secretary Tsao said, 'So long as we poor stand together and follow Chairman Mao's line on agricultural cooperation, we can join forces in co-ops. If we pull together we can make the earth produce gold. Step by step we'll shake off our poverty.'"

"Very good," cried Tu. "I've been wishing we could have a co-op ever since I heard that other districts were trying them. We must make a go of it."

Wang called together all the Party members to pass on Secretary Tsao's advice. Then they went off to try to persuade the villagers to form a cooperative.

This wasn't easy. Why not? Because co-ops were something new. No one had any idea what they were like or what their advantages were. So most of the peasants had doubts.

Some said, "If so many people are thrown together there are bound to be quarrels and fights, even families breaking up."

"Several dozen households farming together? They'll never agree. Everything will be messed up."

"Too many cooks spoil the broth. Too many sons means none support their father. We're better off without co-ops."

But the Party members didn't lose heart. They went on canvassing. And finally twenty-three households agreed to take the cooperative road proposed by the Party.

"Good," said Wang. "We'll start with twenty-three households. If we make a go of it, others will want to join."

A meeting was held to set up the co-op. The twenty-three families who went saw at once that they were all poor peasants, the poorest in the whole village. This really was a Paupers' Co-op. They elected Wang as chairman and Tu as vice chairman.

When they reckoned up their assets, the co-op owned nearly forty acres of land, but no draft animals at all except for three legs of a donkey. Three legs of a donkey? Well, this donkey was the joint property of five households. Four of them had joined the co-op, but not the fifth; so one leg of the donkey didn't belong to the co-op. That meant they had a three-quarter share in this donkey. And not having a single ox or cart, how were they to till the land? . . .

"Of course, we've got hands," said Li. "But where's the money for animals and carts to come from?"

Wang pointed out of the window. "There! Animals, carts, tools—we'll get the lot up there!"

All eyes turned to the mountains ten miles away. They couldn't for the life of them see how they were to provide animals and carts.

"The mountain's covered with brushwood, isn't it?" Wang continued. "Cut some and sell it, and we'll be able to buy all we need.". . .

In twenty days they cut more than twenty tons of brushwood, which they sold in town for 430 *yuan.* Was everyone pleased! These paupers had never handled so much money. . . . Instead of sharing out the money, they went to town and bought an ox, a mule, a cart, and nineteen sheep. The whole co-op exulted over the purchases. . . .

[W]illing as the paupers were to work, they were still hard up, and long before harvest time they ran out of grain. Some cooked a whole basket of greens with a handful of rice; others had nothing at all to put in the pan. When Tai Ming collapsed in the fields from hunger, Wang took him home and made him a broth of the last few beans in their house. He and his wife now had to make do with wild plants.

Hunger affected the co-op members' work and their morale, too.

Li Ying started grousing in the fields, "If I hadn't joined the co-op," he said, "I could have sent my son out as a hired hand. That way I'd have had one less mouth to feed and some cash at the end of the year. Now we haven't so much as a grain of rice, yet he expects us to feed him."

Li Ying's boundary stones were in the way of the plough, and one co-op member started to move them away. But Li growled, "Don't waste your time shifting those. After the autumn harvest I'm leaving the co-op, I'd only have to lug them back again."

Later someone urged Wang, "Let's pick some of our unripe crop, Old Wang, just enough to keep us from starving!"

"And spoil our harvest? No!" said Wang. "We must tighten our belts now to reap more grain later on. We'll find some other way out."

The Party members talked it over and solved the problem again the poor man's way. They could cut brambles, strip the leaves off for compost, and sell the stems to buy grain. . . .

The Longshen terraced fields in the Guangxi Zhuang Autonomous Region.
(From *China*, Beijing: New Star Publishers, 1999, p. 125.)

The Party had taken an interest in this new co-op from the start. When the district Party secretary learned of its predicament, he hurried to Ch'ang-yu Village with a loan.

"Don't worry about us, we're all right," said Wang. "I guarantee no one will die of hunger!"

"All right, are you?" retorted Tsao. "You're as pale as a ghost, man!"

Wang covered his face with his hands and laughed. "That's my natural color. I'm not hungry."

"Not hungry? You haven't eaten a grain of rice for days."

"I don't mind missing a few meals if the co-op can grow strong enough so that none of our members need ever go hungry again. Besides, the Party and the government have much bigger problems to cope with. We don't want to add to their burden."

With Party members like these, who always put others first and work so whole-heartedly for the common good, thought Secretary Tsao, they're bound to make a success of the co-op. "Comrade," he said, "if people have problems, it's up to the state to help. Buy some grain with this fifty *yuan*, and go on finding ways to tide yourselves over. If you succeed, cooperation will take root in this poor mountain valley. And that will be wonderful."

They bought grain for the co-op with the loan. Deeply touched, one member fingered the grain and declared, "They say that nobody is as dear as a mother. But the Party cares for us better than a mother. Just in the nick of time the Party's sent us this loan to see us through."

The co-op's maize grew tall and strong. By harvest time each cob was about a foot long, as plump as a pestle, and covered with symmetrical golden kernels the size of horses' teeth. . . .

Now the harvest was shared out. Li Ying's family of seven owned two acres of land and three of its members worked. The previous year in the mutual-aid team they had harvested six *piculs* of grain; this year in the co-op they got forty-one. Li Ying jumped for joy and caught Wang by the arm. "Let's move those boundary stones away, chairman," he cried. "They use up a furrow or two of land, and get in our way as well."

"Don't let's tire ourselves out shifting those," chuckled Wang. "We'll only have to help you lug them back in a few days."

"Come off it, chairman! My mind's made up. I'm in the co-op for life. You couldn't get me to leave even if you kicked me out."

It had been a tough year, but already the paupers' co-op had shown the advantages of cooperation. After the harvest, sixty new families joined, bringing the total to eighty-three households. Hard work and thrifty management enabled the co-op to forge ahead every year, so that by 1956, three years later, Ch'ang-yu Village had changed out of all recognition. Every household entitled to had joined the co-op, and now they combined with three neighboring villages to form a cooperative of the more advanced type. By now their poor mountain valley had grown rich, the barren hills were smiling; flinty tracks had been transformed into smooth highways, thatched huts into tiled stone houses; and every single family had surplus grain and money in the bank. . . .

Things got better year by year in Ch'ang-yu Village. In 1958, several co-ops merged in the Kuang-ming People's Commune, with Wang as its chairman. Now it is 1962, just ten years after the co-op was set up. What earth-shaking changes these brief ten years have seen! In 1952, they started a co-op with a three-quarters' share in a donkey. Today they've gone a long way toward mechanizing agriculture. They have tractors to plough the fields, electric pumps, motors to hull rice, trucks to transport their produce.

Ten years ago there was more sand than soil on the stony hills, so that the crops were spoiled by flood or drought. In these ten years, they've built reservoirs and canals, changing the sandy hillsides into irrigated fields; they can water the crops in time of drought, and pump out excess water in time of flood. In place of six hundredweight an acre, they now raise one and a half tons or so, and the once barren hills are covered with fruit trees. So Ch'ang-yu Village today has rich mountains, rich water, rich soil, and rich people, too.

Six families out of ten have built new houses. . . .

If you stand on a hill in the evening and look down, the electric lights are like pearls gleaming in the dark, and Ch'ang-yu Village is a beautiful sight!

> *Editor's Postscript:* Not mentioned in this glowing account was the turmoil caused by the Great Leap Forward (1958-62), a national policy, instigated by Mao, that attempted to quicken the pace of socialist development, raise farm production, increase industrial production in the countryside, and decentralize economic decision-making. Communes, such as the one mentioned near the end of the story, were established during this period. Privately owned plots of land, livestock and large farm tools were taken over by the communes and community dining halls and nurseries were established. At the start, rural collectives were reorganized into more than 26,000 communes with approximately 5,000 households each. The Communist Party's Central Committee meeting at Beidaihe in August 1958 declared that:
>
> > The establishment of people's communes with all-around management of agriculture, forestry, animal husbandry, side occupations, and fishery, where industry (the worker), agriculture (the peasant), exchange (the trader), culture and education (the student), and military affairs (the militiaman) merge into one, is the fundamental policy to guide the peasants to accelerate socialist construction, complete the building of socialism ahead of time, and carry out the gradual transition to communism.*
>
> The belief at the time was that with the correct attitude, political "redness," the masses could quickly accomplish any goal regardless of objective conditions.** Specifically, Mao believed that the spirit of individualism could be destroyed and that the barriers between countryside and city, peasants and industrial workers, and manual workers and intellectuals could be eliminated.

---

* Mark Selden, ed., *The People's Republic of China: A Documentary History of Revolutionary Change*, New York: Monthly Review Press, 1974, p. 402.

** Carl Riskin, *China's Political Economy*, New York: Oxford University Press, 1987, p. 139.

During the enthusiastic campaign to create "a new economic man," irrigation systems, dams, reservoirs, schools and clinics were built and peasants learned new skills and created new rural factories. However, haste, lack of coordination and planning, and the lack of objective information reaching central government officials on the results of the new policies soon led to disaster. In an attempt to rapidly increase steel production, for example, hundreds of thousands of small blast furnaces, often referred to as "backyard furnaces," were established throughout rural China. Not only was the quality of the steel abysmally poor but the production process drained millions of peasants from farming during the harvest season. Peasants were also diverted by working in other new rural industries and in transport. In addition, new farming techniques, such as deep plowing and close planting of crops, promoted by Beijing, proved to be dismal failures. Also, the confiscation of private plots and personal property weakened peasant incentives. These policies, plus the flooding and drought that afflicted parts of China during the years of the Great Leap, resulted in severe grain shortages and famine in many parts of China.*

The severity of the crisis was hidden both from the Chinese people and the outside world. Some journals referred to "disaster areas" and reports from Henan province noted the prevalence of "edema," "dropsy," "serious famine" "and starvation."** In 1960 a publication for Party cadres in the People's Liberation Army printed a letter from a soldier reporting that, "At present what the peasants eat in the villages is even worse than what dogs ate in the past. At times dogs ate chaff and grain. Now the people are too hungry to work and pigs are too hungry to stand up. Commune members ask: Is Chairman Mao going to allow us to starve to death?"***

Mao, in a self-criticism acknowledged at the Lushan Conference in July 1959 that "the mass smelting of steel" was "a great catastrophe."+ In addition, Liu Shaoqi (Shao-chi) reported to a top-level conference in January 1962 that "our economy is now on the brink of a complete collapse" and that while 30 percent of the crisis was caused by natural calamities, 70 per cent was attributable to man-made disaster.++

---

* Ibid., pp. 126, 137.

** Kenneth R. Walker, "Grain Self-Sufficiency in North China, 1953-75," *The China Quarterly*, 71 (September 1977), p. 559.

*** Roderick MacFarquhar, *The Origins of the Cultural Revolution: The Great Leap Forward, 1958-1960*, New York: Columbia University Press, 1983, p. 329.

+ Stuart Schram, *Chairman Mao Talks to the People: Talks and Letters, 1956-1971*, New York: Pantheon, 1974, p. 143.

++ Kang Chao, *Agricultural Production in Communist China, 1949-1965*, Madison: University of Wisconsin Press, 1970, pp. 30-31.

THE SPIRIT OF THE GREAT LEAP FORWARD

There is no Jade Emperor in heaven.
There is no Dragon King on earth.
I am the Jade Emperor
I am the Dragon King.
Make way for me.
you hills and mountains,
I'm coming.

Peasant Song, 1958

(The Jade Emperor was the legendary ruler of heaven.
The Dragon King was the ruler of the waters.)

By the early 1960s the Communist Party acknowledged the failure of many Great Leap policies. Although communes were retained, central control of the economy was reimposed, private plots were restored to peasants, communal dining halls and nurseries were eliminated, most of the new rural factories and mines were closed, rural markets based on private production were tolerated, and a new emphasis was placed on expanding agricultural output. (Food grain output, however, did not reach pre-Great Leap levels until the mid-1960s.) Mao, whose policies were discredited, retreated from day-to-day involvement in economic and political affairs and the Party was divided as to the future path of the revolution. However, in spite of all of the debates and speeches, nowhere did the government acknowledge the number of deaths resulting from the Great Leap policies. As late as 1981, the Central Committee of the Communist Party, in its official history, would merely state that during the Great Leap Forward, "our economy encountered serious difficulties between 1959 and 1961, which caused serious losses to our country and people."*

In the early 1980s, however, the Chinese government's State Statistical Bureau began to release, for the first time, statistical and demographic data from the Great Leap Forward period as well as the

---

* Central Committee of the Communist Party of China (1981), *Resolution on CPC History (1941-81)*, Oxford: Pergamon Press, 1981, p. 29.

data from both the 1964 and 1982 census. By analyzing official mortality rates and by reconstructing population trends, several Western and Chinese demographers have concluded that there were between 14 and 30 million excess deaths in China during the period from 1958 to 1961. Although the quality of the statistics has been challenged and the calculations are based on computerized projections, the available data indicates that, in all likelihood, the policies of the Great Leap Forward resulted in a large loss of life.

The Iron Man
of Daqing

Editor's Introduction: Industrial development in China, like agricultural development, relied heavily on labor power. Economists characterized much of China's production as "labor intensive" rather than "capital intensive." In a labor intensive economy humans do much of the work done by machines in a capital intensive economy such as that of the United States. In China, workers were exhorted to be self-reliant and self sufficient, to work hard and overcome all problems through their own efforts. Workers who best exemplified those traits were rewarded and held up as models to inspire others. One such model is "Iron Man Wang," a worker at the Daqing (Taching) oil fields.

The following story was written during the Cultural Revolution. Note the constant use of the language of war to encourage and stimulate industrial production. [27]

ON APRIL 14, 1960, as dawn flushed the rolling grassland, the sun rose slowly over the horizon, red as a ball of flame. The well site was a hive of activity. Wang Chin-hsi, his stained, tattered sheepskin jacket over his shoulders, jumped onto the drilling platform for a final inspection of the preparations. Then be grasped the brake handle in his powerful hands and shouted at the top of his lungs: "Start drilling!" To him, this was not a simple drilling operation but a declaration of war against imperialism, revisionism, and the whole old world.

There followed five days and nights of strenuous work. Then glistening jet-black crude oil—the first Taching oil—came gushing out of the well! The huge oilfield, sealed for thousands of years, began yielding up its treasures. Wang Chin-hsi and his team gathered round, beside themselves with joy at the sight of that spurting column. "Long live Chairman Mao!" they cheered. "Long live Chairman Mao!"

Iron Man Wang Chin-hsi (on the right) with fellow workers. (From *Jen-min hua-pao*, 1971, No. 9.)

It was not all plain sailing from then on, however. Soon after this first well was drilled an accident happened.

At dawn on May Day, under Wan Chin-hsi's supervision, they started dismantling the derrick to "move house." Both arms raised, his eyes on the drill, Wang moved back step by step, shouting directions.

Then, without warning, a drill pipe hurtled down. The team leader, struck on the legs, was knocked unconscious.

When Wang Chin-hsi came to, he saw that the derrick was not yet dismantled but that the political instructor and his comrades had stopped work to gather round and revive him.

"I'm not a clay figure, so easily smashed," Wang protested. With a great effort, he stood up. As he did so, blood soaked through his trouser legs, staining his shoes and socks.

The political instructor tore a strip from his own overalls to bandage the team leader's wound. With amazing tenacity, Wang, both arms raised high, went on directing the work.

Wang's legs became so badly swollen that his mates insisted he go to the hospital. But he would not hear of this. "Norman Bethune came all the way to China to help our revolution, and gave his life here. What's a leg wound?"

he said. He told them on no account to spread word of his injury or report it to those in charge.

Wang's comrades, unable to persuade him to leave his fighting post or rest, made him a pair of crutches. But whenever any of the leading comrades arrived he would hide these crutches in a pile of pipes and stand up unaided to report on the work and ask for new assignments.

Before long, however, those in charge learned what had happened and packed Wang off to the hospital.

Even when lying in bed in the hospital, Wang's heart was in the oilfield. In his mind's eye he saw his mates, strong and active as tigers. This was no time for him to be lying there, while the others battled for oil.

The next day another patient was brought in by truck. Wang seized his chance, when no nurses were about, to limp out on his crutches and clamber onto the truck, which took him back to his post.

To build the oilfield fast and well, Wang Chin-hsi and his comrades battled round the clock. But his legs grew more swollen from day to day, until finally the leadership, backed by his teammates, sent him to a hospital farther away from Taching. They urged the medical staff there to keep a strict eye on him, and he was put in the charge of a young doctor.

To be unable to work is the greatest hardship for a man of Wang's calibre. One hand on his bedside table, the other on a crutch, he propped himself up. Beads of sweat stood out on his forehead.

"My mates are going all out to build the oilfield," he informed the doctor. "How can I lie here idle?"

"You're in no condition to work," rejoined the other. "We're responsible for getting you back into shape."

"It's a serious matter, our country's lack of oil. This scratch on my leg is nothing. Can a few bumps and bruises stop making revolution?" Wang rose painfully to his feet.

"The leadership has entrusted you to my care. This is my fighting post, my job."

"My fighting post is at the oilfield, doctor." Gazing at the young doctor, Wang spoke with feeling. "My job is drilling oil wells for our country. Won't you help me get back to my post, where my duty lies?"

The young doctor, stirred by Wang's revolutionary spirit, went off to consult his leadership. Too impatient to wait for his return, Wang slapped on his cap and stumped out of the ward on his crutches, taking the next train back to the scene of battle. It was dark and pouring with rain when he reached Taching. Too dark to distinguish mud, water, earth, or sky, he slithered along as best he could through the night.

At 1 AM, knocking on the door woke the men of Team 1205. When they lit a lamp and opened the door, they discovered this runaway patient from the hospital, leaning on a crutch. His injured leg was in a plaster cast. He was soaked to the skin and all over mud from his head to his bandaged feet. They hurriedly made up his bed. But by the time they looked round to urge him to rest, Wang had slipped out again behind their backs and limped on his crutches to the oil well.

Some time later, Wang Chin-hsi and his men were seated on some pipes discussing their work when—Wham! The heavy cement lid weighing several dozen pounds was blasted off the top of the drilling machine. A blowout was imminent.

A blowout is the most serious accident that can happen in an oilfield. When the mud specific gravity is too low, the oil and gas in a well burst through the earth to erupt like a volcano, striking sparks from the hurtling stones. The whole oilfield may turn into a sea of flame. A huge towering derrick may sink into the well. Wang held a hasty council of war with his mates and reported what had happened to headquarters.

The usual way of preventing a blowout is to increase the mud specific gravity with heavy spar. But in this newly opened oilfield, where the wells were still few and far between, heavy spar . . . would have to be fetched from far away. It would come too late to avert an accident. With great presence of mind, Wang came to a swift decision: They would pour cement into the mud tank.

This method had never been used before. It meant risking getting the drill stuck in the well. But Wang knew from previous investigations that the water here was too alkaline for the cement to harden immediately. If they took steps quickly to avert a blowout, there would still be time to deal with the cement.

"Pour in cement!" he ordered.

The whole team went into action. It was a tense battle.

Sack after sack of cement and loads of earth were poured into the sump.

A mixer was needed to mix the cement with the mud, but they had none at hand. Wang tried stirring the cement with a crutch, but this proved ineffective. Throwing away his crutches then, he jumped into the waist-deep mud.

Completely oblivious to his own pain, Wang trampled and stirred the mixture with hands and feet, moving swiftly and vigorously. The cement kept sinking to the bottom of the tank. As he stooped to stir it, mud bespattered his face. But simply tossing his head, he went on mixing.

Some young fellows quickly followed his example.

After a battle lasting over three hours they got the blowout under control, saving the oil well and the drilling machine.

By that time, the highly alkaline mud had raised great blisters on their hands. And when his mates helped Wang out of the tank, his legs were so painful that he could no longer stand. Drops of sweat coursed down his face. Nonetheless, he squared his shoulders, reached for his crutches, and struggled to his feet.

"Never mind about me," he ordered. "Go on drilling."

Shortly before this, Aunt Chao had arrived from Ma-chia-yao with a basket of hard-boiled eggs. Tears in her eyes, she gazed at the drill-team leader. His sunken eyes were bloodshot. His prominent cheekbones stood out more sharply than ever. His short beard was caked with mud. Yet he stood his ground on the high drilling platform like some intrepid warrior, his muddy figure transformed by the golden sunlight into a splendid statute of glinting bronze. . . .

In all her sixty-odd years, Aunt Chao had never set eyes on such a sight. With lips that trembled she declared; "Team Leader Wang, you're a real man of iron!"

That is how the name "Iron Man" spread through Taching.

Editor's Postscript: By publicizing the deeds of model workers, such as Iron Man Wang, the Government of China hoped to encourage people to work hard and produce more. Reward would come in the form of praise, publicity, and an increase in collective well-being.

In a capitalist economy, encouragement for hard work and increased production usually takes a more material form—for example, increased wages, profits or bonuses. Such material rewards were denounced in China during the Cultural Revolution as symptomatic of a capitalist mentality. People were encouraged to work selflessly for the good of all, and not for immediate personal gain.

In a socialist economy, some production and price decisions are determined by the market, but many are made by the government. The government might decide, for instance, that the limited resources of a nation should be invested in increasing food production or in housing for the poor. In a market economy, those resources might be invested in the production of luxury apartments or expensive automobiles for the rich because there is a demand for those products by those who have money.

In many third world countries, that is exactly what happens. Production is heavily weighted toward production for the rich or production of goods for sale abroad. In either case, poor people, who are the majority of the population in most third world countries, remain poor. In some market economies, the government intervenes in the market to compensate for inequities by providing services such as social security, unemployment insurance, safety standards, minimum wage platforms, and so on.

Socialism in China was designed to reduce the disparity between rich and poor. There were few private automobiles, and there was little production of luxury goods. But food, medicine and housing, the basic necessities, were all kept rather inexpensive by price controls and by political decisions (rather than market decisions).

If a problem with the market system is that it tends to perpetuate inequalities, there are also problems with the socialist system. Decision making tends to become over-centralized, reducing the freedom of choice and creativity of numerous producers. (Such can also happen when a market system is dominated by monopolies or huge conglomerates.) It is also extremely difficult for the planners to have sufficient data and sufficient wisdom to plan intelligently for the whole society.

In a market economy, each enterprise plans only for itself. Mistakes in a planned, socialist economy tend to have a far wider impact on the whole economy.

Barefoot Doctors

Editor's Introduction: In the years following the establishment of the People's Republic in 1949, a number of measures were taken that greatly improved the general health of the populace. Techniques of mass organization and education, which had been used effectively to bring the Communists to power, were employed in nationwide campaigns to improve sanitation and hygiene, eliminate disease-bearing pests, and immunize the populace against contagious diseases.

As a result of these efforts, epidemics of smallpox, cholera, and plague that had flourished during the long years of war were quickly brought under control; cases of tuberculosis and schistosomiasis (a seriously debilitating disease caused by snails) fell sharply; drug addiction and venereal disease were virtually eliminated, at a time when they were spreading rapidly in other parts of the world.

The government subsidized the cost of medical care, reducing or eliminating direct costs to the patient. For employees of state-run enterprises, such as factories, mines, railroads, and government offices, and for students, medical care was free except for a small registration fee of about 3 cents (U.S. equivalent in 1973). Peasants were covered by cooperative medical plans to which they contributed 25 cents to 50 cents per year. Dependents and other nonworking people who were not covered by these plans paid a very small fee for health care. A chest x-ray cost about 8 cents, a hospital bed cost 25 cents or less per day. The cost for delivering a child was about $1.25, an appendectomy cost $2.00, and the most difficult operations, such as heart or brain surgery, cost less than $8.00.

The cost of medicines was also low and had been reduced continually since 1949. Most prescriptions cost 1 cent or less.

By the mid-1960s, the health of the Chinese people had greatly improved, but a major unsolved problem, which became a central issue of dispute during the Cultural Revolution, was the uneven dis-

An old doctor trains a barefoot doctor to recognize medicinal herbs. (From *China Reconstructs,* November 1972.)

tribution of medical care. As in most countries, doctors and medical supplies were in greater abundance in the cities than in the countryside. In many rural areas, medical care was inadequate or nonexistent. As a result of the Cultural Revolution, much more attention was given to rural areas, where most of the people live. Many doctors were transferred to rural areas to live and work, but because there were too few fully trained M.D.s to service the whole population, the emphasis was on training tens of thousands of paramedical personnel called "barefoot doctors."

The selections that follow describe the function of those barefoot doctors. [28]

THE NAME "BAREFOOT doctor" first appeared in the Chiang-chen People's Commune on Shanghai's outskirts.

In 1965, when Chairman Mao issued the call "In medical and health work, put the stress on the rural areas," a number of mobile medical teams formed by urban medical workers came to Chiang-chen. Though it was near the metropolis, this commune had only one health clinic with about a dozen medical personnel serving a population of 28,000. When the medical teams arrived, the local peasants were glad to see them. While curing and preventing commune members' diseases, the doctors from Shanghai helped the clinic give a group of young peasants some medical training.

Later, when the teams left, these peasants took their place and since then have gradually become full-fledged doctors. Taking medical kits with them, they worked barefooted alongside the peasants in the paddyfields, and they treated peasants in the fields, on the threshing grounds, or in their homes. They were at once commune members and doctors, doing farm work and treating patients. Like other commune members, they receive their pay on the basis of workpoints, and their income was more or less the same as that of able-bodied peasants doing the same amount of work. The peasants warmly welcomed them and affectionately called them "barefoot doctors."
. . .

Generally speaking, "barefoot doctors" are given three to six months of short-term training before starting to work. Training classes with few but well-selected courses are run by the commune's clinic, county hospital, and mobile medical teams from the cities or medical schools. . . . The aim is to give the trainees the ability to do practical work as quickly as possible and to lay the foundation for advanced study. . . .

In 1965, Wang Kuei-chen, who was twenty-one that year, was chosen to attend a training course for "barefoot doctors" run by the commune's clinic.
. . .

During her four months of training, Wang Kuei-chen and twenty-seven other young men and women were taught to cure scores of common diseases and to prescribe some 100 medicines. . . . They learned the fundamentals of acupuncture treatment at thirty major points on the human body. This ABC of medical science was of great use to these young people, who have deep feelings for the peasants.

Back from the training course, Wang Kuei-chen continued doing farm work, such as transplanting rice-shoots, weeding, and harvesting together with the villagers. Wherever she worked, in the fields, at construction sites of water-conservancy projects, or other places, she always had her medical kit at hand. She and two other "barefoot doctors" took charge of handling all the diseases and injuries they could among the more than 1,500 brigade members. After giving prescriptions, she made it a rule to call on the patients and ask them about the effects of the medicine so as to sum up experience and improve her work. As to cases she could not handle, she always went with the patients to the city hospital. . . .

All this was not just for the purpose of learning, but, more important, her aim was to look after the patients still better. In summer, villagers sometimes were bitten by snakes. When she was told that a worker in a factory several kilometers away could treat snakebites with herbal medicine, she immediately went to see him. Combining what she learned from the worker with Western medicine, she has treated more than a dozen snakebite cases in the last two years.

Affectionately called their "close friend" by the villagers, Wang Kuei-chen was elected deputy secretary of the commune Party committee and a member of the county Party committee. Despite the change in her position, she is still a "barefoot doctor."

She has also made rapid progress in medical technique. She and other "barefoot doctors" took turns working in the commune's health clinic or getting further training in advanced courses. Last year, she spent two months studying anatomy, physiology, and biochemistry in a medical college and later went to the county hospital's internal medicine department for advanced study in combination with clinical treatment.

"Barefoot doctor" Chang Hsiang-hua in the countryside . . . in northwest China had only learned some elementary knowledge and technique of Western medicine in a training class. In the course of practice, he found that there were many effective prescriptions of traditional Chinese medicine used by the local people who lived in a hilly village where many medicinal herbs grew. If these traditional methods were put to good use, he thought, it would produce very good results in curing certain diseases and save the patients much expense. So he and his colleagues set about learning from veteran practitioners of traditional Chinese medicine and experienced herbpickers in the locality. As a result, they were able to recognize 240 herbs and learned to give herbal prescriptions and cure diseases by acupuncture. They themselves picked the needed herbs and later planted them. Last year, they went a step further. . . . They processed herbs into easy-to-use pills, powders, and liquid medicines to stop bleeding and coughing, induce lactation, and cure burns.

In 1970, Chang Hsiang-hua had the opportunity to learn from a traditional Chinese doctor of a medical team that had come from Peking for six months. He worked together with this old doctor every day, diagnosing and curing patients. He also spent one to two hours listening to his talks on the theories of traditional Chinese medicine. Studying this way helped Chang quickly increase his ability.

For a period of time, he and other "barefoot doctors" in the brigade cooperated closely with medical teams from Peking, making an over-all investigation of an endemic disease. They learned to give every brigade member a cardiographic check-up and carried out auscultatory and oral investigations from house to house. They gave decoctions of herbal medicine twice a day to twenty-eight patients who had varying symptoms. Carefully observing the effects, they continued studying ways to improve the prescription's ingredients. After 150 days, all the patients were better. In this way, the young "barefoot doctors" learned how to diagnose, cure, treat and prevent this disease.

Study through practice, as shown by the above-mentioned examples, is the basic way "barefoot doctors" are trained. This quick and effective method makes up for the drawbacks owing to medical schools' being unable to train large numbers of doctors in a short time. In a developing country like China, the first step to change backwardness in medical work in the rural areas is, so to speak, "sending charcoal in snowy weather," not "adding flowers to the embroidery." "Barefoot doctors" are a newborn force that has bright prospects.

Every rural people's commune today [1973] has its "barefoot doctors" who are either children of the once-impoverished peasants and herdsmen or city-bred middle-school students who have settled in the countryside. These peasant-doctors are playing an important role in the rural areas where doctors and medicine are in great demand.

The Red Guards

Editor's Introduction: The Communist Party has governed China for many years without permitting any real opposition from other political parties. But there have been serious disputes within the Party itself over what policies to adopt. In 1966, disagreements between rival factions came to a head. The leader of one group was Mao Zedong, Chairman of the Communist Party. Mao accused Liu Shaoqi, then President of the Government of the People's Republic, and also a high-ranking member of the Party, of being the leader of a faction opposed to his policies. Deng Xiaoping, another Communist leader, was also an opponent of Mao at this time.

The dispute between them was settled in a major upheaval known as the Cultural Revolution. Mao was backed by the army, but he did not use it directly to overthrow his enemies. Instead, he called on the students to shut down the schools and attack "people in authority" in the Party and government who were "taking the bourgeois road"—that is, people whose policies tended to favor the more privileged groups in society, contrary to Mao's "mass line."

The students responded to Mao's call with enthusiasm. They formed organizations known collectively as the "Red Guards" and, although they spent most of their time fighting among themselves, they managed to throw many high officials, including President Liu Shaoqi out of office. The following account, by a former Red Guard member—a high school student—indicates the power the students acquired. It describes the arrest by students of Yeh Fei, the first secretary of the Fujian Communist Party Committee and probably the most powerful person in Fujian Province. [29]

AT 9 A.M. SHARP on October 24, to the shrill sound of whistles, more than 1,000 fighters assembled in the compound and piled immediately into more than thirty trucks. We arrived at Yeh Fei's residence in less than ten minutes. The contingent from Amoy (Xiamen) Eighth Middle School was

A criticism meeting at Peking (Beijing) University. (From *China Pictorial*, No. 3, 1969, p. 9.)

directed to guard the front gate, while those from the other schools were posted to keep a lookout for the security detachment stationed nearby for Yeh Fei's protection.

We knew that this No. 1 personage in Fukien (Fujian) had only five members in his family. His two daughters were away in the north attending universities, and at the moment only an adopted son, an orphan whose father had been a revolutionary martyr, was living at home with Yeh and Wang. The residence occupied a large area, with a fishpond, a little bridge, a flower garden, and a bamboo grove. The walls were topped with a barbed-wire fence.

We rushed directly into the living quarters. . . . Yeh Fei, his wife, Wang Yu-keng, their adopted son, and a little girl we did not know were at the breakfast table, with two servants attending. They must have stopped eating on hearing our footsteps, because they sat there motionless. As we entered the dining room, Yeh Fei's face turned white. He seemed to grasp everything at once and tried to feign composure. He took off his glasses and wiped them without a word.

"Yeh Fei, Wang Yu-keng, stand up! You are under arrest! We are the commandos of the 8-29 Revolutionary Rebellion-Making General Headquarters," Piggy shouted. We had never thought the job could be so easy. . . .

Pushing Yeh and Wang aside, we began our search. We neither handcuffed nor beat them; all we wanted was to seize their authority from them, not to take their lives. In our search we tried our best to keep things intact. We took many photographs to use as evidence. . . .

There were eight rooms in the house; the four upstairs consisted of Yeh and Wang's bedroom with private bathroom, Yeh's study, Wang's study, and the adopted son's room, while downstairs were the living room, dining room, a gymnasium, and the two women servants' quarters. An annex contained a kitchen, a bathroom, and three storage rooms. In the garage there were two black limousines. Outside in the garden there were fruit trees and a badminton court.

We divided the residence into ten areas—the eight rooms plus the storage rooms and surrounding garden—and split ourselves into ten small teams to take thorough inventory. Each item was registered, photographed and assessed in value.

We even recorded the reading on the electric meter; the tiniest detail might prove to be revealing and just enough to tip the balance. During the past few months we had seized documents and collected files on Yeh and Wang and interrogated Yeh's close lieutenants, but nothing could be more concrete than what we were doing now.

Those responsible for searching the surroundings measured the total area, the height of the walls, the size of the fishpond, and recorded the number of fish and their probable origin and the kinds of flowers in the garden. They concluded that Yeh and Wang had used their position to build up an unusual collection of fish and plants. They also noted that the space occupied by Yeh and Wang was twenty times that occupied by an average worker. . . .

The first thing that struck us in the living room was the floor, inlaid with an elaborate flower design of different kinds of expensive woods that must have required a lot of people's labor. So we said to Mei-mei, "Imposing hardship on the people and squandering the nation's wealth! Take that down!"

We found more than one hundred bottles of expensive liquor and cigarettes and tea, almost all imported. Wang could not drink because she had high blood pressure. But where did she get all that expensive foreign liquor? When we asked her, she said they were gifts.

A RED GUARD REMEMBERS

Between June and November 1966, we locked up almost every university department head, deputy department head, professor, and lecturer. Every day we rounded them up and read them quotations from the works of Chairman Mao. We marched them off to the student dining halls to eat the same food that the students had to eat. No more fancy meals for them in the special professors' dining halls. No more getting fat on meat and fish while students were eating grain and leftovers. Every day they had to clean the lavatories and carry out the night soil. . . .

Most of them deserved their fate. Chairman Mao was right when he warned us always to be on guard against intellectuals. You can't trust intellectuals. They resist the Party line, become arrogant, develop a bourgeois way of thinking, and worship foreign things. Take old Wang, for example. When the Red Guards went to his place and took it apart, it was full of fancy scrolls and feudal Chinese art. Must have been worth a fortune. We dug out foreign coins and books, and you should have seen the furniture! He had closets full of leather shoes, fancy clothes, and junk like that. He even had a servant living in that apartment doing the cooking and cleaning. How can a socialist society tolerate people like that teaching the young? True, he was a leading specialist in physics and we needed his skills, but was it worth the cost, to keep this stinking bourgeois remnant alive to infect students with his rotten way of life?

Source: B. Michael Frolic, *Mao's People*, Cambridge: Harvard University Press, 1980, pp. 73-74.

"Why did people give these gifts to you and not to me?" Breastbeater asked. Wang Yu-keng would not answer this question.

We had to record the brands of liquor, cigarettes, and tea, but none of us could read English, so we had to ask Yeh Fei to identify the country of origin on the labels. He obliged smilingly; he knew them all. I stared straight into his eyes and said, "What are you smiling for? How can we have time to study English now when we're devoting ourselves to revolution?"

"I don't know English either. It's just that I'm familiar with the brands."

"You ghoul who sucks the people's blood! Do you know how many days' wages of a worker a bottle of this liquor is worth?" Piggy railed at him.

"These were given to me. I never have been able to make myself drink any because I see the toiling masses working so hard. But it would be a waste to throw them away. So I just keep them there."

We ignored his explanation and ordered him to hold a big batch of foreign liquor and cigarettes while we snapped his picture—to bear the caption "Yeh Fei, the ghoul who sucks the people's blood."

Suddenly, somebody upstairs shouted, "Come up and see how corrupt Yeh Fei and Wang Yu-keng are."

We all dashed upstairs to Yeh and Wang's bedroom. It reeked with fragrance, and in the wardrobe there were expensive cloth, high-heeled shoes, and a big stack of French perfumes. Whoever would have thought this old lady close to fifty was still so coquettish?

What really made us wonder was the size of the tub in the bathroom, larger than any we had ever seen.

"This must be where Yeh Fei and Wang Yu-keng bathe together," someone said.

Whereupon Wang was called in and asked whether this was so. She denied it, saying, "We moved into this house only about two years ago and I was then already well over forty years old. Would I still be disposed to do anything like that?"

"I would worry that Yeh Fei might bring a girl secretary here."

"Oh, no. He leads a very austere life. I trust him."

"Dog fart!"

Someone suggested that we ask Yeh and Wang to try out the tub by bathing together now. Instead, we measured it to see how much wider it was than the usual tub, and although we had no solid proof that Yeh and Wang had indeed bathed in it together, we took pictures of the tub anyway as more evidence of their corrupt mode of life. These data were to appear on big character posters that very day, and the bathtub was to become the major attraction for visitors when the house was opened to the public.

Finally, all of us paid a visit to the storage rooms, They looked almost like an exhibition hall; Yeh and Wang had raked together from all over the country many art objects and scrolls of painting and calligraphy, which they had artistically arranged for display. From our interrogations of Provincial Party Committee cadre members, we had learned that Yeh Fei enjoyed bringing people here to see his collections, after which his subordinates would, of course, know what to present to him to win his pleasure.

We helped the team in charge of these rooms record and assess all the items. Although we all were laymen, we did know that the cost of art objects could not be estimated by their weight. Since there was no time to bring in experts, we marked down figures through sheer guesswork—$300 JMP,* $500 JMP—generally higher than we thought the items were actually worth.

It was past noon when we finished; Yeh Fei and Wang Yu-keng had been on their feet for more than three hours. We concluded with an estimate of the total value of his property and compared it with his salary for the past ten years or so (ten times the wage of a worker). More than ten years before, when he had been first transferred from the military to a provincial post, he had come to Fukien (Fujian) empty-handed. Now he was worth several hundred thousand dollars JMP. More than nine-tenths of his property had come from corrupt activities and exploitation.

> *Editor's Postscript:* This Red Guard report points out a major reason for the Cultural Revolution, as well as some of the methods used. Mao wanted to shake up the Party and government because he feared that after seventeen years in power, many officials had lost their revolutionary ideas and were becoming a new class of bureaucrats, who were serving themselves rather than the people. If Yeh Fei is at all typical, Mao's fears seem to have been well grounded.
>
> As for the Red Guards, Mao worried that the youth of China who had been born after the Communists seized power might not be good "successors to the revolutionary cause." Mao felt that they should learn revolution by making it. To a great extent, they directed local activities themselves, and they made many mistakes. They made indiscriminate accusations and attacks and frequently used physical force, contrary to Mao's specific instructions. A number of Red Guard units even attacked the military, which for a while stood by helplessly because Chairman Mao had ordered the troops to "support the Left" and not use weapons.

---

* JMP, Jen-min-pi, Chinese currency. 1 JMP = $.50 U.S.

A Tough Guy

Editor's Introduction: Not all of the victims of the Red Guards were high ranking officials. Many were urban intellectuals. Others were average citizens who had owned land or businesses prior to the 1949 revolution, or whose parents or grandparents had been members of rich families in the prerevolutionary era. The following account relates the experiences of one family as told by a man who was 18 years old in 1966. It was originally published in Beijing in 1990. [30]

WELL, TO TELL the truth, my family suffered pretty badly during those ten years. But I wasn't just some useless wimp. I was a pretty damn tough guy. Usually I'd take on anybody, but in those days even tough guys had to keep their heads down. But you've got to get out your feelings sometime, don't you? I've been holding mine inside for ten years. It's about time I found some release and that's why I'm here.

In 1966 I got through trade school and was assigned to work in a crane equipment factory. I was eighteen. Let me tell you about my family. I had parents, a grandma, two brothers, and a little sister. Grandma was eighty back then. Dad wasn't quite right in the head, not really out of his skull, but not all there either. My older brother had been strong as a bull, but he had a head injury from an accident at work and hadn't been normal ever since. My younger brother and sister were just little kids. So I was the only guy really capable of looking after the family. We were bad enough off to begin with. We sure as hell didn't need the Cultural Revolution.

I was worried from the start about what was in store for us. Because even though my family was pretty poor, we still supposedly didn't have the right class background. Before Liberation, my dad had worked as a traffic police-man for a year. Grandma's parents had some real estate and she and Grandpa became the managers. When they died, Dad took over. There were more than thirty apartments. In the 1950s, in the housing reconstruction period, ten of them were taken by the state. So Dad ended up as manager for about twenty rundown apartments. The "four cleanups'" didn't clear up our family status. We weren't counted as capitalists, but we weren't pure enough to be revolutionary working class either.

When the Cultural Revolution got started, houses were broken into and there was fighting everywhere. No one knew who'd be the next target. I once came across a whole clan, over twenty of them, lined up in the street. They had paper boards around their necks, and their hair was all cut short. You couldn't even tell the men from the women. All of them were being denounced in public by the Red Guards. I got really scared and ran home to sort out and burn everything those bastards might consider old. I didn't want to look for trouble, right?

At first we lucked out. But when the "checkups'" started, everybody got investigated. One midnight some people came pounding at our door. They were the neighborhood committee representatives with a bunch of local activists demanding to see our residence cards. They searched our place and broke all sorts of things. Pretty soon they came up with what they figured was criminal evidence against my dad—his so-called restoration records. It was only the accounts and receipts for the apartments, but those idiots figured they'd struck gold. They dragged my father to their neighborhood committee office and phoned his work unit. His work unit people came that same night and carted him away in a Jeep. They really believed that Dad kept restoration records and was plotting to restore the old order. What's the use of that stuff anyway and what in hell could someone like my father do? He couldn't even talk right. He had to get my little sister to write out his self-criticisms. A guy like him was about to overthrow socialism? Bullshit! Chairman Mao said, "Political power grows out of the barrel of a gun." Dad wouldn't even have known which end goes bang. Well, he still got locked up in the "cowshed." His crimes were being a member of the KMT police and a reactionary householder. He got denounced every day in all his factory's workshops, one by one.

At this point the rest of us just shut ourselves up at home. For days we didn't dare go out and get decent food or anything. Grandma went nuts. The old girl was really terrified. She fell one day and was paralyzed. She spent the rest of her days suffering in bed till she died in 1972.

I went to Dad's work unit, to try to explain his condition. The guy in charge was a real SOB. He started yelling at me even before I had a chance to introduce myself. "Why are you sticking your nose into things?" he said. I figured that if I said one more thing, I'd probably be accused of trying to restore the old order too. And anything I said would make things worse for Dad, so I just shut up and left. Really got pissed off.

Everything wrong got blamed on the Gang of Four, but without a whole lot of other groups all over the place, how could they have done so much damage all by themselves? After my father got into trouble, my family's standing was shot. Overnight our neighbors started acting like they were better than us. The ones that had something or other against us weren't about to miss their chance. Everyone picks on you when you're down. We got shunned and cursed. Sometimes we'd even get a brick through our window while we were eating. Not a damn thing we dared to say or do about it. My mother got hit by a china jar thrown by a neighbor's kid. My fourteen-year-old brother was also hit over the head with a brick by another bastard and have to have nine stitches. His face was covered with blood. I couldn't even see his eyes, nose, and mouth.

We were human beings too. We couldn't put up with the insults and being picked on like this. So we went to the local Public Security Bureau to report. All they did was tell us we were "problematic" and we ended up having to apologize to our neighbors. No matter what we did, we were in the wrong. We were troublemakers because we dared to complain. I was a young man then and knew a little wrestling and kung fu. I had guts and was ready to fight for some justice. At another time I never would have put up with all that, but it was different then.

One night my older brother had a fit and was yelling and screaming. One of our neighbor's visiting country relatives came in and beat the hell out of him with a shoulder pole until he was rolling on the ground and was bleeding like crazy. Another neighbor finally stepped in and told that stupid farmer, "Stop beating him! He is a mental patient!" In spite of that some other bastard was yelling about how the "householder capitalist's" son deserved beating. It all happened while I was working the night shift. When I got home I saw clots of my brother's blood lying there on the ground looking like some rotten bean curd. I just about went out of my mind. I broke down and cried. I don't do that very often. I mean, you know, a man's not supposed to cry. But I couldn't help myself. I got so damn angry—I was breathing fire, the blood vessels on my neck were about to burst. I really wanted to beat the crap out of the bastards, but somehow I managed to hold myself back. I'm not stupid. If I did anything I'd be committing the crime of "class revenge" or some other crap like that. If they hung that rap on me, my dad and my whole family would really have been up the creek. I couldn't let that happen. It was pretty hard to swallow this one, but damn it, I did it.

These days I often think about what happened. My family was actually on pretty good terms with our neighbors. Never did anything bad to them or made any enemies. Why did they treat us so badly? Why did they change like that? It was all because of the goddamn Cultural Revolution!

I figured if I was going to make things any better for us, I'd better get politically progressive and work as hard as I could. So night and day I worked my ass off. I was in the team doing the hardest work. We had about twenty metal lathes and ran two shifts. The production quota was 240 hours a month each. No bonuses. I always managed to put in 300 hours, sometimes even 400. Aside from getting a drink of water or taking a leak, I stood by my lathe all day. Ten years of that. Never got there late or knocked off early. Not even a sick leave or anything. In the summer I worked bare-chested. We'd get red hot steel waste chips flying off the machines going everywhere, sometimes even into your eyes or on your skin. My lathe turned fast and had to be kept going all the time. Even when I got burned I kept on working. I finally convinced my coworkers that I was OK. I was given a bunch of model factory worker awards every year. I bet that if I worked like that now, I'd become a national model worker.

I made out OK at work but back home things were not easy. My brother's brains got more and more scrambled because he was always getting picked on. He was just too crazy. Nobody could get any sleep. No hospital would take him because of our bad family status. Finally, he died at home.

My sister could have stayed in the city and worked because our family was so poor. Even her school agreed. But politics got in the way and she was sent to the Inner Mongolian grasslands, a thousand miles away. Ninety percent of high school graduates with bad family status got sent there. Those who were considered all right went to the Great Northern Wilderness. My sister went through hell out there. She was really suffering from the climate, and the political pressures were pretty bad too. When she came back at twenty-seven after eleven years of that, she was totally wasted—her hair had even turned white. She only began to look normal again just lately. Can you imagine how I feel about it?

My father was now working as a boiler room janitor. After his shift he went around collecting the wasted coal bits to show his revolutionary conscience. He wouldn't get home until midnight. Some young [punks] often took advantage of my dad's weirdness and would knock him around and throw him on the ground. He was mentally ill and even the constitution said he should be protected, but who gave a hoot about the law in those days? I couldn't stand my dad being treated like that. I wanted to find those guys and take them apart. But it wouldn't have done my family any good. Not a damn thing I could do.

Once a military unit came to my factory to recruit young people. To show my patriotism I wrote a letter in my own blood. It went something like this: "Resolutely vowing to safeguard Chairman Mao and the Party Central Committee and to defend our motherland to the death, I earnestly request to join the army." I figured that if I got to be a soldier, my family would be military dependents and their political status would get a lot better. I passed the physical and the army wanted me since I'd already shown myself to be a model worker. But again I got the boot because of our family background. The army just couldn't risk it. I didn't get anywhere that time either.

My factory leaders were touched by how hard I'd been working. They went to my father's factory over and over to try and sort out this family background business but got nowhere. We were stuck with this damn background crap for ten years. I lost a hell of a lot of weight and turned into a nervous wreck. Half of my stomach had to get cut out in an operation. Nothing worked. I just couldn't do anything to help my family. I felt so useless!

After the Gang of Four fell, my father was finally let off the hook. He was still the same guy as always but they no longer considered him "problematic." . . . It's . . . absurd! I demanded that those bastards at his factory give him rehabilitation and compensation, but they told me the "cowshed" and the rest of the crap he went through was the fault of the "mass movement." He'd never officially been called a capitalist so there was nothing to rehabilitate him for. Those bastards just dismissed the whole thing with a few words. No worries for them. I really wanted to beat them to a pulp but a real man has to control himself. All right, even if you figured you were a tough guy, what the hell could you have done in that situation? So, that was my ten years.

Editor's Postscript: The Red Guards left chaos in their wake. They were inexperienced and so divided among themselves that they could not possibly create new institutions to take the place of the ones that they had destroyed. Eventually the army was commanded to restore order. It then took the lead in establishing "revolutionary committees" to replace the old administrative institutions that had been destroyed by the Red Guards. Gradually, the Party and government were reformed on Maoist lines, and the role of the army in administration declined.

Maoism as Religion

The gods? Worship them by all means. But if you had only Lord Kuan and the Goddess of Mercy and no peasant association, could you have overthrown the local tyrants and evil gentry? The gods and goddesses are indeed miserable objects. You have worshipped them for centuries, and they have not overthrown a single one of the local tyrants or evil gentry for you! Now you want to have your rent reduced. Let me ask how will you go about it. Will you believe in the gods or in the peasant associations?

—*Mao Zedong, 1927*

Editor's Introduction: Changing the way people think requires more than a transformation of secular values. It also means changing religious ideas and institutions.

The Communists are atheists; they do not believe in any god or supernatural force. Rather, they assert that only living beings have ideas, and that those ideas did not exist before life on earth. In other words, they do not believe in a Grand Idea or master plan of God that existed before material reality and shaped it. Furthermore, they assert that there are no gods to help or to punish human beings. They believe that people make their own history in accordance with material reality. History and environment are what influence ideas and actions.

Karl Marx, after studying history, concluded that human society is moving toward Communism—that is, toward a system in which everyone is equal and no person or group exploits another. The future can be foreseen to some extent, Marx felt, because of trends apparent in historical development so far, not because of a divine plan.

Mao Zedong among all the followers of Marx, has particularly stressed that Communism is not predetermined. There is no mysterious force that makes the realization of Communism certain. And while firmly believing that Communist egalitarianism is good and worth struggling to achieve, he constantly reiterates that only humans can bring it about. To do so, they must get rid of all their superstitions and traditional ideas about gods and fate.

During the Maoist era, many places of worship were closed, believers harassed, and priests mistreated. Freedom to practice religion was never extended to the foreign missionaries, who dominated the Christian Church in China. Like other foreigners, most were expelled from China. A few were convicted of espionage and subversion, and were jailed.

The Communists' main effort, however, was to change old practices gradually through education and by providing beneficial alternatives to old religious practices. For example, better medical facilities and care greatly reduced reliance on spirit mediums; the removal of ancestral remains from family plots to common graveyards had increased the amount of land available for agriculture; and the encouragement of less expensive funerals had lifted a heavy financial burden once considered necessary to honor dead ancestors properly. (Many of these accomplishments, however, were reversed during the post-Mao years.)

In addition, as many people have pointed out, Maoism itself is like a religion in many respects. It has a concept of future paradise (on earth), a savior (Chairman Mao), a set of sacred books (Mao's works), saints (revolutionary martyrs), hymns, and proselytizing missionaries (Party cadres). And last, but by no means least, it has a distinct set of moral principles.

In this regard, a statement from the Vatican in Rome in April 1973 is interesting. It asserts that Maoist doctrine contains some directives that "find authentic and complete expression in modern social Christian teaching." The statement goes on to say that "Christian reflections" are present in the thoughts of Mao, and that present-day China, like Christianity, "is devoted to a mystique of disinterested work for others, to inspiration by justice, to exaltation of simple and frugal life, to rehabilitation of the rural masses, and to a mixing of social classes." *

Obviously there are many important differences between Christianity and Maoism, but the Catholic Church found in Maoist moral principles the basis for reconciliation between the Vatican and the People's Republic.

As a demonstration of the analogy between Maoism and religion, consider the following poem. It was written in 1969 when the cult of Maoism was at its height in China. [31]

---

* Reported in *The New York Times*, April 18, 1973.

LONG LIFE TO YOU, CHAIRMAN MAO

OVER THE SURGING waters
Of the great Yangtse,
Ten thousand *li*, and more,
Rises a bright red sun,
Riding over the waves,
Shaking the earth!
The bold and stately mountains
Straighten out;
The rippling waters
Sing a joyful song:
Chairman Mao!
Our most respected and beloved leader
Chairman Mao
Enjoys good health;
Enjoys good health!
Chairman Mao
You give us
Faith and strength illimitable;
With your encouragement
Comes the realization of our great ideals;
We give of our best,
Aim high;
We will follow you forever!
We will advance
Through storm and hurricane!
We bless you, Chairman Mao;

Editor's Postscript: The cult of Mao was particularly a feature of the early years of the Cultural Revolution, when the aging leader made his most vigorous attempt to transform the habits and traditional thought patterns of the Chinese people. No work on any topic was published without obligatory quotations from The Chairman.

REVOLUTIONARY APHORISMS
IN PRAISE OF MAO ZEDONG

Editor's note: Aphorisms form an integral part of Chinese folk literature. The people compose them whenever they want to state a general truth derived from their own experience of life. The following is a selection of new [1966] aphorisms widely circulated among the men of the Chinese People's Liberation Army.

Chairman Mao's works shed a golden light,
Like the red sun, forever bright.

Relying on mere physical strength is of little worth,
But relying on Mao Zedong's thought we can make a new heaven and earth.

All rivers in the world flow to the sea,
All truths are found in the works of Mao Zedong.

Bullets and shells
Are no match
For the spiritual atom bomb of Mao Zedong's thought.

Difficulties by thousands may hedge us around,
But with Chairman Mao's thought a solution is found.

Learn from Chairman Mao to keep a firm class stand,
Or you may betray the Party in the end.

Read Chairman Mao's works every day,
You'll not lose your way but see clear;
Read Chairman Mao's works every day,
And you'll have drive to spare;
Read Chairman Mao's works every day
And you'll overcome hardships of every kind;
Read Chairman Mao's works every day
And nothing can poison your mind.

Source: Michael Schoenhals, ed., *China's Cultural Revolution, 1966-1969: Not a Dinner Party*, Armonk, NY: M.E. Sharpe, 1996, pp. 188-192.

The Disillusionment
of Youth

Editor's Introduction: It is probably fair to say that the great majority of students who participated in the Cultural Revolution acted out of idealism. They were convinced that they were in the vanguard of a movement to purge China of corrupt officials and "feudal" ideas and move a step closer to the ideal egalitarian society. When government institutions and the Communist Party itself collapsed as a result of their actions, the People's Liberation Army finally moved in to restore order.

The army had always been the decisive factor in the struggle. Under its commander, Lin Biao, the army had supported Mao's Cultural Revolution, allowing the students free rein for a while. When it took the initiative from the Red Guards, it became the nucleus of "revolutionary committees" formed to replace fallen government institutions. But Lin Biao had ambitious plans of his own. The Chinese now say that in his quest for power, he tried to assassinate Chairman Mao in 1971 and establish a military dictatorship. They report that he was killed when his plane crashed en route to the Soviet Union where he tried to flee after his plot was discovered.

Following Lin's death, Party and government agencies were reestablished, but a ferocious power struggle continued behind the scenes. The faction that was dominant most of the time until Mao's death, in 1976, was led by Mao's wife, Jiang Qing. She and three others, subsequently known as "The Gang of Four," favored the policies of the Cultural Revolution, particularly the vigorous promotion of class struggle. Immediately following Mao's death, they were arrested by Mao's replacement, Hua Guofeng, who accused them of high crimes against the state. At their trial in November 1980, they were charged with murdering or "persecuting to death" 34,800 people in their quest for power. All four were found guilty. Jiang Qing was given a death sentence, suspended for two years, pending a change of attitude and behavior. Her sentence was subsequently commuted to life imprisonment. She reportedly committed suicide in 1991.

The other faction, led by Deng Xiaoping, became ascendant after Mao's death and immediately set about reversing most of the policies and programs of the Cultural Revolution. All of China's problems were now blamed on Lin Biao and the Gang of Four, and even Mao was subject to considerable criticism and blame. Lin and the Gang were held responsible for distorting Maoism and making it a religion which no one dared contradict. The new leadership called for demystification of the cult of Mao under the slogan "seek truth from facts," but at the same time, it put its own limits on truth seeking by restricting the factual data that one could consider. For instance, few would dare to suggest openly that the activities of the Gang of Four were motivated by any but the basest motives.

It is little wonder that these events left many people, particularly young people, cynical about politics and about life in general. The general disillusionment of youth in China was of great concern to the leadership in the 1980s. Illustrative of the problem is a series of letters on "the meaning of life" published in the journal *Chinese Youth*. The series was initiated by a once idealistic young woman, Pan Hsiao, who had lost all faith in the Communist Party and the Chinese government and had come to view life as a selfish struggle for personal gain. Her letter to the journal was answered by thousands of others expressing both agreement and disagreement with her position. The following selection is from one of those letters. It reads like the collective biography of the youth of the Cultural Revolution generation. The author, contrary to Pan Hsiao, has regained his idealism. [32]

DEAR COMRADE PAN Hsiao:

How are you?

I am the author of the short story "Maple." I don't know whether you have read it or not. The story depicts the younger generation's idealism and heroism tinted with modern religious superstition during the Cultural Revolution. It can be said that it epitomizes the spirit of that era. The story is not well-written, but I can guarantee one thing: it is true to life.

This generation of ours spent our early youth in a comparatively stable society. With their exploits, heroes like Lei Feng and other models for young people imbued our crystal-like hearts with the lofty and magnificent idea of "revolution." With great eagerness, we studied Mao Tse-tung's (Mao

Zedong's) Thought and were ready at any time to dedicate all we had to the Chinese revolution and the world revolution.

When the Cultural Revolution got underway, our revolutionary enthusiasm erupted like a volcano. Swimming with the tide and obeying the orders of the proletarian headquarters, we plunged into the whirlpool of struggle. Finally, however, history mercilessly displayed before us the harsh reality. In the face of these bloody facts, all the lies and deceptions became obvious one after another. The myth about the sanctity of Mao Tse-tung's (Mao Zedong's) Thought exploded, and so did the deity himself. Ideas, life, hope, and courage were all ruined.

I had been most eager to pitch into the struggle. Being concerned about the nation's destiny, I ran across several provinces and municipalities, joining the youthful forces of the Cultural Revolution. But I saw the killing of more than 2,700 people in the so-called struggle by violence in a small prefecture called Luzhou. In addition dozens of boats and ships were sunk or destroyed. Could this have been done for the sake of "revolution" as conceived by the people?

Like you, we were seized by all kinds of anxiety and misgivings. But as we studied Chairman Mao's exhortations to "combat selfishness and criticize revisionism," we piously criticized our hesitation and wavering as simply a manifestation of a *petit bourgeois* mentality. Therefore as soon as we young people were called upon to resettle in the countryside, we all eagerly signed up without any reluctance. Everyone was determined to integrate himself with the worker and peasant masses and to reform the "deep-rooted bad habits of the *petit bourgeoisie*" by doing arduous labor.

Among my schoolmates who went to Taigu County, Shansi (Shanxi) Province, some had deformed legs, some had chronic diseases, and others were under the age requirement for living and working in the countryside. They had applied many times before they were approved. Some even wrote application letters with their blood. A batch of us, some thirty in number, were assigned to a commune named Pingchuan. We did not accept the assignment, but went to see the leader in charge, asking her to send us to a commune where conditions were the most difficult. At first, she mistook our request as an expression of dislike for the commune to which we were assigned. She explained to us again and again that the commune was not bad and one could get high bonuses there. When she finally understood our intention, she was so moved that for a while she was unable to utter a word.

In this way we came to a mountainous commune in the remotest part of Taigu County, the only commune that did not have electricity. As soon as

Comic books were a popular means of publicizing information and ideas in China. The cartoon illustrates Mao's assertion that: "The day the women of the whole country arise is when the Chinese revolution will be victorious." The young woman in the picture is suggesting to her Party Secretary that a women's militia unit be established during the Chinese Civil War.

we put down our luggage, we went through the village, visiting the poor peasants and presenting to every household Chairman Mao badges and his works. Braving the coldest weather in a year in that highland, we took up our hoes early the next morning to dig up the earth and fill the gullies in order to reclaim land for agriculture. Thus, in a little mountainous village of only nine families located in the chain of Taihang mountains, we started our difficult life as rusticated youths with high spirit and vigor.

My friends and I were deeply grateful for being resettled in the countryside. It brought us from the dazzling blue sky of idealism down to the cold and harsh earth of reality. Rustication opened our eyes for the first time to the real countryside in China not to be found in propaganda, and to the peasants' real feelings of joy, anger, sorrow and happiness.

With the courage of being ready to gulp down all the sufferings of the world at once, we pitched into the struggle to remake nature. On the first day alone I broke several hoe handles while digging with all my might. At the risk of my life, I used a wire only ten meters long as a detonating cord for dynamiting rocks. In spite of the production team leader's dissuasion, another schoolmate and I jumped into the mountain torrents to salvage timber owned by the collective. Some schoolmates experimented in growing rice in the mountainous region despite the difficulties. Even our girl schoolmates carried on their shoulders rocks and manure buckets, and so did the schoolmates with deformed legs. Instances like this are too many to enumerate.

Nevertheless, our blood and sweat were of little avail. Our ideal of building a socialist new countryside suffered severe setbacks under the "left" deviationist line which called for "evaluating one's work according to political performance" and "conducting agricultural production by exercising proletarian dictatorship."

Resettlement also helped us to sober down for the first time and reflect on the Chinese Revolution. When looking at Peking (Beijing) from afar, we were pained to find that the end result of the Cultural Revolution was not a much better society as had been promised. The so-called "capitalist roaders" were toppled, but in their place emerged a feudal, fascist dictatorship we had never seen before. Lin Piao's (Lin Biao's) attempted coup especially shocked us like a thunderbolt. Any apology or excuse could in no way cover up the lightning that made our souls tremble. We were faced with a deep spiritual crisis!

Some schoolmates were unable to stand a life of deception and loss of faith. They committed suicide as a protest, though a thin voice it was against society. Some sank into degradation, engulfed in the turbid waves of life. However, there were still quite a few comrades who started thinking things out on their own; they were searching for answers from the realities of society and Marx's works. We did physical labor in the daytime and conducted extensive and in-depth social surveys. At night we read and studied. For a period of time, we had only one kerosene lamp and had to make do by reading in three shifts. Some read while others went to sleep. In the dimly-lit cave, we took turns studying until daybreak.

I had been the most pious and therefore was also the most disappointed. Confronted with harsh realities, my girl friend nearly committed suicide, and I went to the north of the Shanhai Pass and roamed about in the forests of the Xing-an Mountains and in the prairies of Hulunbeier. I took up odd jobs and did hard labor. I carried with me a set of carpentry tools and wrapped myself in a worn-out dog hide. My satchel was filled with works by Marx, Feuerbach and Huxley. I wanted to see the world, I wanted to find out from my 3,000-mile journey and from the sweat and toil I spent in dozens of towns and villages something true and reliable.

"A Newcomer," painting utilizing traditional brush technique by Yang Chih-kuang. (From *Chinese Literature*, No. 3, Peking: Foreign Languages Press, 1972, p. 48.)

Some of my friends wrote economics essays to criticize theories advocated by Lin Piao (Lin Biao) and the "Gang of Four" concerning the basic economic law of socialist society, and because of this they were placed under surveillance for quite a few years. Still others took up the pen, broke through literary blockades, and produced a number of poems and articles opposing Lin Piao (Lin Biao) and the "Gang of Four." These hand-copied manuscripts soon got around and became "underground literature" of considerable influence at that time. In this way the old religion fell apart like an avalanche, while a new faith was still in the difficult process of being conceived.

There has never been a generation, I dare say, that has experienced such terrible spiritual collapse and mental torture as we have. Our revolutionary predecessors, once they discovered the truth of revolution, threw themselves into the people's cause, courageously and faithfully carrying on the struggle. They did not have the pain of wavering and losing faith that we have experienced. To whom could we turn? The "Gang of Four," by stealing the name of the leader and the Party, had everything under their control and monopolized the right to interpret Marxism-Leninism and Mao Tse-tung (Mao Zedong) Thought. In the darkness we could only explore Marxist theories on our own, groping forward in a painful mood of negating the past.

We are grateful to the vast expanse of life in society. At the bottom of society we experienced an acute and complex struggle marked with the characteristics of the new era. We were maturing, embracing again the great truth of Marxism. We are now espousing a Marxism that is no longer superstition shrouded in the halo of myth, nor the means and tool which certain conspiratorial cliques employed to exercise an "all-round dictatorship" over the people in order to strengthen their rule of feudal fascism. It is a scientific world outlook, the truth for the emancipation of all mankind! We are grateful to the deep ocean of the people! They are like a mother to us and it is in their arms we have healed our wounds, returned to life and drawn courage and strength.

This is the history of how we changed from a generation of blind and pious faith to a generation of tenacious thinking. Some older comrades understand this, but some news media and leadership just make endless accusations against us. I have no intention of defending our conduct; rather, I only want to make a relatively objective review of history. True, there are hoodlums, thieves and murderers among us. But whenever I call to mind this generation of ours, first to appear before my eyes are a group of kind and generous laborers. I cannot go against my conscience and show disappointment in them. This is because I understand them. I know for sure they hate evil like an enemy, and behind their sometimes extremist language is a child's innocent heart beating for the motherland, the people and the Party.

Just as every generation has its own merits and shortcomings, we, too, have many drawbacks and problems. For example, we lack a sense of duty, a sense of being the masters of the country. We are not constructive in nature and are short of cultural cultivation. We have done more destruction than construction, and we are skeptical about more things than we affirm. But if we analyse the matter in a materialist perspective and assume that all this came as a result of a social life which had been turned upside down, then after having smashed the "Gang of Four," we have reason to believe that in a stable and united social environment all these problems can be solved step by step under positive guidance.

Comrade Little Pan, it is my feeling that you have not truly seen through life. For thousands of years humans have tenaciously searched for the value of existence; they seek the truth of life, pursuing the true, the good and the beautiful. You are only 23 years of age and your experience cannot be regarded as profound and mature. It is inappropriate for you to blurt out that you "see through" everything, Your understanding at this stage is only one phase of your life. You will not stop at this point and your path is by no means narrowing. Precisely because you are persistently exploring and are not fearful of hardships, you are standing at the threshold of truth. It is possible for you to find a valuable life and thus become a most enthusiastic and valiant fighter. Of course we cannot rule out the other possibility. Don't hide yourself in love, and don't evade the crisis of your faith, but move forward to meet it head-on. Your age is the best time to solve the problem of your outlook on life. If you turn from it, you will achieve nothing in your whole life. If you step up to it and find a good solution, you will sweep forward irresistibly like water pouring from a steep roof.

The Results of the
Cultural Revolution

Editor's Introduction: The official position of the Chinese government is that the Cultural Revolution lasted from the Spring of 1966 until the death of Mao in 1976. The policies of Mao and his followers, the Gang of Four, were blamed for creating ten years of chaos that ruined China economically, culturally and socially. Here is an account of this momentous period from an officially produced history book. [33]

MAY 1966 MARKS the beginning of an event unprecedented in the international Communist movement, the "Great Proletarian Cultural Revolution." During the decade that followed, China was thrown into a period of turmoil and destruction that caused the severest setbacks that the Communist Party and the nation had ever experienced since the founding of the People's Republic.

The theoretical rationale for the "cultural revolution," formulated largely by Mao Zedong, the initiator and leader of the movement, was complex and at times confusing. Mao believed that representatives of the bourgeoisie, called counterrevolutionary revisionists, had infiltrated the Party, the administration, the army and academic and cultural circles in large numbers. This meant that leadership in a majority of organizations was no longer in the hands of Marxists and of the people. The Chairman insisted that powerful Party members with capitalist leanings had formed a bourgeois stronghold within the Party Central Committee that pursued revisionist policies and had agents in all provinces, municipalities and autonomous regions as well as central government departments. Since all previous forms of struggles had proved incapable of solving this problem, Mao believed that the power usurped by those with capitalist tendencies could be recaptured only by carrying out a great cultural revolution, by publicly and unequivocally encouraging a mass movement from below to expose the dangers threatening socialism. The "cultural revolution," then, was not thought of as a political revolution, in which one class would overthrow another, but as just one of many such revolutions necessary to prevent political-ideological retrogression.

These theses underlay the overriding "theory of continuing the revolution under the dictatorship of the proletariat," which Mao was later to incorporate into his political philosophy. However, the history of the "cultural revolution" showed that such thinking conformed neither to the principles of Marxism-Leninisin nor to the reality of the situation in China at that time. It not only represented a misdirected appraisal of prevailing class relations and of the political climate in the Party and the state, but suggested inappropriate means for solving any problems that did exist . . . .

In the late 1950s Mao Zedong's prestige among the people reached its peak. The Chinese people's gratitude for his leadership in the revolution and their admiration for his dedication to socialist reconstruction developed into a cult that grew beyond all reason. In the circumstances, Mao began to make arbitrary decisions, sometimes ignoring or acting against the consensus of the Party Central Committee. The result was a steady weakening of the principle of collective leadership and democratic centralism in the Party and in the state mechanism. It was precisely this complex of ideological misformulations that Lin Biao, Jiang Qing, Kang Sheng and others were to encourage and manipulate to their own political advantage.

The overthrow of the Jiang Qing clique brought to a close the ten most chaotic years in the history of the People's Republic of China and marked the beginning of a new era of national development. What transpired in this period showed that it was neither a cultural revolution nor a true revolution in any sense. Instead of social progress, it only brought chaos, losses and retrogression to the Party, the state and the Chinese people.

The main responsibility for the serious "Left" errors that left the nation in a shambles rests with Mao Zedong. However, his error was, after all, the error of a great proletarian revolutionary.

> This view still represents the position of the Chinese government. However, several scholars, both in China and abroad, have challenged this view. The first bone of contention pertains to the length of the Cultural Revolution. China scholar Jonathan Unger, who conducted numerous interviews for his studies of rural China, noted that, "For its own reasons, the Chinese government declared in 1977 that the Cultural Revolution had lasted

until Mao's death, and many foreign and Chinese authors have adopted the Chinese government's new periodization of the term. Doing so obfuscates what occurred in China." He claimed that if one is writing about "leadership turmoil and violent mass purges among the Party elite," these were ended at the Ninth Party Congress in 1969. However, if one is discussing the situation "at the grassroots in the provinces," the Cultural Revolution was forcibly ended in late 1968.*

By claiming that the Cultural Revolution lasted for ten years, the new post-Mao government was able to demonize all of the radical policies of the 1970s by associating them with the most disruptive ones of the 1966 to 1968 period.

Other scholars pointed out that many of the Cultural Revolution's policies had a positive impact on millions of Chinese. Mobo C. F. Gao, who lived and worked in China during the period, wrote that the "positives" should include, "developments in military defense, industry and agriculture. The politically correct line argues that the Chinese economy was brought to the brink of collapse during the Cultural Revolution. However, documentary evidence and special studies of the period ... all demonstrate that that was not the case. True, China's economy was disrupted in 1967 and 1968, but throughout the rest of the 1960s and throughout all of China's 1970s the economy showed consistent growth."**Similar views on the economy were put forward by Philip C.C. Huang, who undertook a comprehensive study of Songjiang county in the Yangzi delta. He concluded that, [34]

THE STATISTICAL RECORD bears out the overall impression of stability and growth in agriculture. Crop yields advanced steadily, and in some cases dramatically, in both Songjiang and the nation as a whole between 1962-66 and 1972-76. That is why peasants and technical cadres alike emphasize that the Cultural Revolution was a Political movement that had little impact on crop production.

In the realm of sidelines, the Cultural Revolution . . . let private plots, at least in Songjiang, untouched. . . . In industry the Cultural Revolution years saw new advances. . . . This is not to deny the great human toll that

---

*   Jonathan Ungar, *The Transformation of Rural China*, Armonk, NY: M.E. Sharpe, 2002, p. 41.

**   Mobo C.F. Gao, "Debating the Cultural Revolution: Do we only know what we believe?" *Critical Asian Studies*, Vol. 34, Issue 3, 2002, p. 424.

the Cultural Revolution took in its indiscriminate attacks on innocent victims, especially in the cities. It is only to point out that the political radicalism of the Cultural Revolution was not accompanied by extremist economic policies in the countryside.

> Critics of the official view also emphasized the dramatic increase in educational opportunity available to the average Chinese during the Cultural Revolution. While colleges and universities were shut down for several years, elementary and middle school was expanded. Elementary school enrollment went up from 116.2 million in 1965 to 150.0 million in 1976, and middle school enrollment jumped from 9.3 million in 1965 to 67.8 million in 1977. The curriculum in these schools ignored elitist subjects and concentrated on practical knowledge that was relevant to the lives of peasant farmers. Han Dongping, who lived in Jimo County, Shandong Province, during the Cultural Revolution, noted that in his area many new schools were built and that almost every child was enrolled in primary school. [35]

IT IS TRUE that the students of the village school did not learn as many new words and scientific principles as the graduates of the former elite schools did. The students of the village school devoted more time to practical knowledge than the former elite school. . . . In terms of bookish knowledge, graduates of the village school were inferior to graduates of the former elite middle school. But in terms of practical knowledge we were inferior to none. Most of my old classmates from the village school played a very important role later in the village life. Several of them became heads of production teams, construction teams, and technicians in village factories. . . .[T]he fact that more than half of villager's kids who finished junior high school could go to senior high school was revolutionary. It helped reduce the gap in the living standards between the social elite and common villagers.

> Han also claimed that the debates and discussions in the rural areas gave "common villagers some sense of power that they never had before, and it changed the common farmers' mentality." This new sense of power and liberation affected relations within his own family. He wrote that, [36]

EVERYBODY WAS EQUAL on the basis of Mao Zedong's works. My father, for example, who had never allowed me to speak with him on an equal basis before, had to tolerate my arguing with him about our political differences, thanks to the political climate of the time. The absolute authority he held over me was broken for no other reason than that Mao said that everybody inside the revolutionary rank was equal. What we argued may not have been of significance now, but the fact that I could argue on an equal basis with my father and my teacher was nothing short of personal liberation for me.

The same was true with the different groups of red guards in the whole county or whole village. One can dismiss the fighting and arguments among the different red guards groups as much ado over nothing or over trifle things only. But one can never deny that these arguments and fighting per se was part of a process of personal awakening and personal liberation for common villagers who had never been active in politics ... a kind of political maturing for the common villagers.

> Finally, Mobo C.F. Gao noted that while there were many instances of Red Guard attacks on traditional Chinese culture, including the destruction of books, historical relics and temples, there was at the same time, a flowering of culture among rural peasants. [37]

I WITNESSED AN unprecedented surge of cultural and sports activities in my own home village, Gao village (in Jiangxi province). The rural villagers, for the first time, organized theater troupes and put on performances that incorporated the contents and structure of the eight model Peking Opera with local language and music. The villagers not only entertained themselves but also learned how to read and write by getting into the texts and plays. They also organized sports meets and held matches with other villages. All these activities gave the villagers an opportunity to meet, communicate, fall in love. These activities gave them a sense of discipline and organization and created a public sphere where meetings and communications went beyond the traditional households and village clans. This has never happened before and it has never happened since.

> Gao also noted that during the Cultural Revolution thousands of unofficial newspapers and pamphlets were published by *laobaixing* (ordinary people), four national fine arts exhibitions were held in Beijing attracting an audience of 7.8 million, and the number of cinemas, cultural clubs, public libraries and museums all increased.

The Official
Legacy of Mao

Editor's Introduction: Since the death of Mao in 1976, his role in the Chinese revolution has been reassessed. As the following excerpt from a 1980 article in a Communist Party journal indicates, the cult of Mao has been repudiated.

OPPOSING PERSONALITY CULT

IS IT POSSIBLE for the Party Central Committee to make mistakes? Is it possible for responsible comrades of the Central Committee to make mistakes? Yes, it is in both cases.

In the late 50s, due to lack of normal, democratic life inside the Party, and due to lack of properly conducted criticism and self-criticism, the responsible comrade of the Central Committee (Chairman Mao) deviated from his own correct thinking and made mistakes. For many years ... the personality cult prevailed, so that a particular person was deified and it was assumed that whatever he said or did was one hundred per cent correct and there couldn't possibly be any doubt about it.

There were many other things that smack of feudalism and ignorance, things like: he understands the situation to the last detail, he sees right through everything, and he is our saviour.

The consequences of this were: firstly, democratic centralism which is a Party tradition disappeared completely; secondly, it was utterly impossible to seek truth from facts; thirdly, it was utterly impossible to emancipate the mind; and fourthly, it inevitably led to feudal autocracy under which one person had all the say and patriarchal practices prevailed and this was exploited by some bad elements, who engaged in fascist practices.

So the personality cult, something which is so completely anti-Marxist, must be repudiated in all seriousness and it must never be revived again in future.

> The following year, in the Resolution on *CPC History 1949-1981*, the Communist Party noted that Mao made "gross mistakes during the 'cultural revolution'." It also stated that it is wrong: "To adopt a dogmatic attitude towards the sayings of Comrade Mao Zedong, to regard whatever he said as immutable truth which must be mechanically applied everywhere, to be unwillingly to admit honestly that he made mistakes in his later years, and even to try to stick to them in our new activities."*

---

* Central Committee of the Communist Party of China, *Resolution on CPC History (1949-81)*, Oxford: Pergamon Press, 1981, p. 29.

PART V
THE ERA OF REFORM

Introduction

The policies of Deng Xiaoping ushered in a new era in modern Chinese history. China would no longer be dominated by Maoist ideas and the influence of the government in economic, cultural and social matters would be diminished. The communes were broken up and peasant families were allowed to control plots of land for private use. Capitalism was no longer seen as a totally negative system, private businesses were established, and workers could opt for private or public employment. Privately produced books, magazines and newspapers were published. Foreign investment grew exponentially and Western products and culture spread throughout China. Rates of economic growth soared. Criticism of some government policies and of local officials involved in corruption was tolerated (as long as critics did not directly attack the Communist system or advocate the formation of non-Communist political parties). In short, while the Communist Party remained the dominant force in society and dissidents continued to be detained or imprisoned, China became a much more open, free and tolerant society than it had been at any time since the 1949 Communist Revolution.

However, the rapid change in society had, and continues to have, negative consequences. Many new problems arose, and many old problems, which had been eliminated after the revolution of 1949, returned to plague the country. A new class of millionaires has emerged wielding enormous economic power, tens of millions of rural peasants are migrating to the cities in search of jobs and money, corruption is rampant in all levels of society, inflation has become a serious problem, the values of consumerism, commercialism and individualism have become embedded in everyday life, and Western culture has overwhelmed traditional Chinese forms of high culture as well as popular culture.

The enormous changes resulting from the reform policies initiated by Deng, and continued by his successor, Jiang Zemin (Party General Secretary, 1991-2001), and later by Hu Jintao (Party General Secretary, 2002–), are widely discussed in China. They are among the topics highlighted in this chapter.

The Call for Change

Editor's Introduction: Deng Xiaoping came to power in 1978 advocating policies opposed to those which dominated China during the Maoist era. A pragmatist who downplayed the role of ideology, he became well-known for saying "it doesn't matter whether the cat is white or black as long as it catches the mice."

He believed that the major role of the Chinese Communist Party was to develop the country economically in order to make China a prosperous and powerful nation. For him, class struggle had ended and polarization between rich and poor would not be a problem "so long as we keep our socialist public ownership predominant." Claiming that, "to be rich is glorious," he broke up the rural communes to allow peasant families to utilize the land for their private enrichment and he encouraged private businesses to be established in the cities and in the countryside. He also encouraged foreign investment to build up the economy.

Deng summarized his views in 1985 remarks to Robert Mugabe, prime minister of Zimbabwe, which are excerpted below. [38]

WHAT IS THE essence of Marxism! Another term for Marxism is communism. It is for the realization of communism that we have struggled for so many years. We believe in communism, and our ideal is to bring it into being. In our darkest days we were sustained by the ideal of communism. It was for the realization of this ideal that countless people laid down their lives. What is a communist society? It is one in which there is no exploitation of man by man, there is great material abundance, and the principle of "from each according to his ability, to each according to his needs" is applied. It is impossible to apply that principle without overwhelming material wealth. In order to realize communism, we have to accomplish the tasks set in the socialist stage. They are legion, but the fundamental one is to develop the productive forces so as to provide the material basis for communism.

Socialism, whose ultimate aim is the realization of communism, should develop the productive forces and then demonstrate its superiority over capitalism. For a long time we neglected the development of the socialist productive forces. From 1957 on they grew at a snail's pace. In that year the peasants' average annual net income was about 70 yuan, which meant that they were very poor. That figure was about the same as what a factory worker earned in a month. In 1966, when the "Cultural Revolution" was launched, the peasants' annual net income rose only slightly. Although peasants in some areas were better off, those in many other areas could barely manage to live from hand to mouth. Of course, even that was progress, compared with the old days. Still, it was far from a socialist standard of living. During the "Cultural Revolution" things went from bad to worse.

By setting things to right, we mean developing the productive forces while upholding the Four Cardinal Principles. [Ed. "upholding the socialist road, the dictatorship of the proletariat, the leadership of the Communist Party and Marxism-Leninism-Mao Zedong Thought"] To develop the productive forces, we have to reform the economic structure and open to the outside world. It is in order to assist the growth of the socialist productive forces that we absorb capital from capitalist countries and introduce their technology. After the third plenary session of the Eleventh Central Committee we began our reform step by step, starting with the countryside. The rural reform has achieved good results, and there has been a noticeable change in the countryside. Drawing on our successful experience in rural reform, we embarked on urban reform. Urban reform, a comprehensive undertaking involving all sectors, has been going on for a year now, ever since the second half of last year. Since it is much more complicated than rural economic reform, mistakes and risks are unavoidable, and that's something we are quite aware of. But economic reform is the only way to develop the productive forces. We have full confidence in urban reform, although it will take three to five years to demonstrate the correctness of our policies.

In the course of reform it is very important for us to maintain our socialist orientation. We are trying to achieve modernization in industry, agriculture, national defense, and science and technology. But in front of the word "modernization" is a modifier, "socialist," making it the "four socialist modernizations." The policies of invigorating our domestic economy and opening to the outside world are being carried out in accordance with the principles of socialism. Socialism has two major requirements. First, its economy must be dominated by public ownership, which may consist of both ownership by the entire people and ownership by the collective. Our publicly owned economy accounts for more than 90 percent of the total. At the same time, we allow a small proportion of individual economy to develop, we absorb foreign capital and introduce advanced technology, and we even encourage foreign enterprises to establish factories in China. All that will serve as a supplement to the socialist economy based on public ownership; it cannot and will not undermine it. While half the investment in a joint venture comes from abroad, the other half comes from the socialist sector, which will therefore also benefit from the growth of the enterprise. Half its profits go to the socialist sector, and the state collects taxes on all of them. An even more important aspect of joint ventures is that from them we can learn managerial skills and advanced technology that will help us to develop our socialist economy. We are also happy to have foreign businessmen launch wholly foreign-owned enterprises, on which we can also levy taxes and from which we can also learn technical and managerial skills. They will bring no harm to socialist ownership. As of now, there has been only limited foreign investment, far less than we feel we need. The second requirement of socialism is that there must be no polarization of rich and poor. If there is, the reform will have been a failure. We have given much thought to this question in the course of formulating and implementing our policies. Is it possible that a new bourgeoisie will emerge? A handful of bourgeois elements may appear, but they will not form a class. There will be no harm so long as we keep our socialist public ownership predominant, and so long as we guard against polarization. In the last four years we have been proceeding along these lines. In short, we must keep to socialism.

Manifestations
of Discontent

Editor's Introduction: The rapid changes in society, based on policies which were vilified and forbidden for decades, caused a great deal of confusion and apprehension. While some felt economically liberated, others lost their jobs and felt victimized by the new phenomena of inflation and crime. While some were emboldened to criticize the government, others feared that the new open policies would be reversed and became apolitical. Some concentrated on making money and other individual pursuits while others bemoaned the loss of communal values and social concerns. Many felt totally alienated from society and expressed their views in plays, novels and short stories. Female writers produced works that described the continuing subordination of women in Chinese society, countering the official view that women had achieved equality since the Communist Revolution. Indirect criticism of the Communist system appeared in television shows and reached the public through a new medium, rock and roll. Thus, economic growth and social ferment characterized Chinese society during the period of reform from the late 1970s through the 1980s.

One of the first manifestations of protest against the government appeared (December 5, 1978) in the form of a Beijing wall poster written by Wei Jingsheng. He was a leader of the Democracy Movement, a group of youthful political activists seeking to transform the Communist political system. Wei's treatise, "The Fifth Modernization—Democracy," condemned Chinese communism, likening it to a feudal monarchy, and advocated the establishment of a democratic government. In referring to democracy as the "fifth modernization," Wei was alluding to Premier Zhou Enlai's famous 1975 report to the National People's Congress in which he called for the rapid modernization of China's agriculture, industry, science and technology, and national defense, which were subsequently referred to as the "four modernizations." Wei believed that only with a truly democratic system could China become a modern society. Although Wei was arrested (and served nearly 20 years in prison) and the Democracy Movement was suppressed, his views undoubtedly represented the aspirations of a significant segment of the Chinese population. Below are excerpts from Wei's well-known manifesto. [39]

WHAT IS DEMOCRACY? True democracy means placing all power in the hands of the working people. . . . What is true democracy? It is when the people, acting on their own will, have the right to choose representatives to manage affairs on the peoples' behalf and in accordance with the will and interests of the people. This alone can be called democracy. Furthermore, the people must have the power to replace these representatives at any time in order to keep them from abusing their powers to oppress the people.

Is this actually possible? The citizens of Europe and the United States enjoy precisely this kind of democracy and can run people like Nixon, de Gaulle, and Tanaka out of office when they wish and can even reinstate them if they so desire. No one can interfere with their democratic rights. In China, however, if a person even comments on the "great helmsman" or the "Great Man peerless in history," Mao Zedong, who is already dead, the mighty prison gates and all kinds of unimaginable misfortunes await him. . . .

Will the country sink into chaos and anarchy if the people achieve democracy? On the contrary, have not the scandals exposed in the newspapers recently shown that it is precisely due to an absence of democracy that the dictators, large and small, have caused anarchy? The maintenance of democratic order is an internal problem that the people themselves must solve. It is not something that the privileged overlords need concern themselves with. Besides, they are not really concerned with democracy for the people, but use this as a pretext to deny the people their democratic rights.

Of course, internal problems cannot be solved overnight but must be constantly addressed as part of a long-term process. Mistakes and shortcomings will be inevitable, but these are for us to worry about. This is infinitely better than facing abusive overlords against whom we have no means of redress. Those who worry that democracy will lead to anarchy and chaos are just like those who, following the overthrow of the Qing dynasty, worried that without an emperor, the country would fall into chaos. Their decision was to: patiently suffer oppression because they feared that without the weight of oppression, their spines might completely collapse!

To such people I would like to say, with all due respect: We want to be the masters of our own destiny. We need no gods or emperors and we don't believe in saviors of any kind. We want to be masters of our universe; we do not want to serve as mere tools of dictators with personal ambitions for carrying out modernization. We want to modernize the lives of the people. Democracy, freedom, and happiness for all are our sole objectives in carrying out modernization. Without this "Fifth Modernization," all other modernizations are nothing but a new lie.

> As the reforms intensified, so did expressions of discontent. Several writers and social critics described the re-emergence of the liumang, a Chinese term referring to alienated, anti-social, rootless and criminal elements of society. These writers argued that the "liumang mentality" had pervaded Chinese social, intellectual and political life. For example, an article that appeared in a Beijing weekly in 1989 noted that: [40]

FEUDALISM IS PARTICULARLY to blame [for immoral business dealings], for such nefarious activities are one of the specialties of the liumang, the rootless and the dregs of society. I'm afraid they have a lot more to do with the proletariat than the bourgeoisie.

The lumpen or liumang proletariat despises labor; it is nonproductive and parasitical. Its members do not create wealth for the society, they only consume and destroy. . . .

In the age of reform, they have appeared once more in the guise of the most unscrupulous [entrepreneurs], utterly without conscience and contemptuous of the law. They take what they can and squander what they get. Unlike the bourgeoisie, who reinvest their profits and expand production, the *luimang* proletariat eats and spends until there is nothing left. They are wasteful and extravagant in the extreme and live as if there were no tomorrow.

This social stratum is adventurous, vengeful, opportunistic, and destructive.

This *liumang* mentality has already insinuated its way into some party and state organs, companies, and industries. Creaming off a percentage of whatever passes through their hands, they take every advantage of their position to eat and drink for free, exploit every bit of power they have, and use whatever resources are available to them—be it land, means of transportation, even official seals—for their personal benefit. . . .

. . . Acting as though their workplace is a piece of turf in some mafia network, doing whatever they please, and ignoring all laws and principles, these things are all part and parcel of the *liumang* mentality.

Other writers concentrated on the plight of women, pointing out that in spite of decades of Communist rule, traditional ideas regarding sexual roles were rampant and women were still subordinate to men in Chinese society. Essays, poems and plays written from a feminist perspective proliferated and were widely discussed. Two examples are presented below. [41]

FOUR QUESTIONS

TIMES HAVE CHANGED,
Men and women are equal.
Then why, in a certain production brigade,
Are men and women not treated equally?
They get different pay for the same work.
So men and women are different.

Times have changed,
Men and women are equal.
Then why in a certain factory
That is recruiting workers are they not treated equally?
If a man is hired the terms are flexible,
If a woman is hired the terms are strict.

Times have changed,
Men and women are equal.
Then why in a certain family
Do they respect boys and look down on girls?
If a baby boy is born the mother is happy,
If a baby girl is born she does not like it.

Times have changed,
Men and women are equal.
Then why is it that when a certain school
Admits students they are not treated equally?
To admit women they look at the score,
To admit men the score can go down.

Times have changed,
Men and women are equal.
It is natural to have both men and women.
The old feudal thinking
Must be eliminated to the core!

WOMAN IS NOT THE MOON

The play "The Return of an Old Acquaintance on a Rainy Night" (*Fengxue guren lai*) contains the following words: "Woman is not the moon. She cannot depend on the brightness of someone else to make herself shine." This is a verse that comes from real-life experience. It is a general philosophy that expresses what a large number of women feel in their hearts. Many people know this truth, but there is no better way to express it than these words. It is a pure truth.

Woman is not the moon. It is true, a woman is not an appendage of a man. As a member of society she has independent qualities; she has all the behavior, morality, intelligence, and ability of a human being. She can work and be creative. Isn't that true? Take Madame Curie—everyone has heard of this famous scientist—her contribution to society is certainly no less than that of her husband, Pierre Curie. In the scientific sky full of so many shining stars, hers is one shining all by itself, beautifully and brilliantly. Nothing can compare to it, and it will shine eternally.

Didn't our own country's contemporary woman writer Ding Ling *(The Sun Shines Over the Sanggan River)* win the Stalin Prize for Literature? The famous scientists Ling Lanying and Xiu Ruijian, the gynecologist Lin Qiaozhi, the singer Zhu Mingying—aren't they all women? Who among them did not depend on her own hard struggle and self-sacrifice to contribute to society and thus make herself shine?

These are things that many of us women understand. The problem is that many people are oppressed by old ideas and the old consciousness. They believe that as women, we don't have to be strong. They think that as long as one finds a good husband to depend on, it will be enough to just live out one's days. Old ideas such as "Woman is one of man's ribs," "if a woman does not have a husband, her body does not have an owner," etc., still influence some people. [Many believe that] man is the supporter of the family; the only thing that a woman can do is help him at home as a virtuous wife and good mother; getting ahead is something for men to do. History and present circumstances make many of us women comrades oppressed and constrained. This makes it impossible for us to display our talents, intelligence, and creativity. We just become men's servants or their burden.

Woman is not the moon. She must rely on herself to shine. These are words that many pioneers of the women's liberation movement, valiant women, and heroines have inscribed with their own actions, tears, and blood. Let us treasure these words, remember them, and act on them. Hopefully each person can find her own path in life and develop her own brilliance.

During this same period, a home-grown version of rock-and-roll emerged and quickly came to represent growing numbers of disaffected youth. Singer and composer Cui Jian, the most prominent and popular of the young musicians, wrote numerous songs whose ambiguous lyrics were interpreted as criticism of Communist society by his fans as well as by government censors. Although he was frequently banned by the government, his songs became known throughout China. Three of his best known compositions are "Nothing to My Name," "It's Not That I Can't See," and "A Piece of Red Cloth." [42]

NOTHING TO MY NAME

IT'S AGES NOW I've been asking you:
When will you come away with me?
But all you ever do is laugh at me, 'cause
I've got nothing to my name.

I want to give you my hope
I want to help make you free
But all you ever do is laugh at me, 'cause
I've got nothing to my name.

When will you come away with me?

The ground is moving under your feet
The waters of life are flowing free
But all you ever do is laugh at me, 'cause
I've got nothing to my name.

Why do you always laugh at the pack on my back?
Why do I always keep on going?
The old horse stands before you; here I am
With nothing to my name.

When will you come away with me?

Tell you this—I've been waiting a long time.
Tell you this—my final plea:
I want to grab you by the hands
And have you go away with me.

Your hands they are a-shaking
Your eyes awash with tears
Do you really mean to tell me
You love me as I am?

Come with me then

Come with me then

IT'S NOT THAT I CAN'T SEE

Never used to know what it meant to take it easy,
Just couldn't see how weird the world was growing.
The future I'd been seeing sure isn't here today,
But now I think I know which way it's going.

Of everything that's said and done,
I can't tell good from bad,
Which year was which, the times I've had.
The things I thought were simple.
Makes me feel like I've been had.
Suddenly it seems as if the world's no place for me.

Twenty years and all I've learnt is patience, holding on.
No wonder all the comrades said my head was in the clouds,
I got myself together, made myself stop dreaming,
Now I'm awake and I can see
This world's as weird as weird can be.

Looking out at all the highrise buildings there
    like fields of rice and wheat,
Looking out and all I see is waves of people
    traffic in the street.
Looking left now right, front, back,
I'm so busy I can't keep track.
This 'n' that, that 'n' this
    the more I see the weirder it is.

Never used to know what it meant to take it easy,
Just couldn't see how weird the world was growing.
The future I'd been seeing sure isn't here today,
But now I think I know which way it's going.

It's not that I can't see,
The world's too weird for me.

It's not that I can't see
The world's too weird for me.

A PIECE OF RED CLOTH

That day you used a piece of red cloth
to blindfold my eyes and cover up the sky
You asked me what I had seen
I said I saw happiness

This feeling really made me comfortable
made me forget I had no place to live
You asked where I wanted to go
I said I want to walk your road

(saxophone solo)

I couldn't see you, and I couldn't see the road
You grabbed my hands and wouldn't let go
You asked what was I thinking I said
I want to let you be my master

I have a feeling that you aren't made of iron
but you seem to be as forceful as iron
I felt that you had blood on your body
because your hands were so warm

This feeling made me comfortable
made me forget I had no place to live
You asked me where I wanted to go
I said I want to walk your road

(saxophone solo)

I had a feeling this wasn't a wilderness
though I couldn't see it was already dry and cracked
I felt that I wanted to drink some water
but you used a kiss to block off my mouth

I had a feeling this wasn't a wilderness
though I couldn't see it was already dry and cracked
I felt that I wanted to drink some water
but you used a kiss to block off my mouth
I don't want to leave and I don't want to cry

Because my body is already withered and dry
I want to always accompany you this way
Because I know your suffering best

Du la, du du du la la, du la...

(saxophone solo)

That day you used a piece of red cloth
blindfolded my eyes and covered up the sky
You asked me what I could see
I said I could see happiness

> Thinly veiled criticisms of the Communist system also appeared
> in the widely watched and hotly debated multi-part television
> series *River Elegy*. Devoted to the history of the Chinese state, the
> 1988 documentary seemed to equate elements of the Communist
> system to elements of the Confucian culture and the feudal polit-
> ical system. The program, which was officially denounced by the
> Communist Party in 1989, called for a break with the past and
> for increasing contacts with foreign countries. The following are
> excerpts from the series: [43]

AN ULTRASTABLE SYSTEM

Episode Five: Anxiety

WHAT POWERFUL FORCE has bound this nation together for over two
thousand years? The enigma of the Great Unity has taxed the minds of
Chinese and foreign scholars alike. . . . In ancient China small agricultural
producers were as numerous as the stars in the summer firmament; they were
like a plate of loose sand. The Confucian intellectuals, who created a coher-
ent social structure with their unified belief system, were able to bring these
disparate farmers together effectively to form a society.

This unique social structure once created great prosperity for China.
However, within the miracle of the Great Unity, under the dazzling surface
of its glorious culture, behind the swirling mists of incense burning on
ancestral altars, and despite the homage paid to the emperor, the sages, and
the elderly, the social system was slowly rotting away at the core—just as the
pillars of the dikes along the Yellow River were being slowly gnawed away by
rats and termites! The Confucian bureaucracy lurched irrevocably toward
decay; power itself was a corrosive. The prosperity of each dynasty presaged
its collapse.

The end of one dynasty would quickly lead to the establishment of another; the social structure would soon regain its original contours and start on a fresh path to collapse. So too it has been with the Yellow River, the dikes bursting only to be restored by human labor, then bursting again. Why are we condemned to this cycle of fate?

The mysterious ultrastable system has controlled us for two thousand years. Today the Golden Phoenix Throne in the Forbidden City is nothing more than an antique; the massive network of Confucian bureaucracy has turned to dust. However, the specter of the Great Unity still prowls our land. The nightmare of social tremors still haunts our waking hours. And bureaucracy, the mentality of privilege, and corruption are undermining our grand plans for the "Four Modernizations." These chronic, ancient ailments are not unlike the daily accumulation of silt in the Yellow River, forever building up to a new crisis. . . .

Perhaps we should be concerned by our eternally ultrastable system, just as we feel unsettled by the ever-increasing height of the dikes along the river. Hasn't history provided us with more than adequate lessons? . . .

One reassuring thing is that following the inception of economic reform, we are now finally beginning to experiment with political reform . . . no matter what type of resistance and threats this reform may face, we have no choice but to move ahead. For behind us are surging floodwaters and ceaseless turmoil. We must move on and break out of the vicious cycle of history.

ENTREPRENEURS

Episode Six: The Color Blue

Perhaps the new entrepreneurs, people of average appearance who have nothing surprising to say, are the ones with the real power [to change things]. Small shopkeepers, businessmen on the move, even peasants who travel around looking for work: Perhaps among them a new force is gathering, an energy that can be directed toward social change. We must not underestimate them.

REFORM

Episode Six: The Color Blue

The greatest obstacle to Reform seems to be that we're always worrying whether the Chinese will remain Chinese. Nobody seems to realize that in the West, no one ever agonized over whether the Renaissance, Reformation, or Enlightenment would make them any less Italian, German, or French. But in China, this is the greatest taboo of all.

Perhaps this is both the weightiest and most shallow aspect of our Yellow Civilization.

> More direct criticism of government policies appeared in the press as unemployment increased. The following angry article decried the fact that the "iron rice bowl" (guaranteed employment for state workers) was being eliminated.[44]

AN UPSURGE OF unemployment is coming from heaven! . . . Thirty-odd years ago, we were happy and excited at giving every urban citizen an "iron rice bowl," but now we have to use our own hands to smash some people's iron rice bowls.

- In 1987, within one year the state-operated enterprises in Hubei Province discharged fourteen thousand permanent state employees.
- By mid-summer 1988, there were already thirty thousand persons receiving unemployment benefits in Shanghai.
- In Zhuzhou [Hunan], the reform has forced forty thousand "excess workers" out of their jobs ...

According to the most recent news, issued ... by the state's Xinhua News Agency, by the end of August 1988, nationwide at least three hundred thousand permanent state employees had been removed from their jobs. They have become the first group of people openly unemployed in new China....

What is left are many puzzling questions.

- Isn't it true that unemployment only belongs to capitalism? Why is there also unemployment in a socialist country?
- Aren't we the masters of the country? Why smash the rice bowls of the masters?
- Aren't the directors of the factories public servants? On what grounds can they dismiss workers?

For more than thirty years, didn't people have a comfortable life with the "iron rice bowl"? Why is it now necessary to break their "rice bowl"? . . .

During the four years between 1984 and 1987, the trade unions in large, middle, and small cities in China . . . conducted large-scale surveys among the workers. Fifty-six percent of the workers surveyed believed that the status of the Chinese workers as the masters of the country had declined. The interests of the workers are hurt.

The Tiananmen Crisis

Editor's Introduction: The tensions that were building up in China during the 1980s came to a head in the Spring of 1989. Although the economy was growing rapidly and many Chinese benefited from the reforms, others lost their jobs and faced an insecure future. Many complained about rampant corruption and others demanded increased political freedoms. On April 17, 1989, several hundred young people, mostly students from Beijing University and other universities in the capital, marched to Tiananmen Square to honor the memory of former Communist Party Secretary-General Hu Yaobang, who had died two days earlier. Dismissed by Deng Xiaoping in January 1987, Hu had alienated many of the top leaders of the Communist Party for his attempts to democratize the Party, for his efforts to curb corruption among family members of high Party officials, and for his support of intellectuals who favored democratic reforms. Reform-minded students saw Hu's death as not merely an opportunity to peacefully honor one of their heroes but an unusual opportunity to demonstrate for the right to freely organize, for freedom of the press, for higher education budgets and for an end to corruption by government officials.

Following the march, about 1,000 students staged a sit-in at the Square and they were joined the following day by more than 10,000 additional demonstrators. Defying government orders, more than 100,000 Beijing citizens flocked to the Square on April 22, the day set aside for a memorial service and funeral for Hu. The following day a loosely-organized independent union of Beijing University students was organized and on April 24 representatives from 21 Beijing colleges and universities declared a student strike and urged workers and other citizens to join them. Demonstrations continued for the next few days and on April 26 an editorial in the *People's Daily* called the protests "an organized conspiracy" opposed to the "leadership of

the Chinese Communist Party and the socialist system" whose purpose was to "sow dissension among the people, plunge the whole
country into chaos, and sabotage the political situation of stability
and unity."*

The government banned unauthorized marches, demonstrations, speechmaking and the passing out of leaflets on Beijing streets.
Rather than complying, angry students defied the order and on April
27 organized a march to Tiananmen Square which drew an estimated 150,000 people.

On May 4, the students were joined by numerous groups,
organizations and hundreds of thousands of ordinary citizens in commemorating the seventieth anniversary of the May Fourth
Movement. Student leader Wu'er Kaixi read the following New May
Fourth Manifesto at Tiananmen Square. It summarizes the goals of
the protesters. [45]

FELLOW STUDENTS, FELLOW countrymen:
Seventy years ago today, a large group of illustrious students assembled in
front of Tiananmen, and a new chapter in the history of China was opened.
Today, we are once again assembled here, not only to commemorate that
monumental day but more importantly, to carry forward the May Fourth
spirit of science and democracy. Today, in front of the symbol of the Chinese
nation, Tiananmen, we can proudly proclaim to all the people in our nation
that we are worthy of the pioneers of seventy years ago.

For over one hundred years, the pioneers of the Chinese people have
been searching for a path to modernize an ancient and beleaguered China.
Following the Paris Peace Conference, they did not collapse in the face of
imperialist oppression, but marched boldly forward. Waving the banners of
science and democracy, they launched the mighty May Fourth Movement.
May Fourth and the subsequent New Democratic Revolution were the first
steps in the patriotic democracy movement of Chinese students. From this
point on, Chinese history entered a completely new phase. Due to the
socioeconomic conditions in China and the shortcomings of intellectuals,
the May Fourth ideals of science and democracy have not been realized.
Seventy years of history have taught us that democracy and science cannot
be established in one fell swoop and that impatience and despair are of no
avail. In the context of China's economy and culture, the Marxism espoused
by the Chinese Communist Party cannot avoid being influenced by remnants of feudal ideology. Thus, while New China has steadily advanced

---

* Maurice Meisner, *The Deng Xaoping Era*, New York: Hill and Wang, 1996, p. 410.

TIANANMEN PROTEST SONG

In 1989, during the Tiananmen Square protests, slogans condemning corruption were more frequently seen and heard than those related to any other concern. One song particularly relished by the demonstrators was one that began with the words "Dadao guandao [down with profiteering officials], dadao guandao, fan fubai [oppose corruption] fan fubai," sung to the tune of the nursery rhyme Frère Jacques. Protesters said they felt corruption had become increasingly rampant since Deng Xiaoping launched his economic reforms.

Source: James A.R. Miles, *The Legacy of Tiananmen*, Ann Arbor: University of Michigan Press, 1996, p. 147.

---

toward modernization, it has greatly neglected building a democracy. Although it has emphasized the role of science, it has not valued the spirit of science-democracy. At present, our country is plagued with problems such as a bloated government bureaucracy, serious corruption, the devaluation of intellectual work, and inflation, all of which severely impede us from intensifying the reforms and carrying out modernization. This illustrates that if the spirit of science and democracy, and their actual processes, do not exist, numerous and varied feudal elements and remnants of the old system, which are fundamentally antagonistic to large-scale socialist production, will reemerge in society, and modernization will be impossible. For this reason, carrying on the May Fourth spirit, hastening the reform of the political system, protecting human rights, and strengthening rule by law have become urgent tasks of Modernization that we must undertake.

Fellow students, fellow countrymen, a democratic spirit is precisely the absorption of the collective wisdom of the people, the true development of each individual's ability, and the protection of each individual's interests; a scientific spirit is precisely respect for individual nature, and the building of the country on the basis of science. Now more than ever, we need to review the experiences and lessons of all student movements since May Fourth, to make science and rationalism a system, a process. Only then can the tasks the May Fourth Movement set before us be accomplished, only then can the spirit of May Fourth be carried forward, and only then can our wish for a strong China be realized.

Fellow students, fellow countrymen, the future and fate of the Chinese nation are intimately linked to each of our hearts. This student movement has but one goal, that is, to facilitate the process of modernization by raising high the banners of democracy and science, by liberating people from the constraints of feudal ideology, and by promoting freedom, human rights, and rule by law. To this end, we urge the government to accelerate the pace of political reform, to guarantee the rights of the people vested in the law, to implement a press law, to permit privately run newspapers, to eradicate corruption, to hasten the establishment of an honest and democratic government, to value education, to respect intellectual work, and to save the nation through science. Our views are not in conflict with those of the government. We only have one goal: the modernization of China.

> In the weeks following the May 4 demonstration, increasingly large numbers of Chinese, from every walk of life, were emboldened to join the protesters in Tiananmen Square. The government's response to the students' demands for a meaningful dialogue, for recognition of their independent "autonomous" organizations, and for an official retraction of the despised April 26 *Peoples' Daily* editorial was one of delay and avoidance. Finally on May 13 a group of more than 400 student protesters began a hunger strike, vowing not to eat until the Party leaders started a "substantive, concrete and equal dialogue" and acknowledged that the student movement was "patriotic and democratic". *
>
> On May 15 and again on May 17 more than one million Beijing residents marched to Tiananmen Square to support the protest movement. A May 18 nationally televised "dialogue" between government leaders and student protest leaders featured Wu'er Kaixi challenging and berating Premier Li Peng. This astonishing broadcast was followed the next day by the students voting to call off the hunger strike. However, on the evening of May 19 the government declared the imposition of martial law and banned all public protests effective the following morning. The decree was met with defiance by hundreds of thousands of demonstrators during the next few days and advancing soldiers were peacefully blocked by huge crowds on Beijing's major thoroughfares. The soldiers did not attack the crowds and retreated.

---

* Orville Schell, *The Mandate of Heaven*, New York: Simon & Schuster, 1994, p. 81.

At this point many students from Beijing universities, fearful of a bloody confrontation, felt that they should leave the Square and return to their schools to prepare for a protracted peaceful struggle to bring about democratic reforms. Their leaders decided to hold a final giant rally on May 30. At that gathering a 37-foot plaster and styrofoam "Goddess of Democracy," which resembled the Statue of Liberty and was created by students at the Central Academy of Fine Arts in Beijing, was unveiled directly opposite the giant portrait of Mao at Tiananmen Gate. The appearance of the statue briefly reinvigorated the protest movement. Although almost all of the Beijing students had left the Square by the end of May, students from outside the capital formed their own organization and voted to remain in the Square until the Standing Committee of the National People's Congress was scheduled to meet on June 20. Meanwhile, the government was planning to use the military to retake the Square and forcibly end the protests.

On the night of June 3, approximately 40,000 troops invaded Beijing from both the east and the west and headed for the Square. Immediately, city residents tried to block the soldiers but unlike the situation two weeks earlier, they did not retreat. Battles broke out throughout the city and many soldiers and civilians were killed during these encounters. Within a few hours soldiers surrounded Tiananmen Square. A last-minute rapidly-negotiated agreement between leaders of the roughly 4,000 to 5,000 protesters left in the Square and local military commanders enabled the protesters to leave the Square just before dawn on June 4. Although controversy surrounds the final chaotic hours of the Tiananmen protests, it seems as if few if any protesters were killed in the Square itself. However, hundreds if not thousands were killed on streets leading to the Square and in neighborhoods adjacent to it.

Officially the Chinese government claimed that "more than 6,000 martial law soldiers, armed police and public security officers had been injured, and the death toll was more than 10. More than 3,000 civilians had been wounded and over 200 had died, including 36 students."* However, almost all independent observers, including eyewitnesses, judge these death figures to be impossibly low. The Chinese Red Cross reported early on June 4 that 2,600 people had died and Amnesty International estimated

---

* Chu-yuan Cheng, *Behind the Tiananmen Massacre*, Boulder, CO: Westview Press, 1990, p. 138.

THE DISEASE OF "BOURGEOIS LIBERALIZATION"

In October 1989 . . . a telling commentary in the *Economic Daily* . . . compared the spread of "bourgeois liberalization" and the creeping process of "peaceful evolution" to the transmission of the AIDS virus. The transliteration in Chinese for AIDS is a*izibing*, literally "AIDS sickness." However, *aizibing* also happens to be a homophone for the Chinese characters which mean "the sickness of loving capitalism." It was a perfectly ambiguous term for Party hardliners to latch on to in their efforts to equate the contamination of Chinese society by Western, bourgeois values with contracting this deadly and alien biological disease.

Aizibing is a sickness that "destroys a person's ability to distinguish, remember, and compare," the dire commentary warned. This "infectious disease" makes people believe that if "something is called capitalism, everything will be good; that commodities from foreign countries are good; that white skin is smarter than yellow skin; and that individualism that ignores national interest should be called freedom and human rights. . . . The turbulence that has just passed can be said to show the enormous impact of *aizibing*, the 'sickness of loving capitalism.'"

Source: Orville Schell, *The Mandate of Heaven*, New York: Simon & Schuster, 1994, pp. 181-182.

that there were 1,000 fatalities. Other reports of the death toll ranged from 400 to 10,000. The precise figure will probably never be known.

The man most responsible for authorizing the use of armed violence to end the Tiananmen protests was Deng Xiaoping. Less than a week after the protest movement was crushed he defended his actions in a televised address before military and Party leaders. He declared that, "what we faced was not just some ordinary people who were misguided, but also a rebellious clique and a large quantity of the dregs of society...Their goal was to establish a bourgeois republic entirely dependent on the West...Their real aim was to overthrow the Communist Party and topple the socialist system." *

The government subsequently published numerous explanations for its actions. The following account appeared in the *People's Daily*. [46]

PEOPLE WILL ASK: If everything is so good, why did the disturbance start at all? This is not hard to understand, and with the passage of time, we can see it more clearly. Those who planned and whipped up the disturbance behind the scenes were so-called elites protected by reactionary forces in and outside China. They had without reservation accepted Western liberal thinking and tried to overturn socialist China. Naturally, there have been many faults and unsatisfactory performance in the work of our party and government. Those "elites" manipulated them and tried to confuse and poison the people's minds. They spread rumors in and outside China and stirred up some simple-minded, childish students and masses who did not know the truth. The bad elements that hit, smashed, looted, and burned were only a small handful of thugs and scum in the crowd. . . . Now some of the "elites" have fled abroad to beg pity from reactionary forces. They pass their days by condemning their motherland. They are no more than a few flies that meet failure everywhere.

The lesson from this disturbance is bitter. Because we had abandoned our ideological base, bourgeois liberalization flooded to the point of calamity. A microclimate was even formed in China that echoed the international microclimate. Together they set off this storm in our capital and caused undue damage to our nation and people who try hard to maintain stability and prosperity. However, genuine gold is forged in fire, and the hero is born from adversity. It is in this riot and under new historical conditions that we know better how trustworthy and reliable our Army, people, and students are. This is a firm guarantee for China to continue its stability and unity, to adhere to the Four Cardinal Principles and the deepening of reform, and for the socialist banner of China to flutter.

---

* Pei-kai Cheng and Michael Lestz with Jonathan Spence, eds., *The Search for Modern China: A documentary collection*, New York: Norton, 1990, p. 502.

The Intensification
of Reform

Editor's Introduction: The government's brutal ending of the Tiananmen demonstration was followed by severe political and intellectual repression. However, rather than curtail or reverse the economic reforms, the government intensified them, particularly during and after 1992. In January and February of that year, Deng Xiaoping embarked on a southern tour which included visits to Wuchang and Shanghai as well as to the special economic zones of Shenzhen and Zhuhai. In speeches on the tour he praised market reforms and called for their acceleration in order to increase production and raise living standards. Deng's comments were collected, became required reading and served as the basis of official Communist Party policy. His main points included the following: [47]

II

WE SHOULD BE bolder in carrying out reforms and opening up to the outside world and in making experimentations; we should not act like a woman with bound feet. For what we regard as correct, just try it and go ahead daringly. Shenzhen's experience means daring to break through. One just cannot blaze a trail, a new trail, and accomplish a new undertaking without the spirit of daring to break through, the spirit of taking a risk, and without some spirit and vigor. Who can say that everything is 100 percent sure of success with no risk at all? One should not consider oneself always in the right—there is no such thing.

Failing to take bigger steps and break through in carrying out reforms and opening to the outside world is essentially for fear that there may be too much capitalism or that the capitalist road is followed. The question of whether a move is socialist or capitalist is crucial. The criterion for judging

Deng Xiaoping (second from left) inspected the Shenzhen Special Economic Zone in
Guangdong Province in 1992. (From *China*, Beijing: New Star Publishers, 1999.)

this can only be whether or not a move is conducive to developing the productive forces in socialist society, increasing the comprehensive strength of
the country, and improving the people's living standards. There were differ-
ing views on setting up special economic zones from the beginning, and people feared that they might involve the practice of capitalism. The achievements made in the construction of Shenzhen provide clear answers to people with various misgivings. The special economic zones are socialist, not
capitalist. Judging from Shenzhen's situation, public ownership is the main
system of ownership, and the investment by foreign businessmen accounts
for only one-fourth of the total amount of investment in the zone. As for foreign investment, we can also benefit from it through taxation and by providing labor services. There should be more three kinds of partially or wholly foreign-owned enterprises [joint ventures, cooperative enterprises, and
wholly foreign-owned enterprises], and we do not have to be afraid of them.
We do not have to be afraid so long as we keep a clear head. We have advantages, such as large and medium-sized state enterprises, and village and town
enterprises. More important, the political power is in our hands. Some people hold: The more foreign investment, the more capitalism; the more three
kinds of partially or wholly foreign-owned enterprises, the more capitalist
things—that means the development of capitalism. Those people do not
even have basic common sense. In accordance with current laws, regulations,

and policies, foreign businessmen running such enterprises always make some money. But the state taxes them, and they pay our workers; we can also learn from their technology and managerial expertise and get information to open up markets. So the three kinds of partially or wholly foreign-owned enterprises that are restricted by our political and economic conditions are a beneficial supplement to the socialist economy. In the final analysis, they are advantageous to socialism.

Whether the emphasis is on planning or market is not the essential distinction between socialism and capitalism. A planned economy is not socialism—there is planning under capitalism, too; and a market economy is not capitalism—there is market regulation under socialism, too. Planning and market are both economic means. The essence of socialism is to liberate and develop productive forces, to eliminate exploitation and polarization, and to finally realize common prosperity. This is the truth I want to explain to you all. Are negotiable securities and stock markets good stuff after all? Are they risky? Are they peculiar to capitalism? Can they be used in socialism? Try them out, but try them resolutely. If they prove to be correct after one or two years, let's open them up; if they prove to be wrong, let's take corrective action by closing them. Even if we want to close them, we can close them quickly or slowly; and we don't have to close them completely. There are no grounds for fear. If we persist in such an attitude, we will be all right and will not commit major blunders. In short, in order to win a relative edge of socialism over capitalism, we must boldly absorb and draw on all fruits of civilization created by the society of mankind, as well as all advanced management and operational methods and modes reflecting the law on modern socialized production in various countries of the world today, including developed capitalist countries. . . .

III

To seize the opportunity and develop ourselves, the key lies in economic development. At present, the economies in some of our neighboring countries and regions are developing faster than ours. If we do not develop our economy or if we do it too slowly, the people will complain after making comparisons. Therefore, if development is possible, we should not block the way. Localities with conditions should carry out development as quickly as they can. As long as attention is paid to economic efficiency and product quality, and as long as the economy is export-oriented, we need not be worried about anything. Low-speed development is equal to stagnation or even retrogression. We should grasp the opportunity. The present is precisely a good opportunity, I am afraid that the opportunity may be lost. If you do not grasp it, the opportunity in sight may still slip away, and we may lose time easily.

> *Editor's Postscript:* As a result of the expansion of economic reforms, the economy grew at an unprecedented pace. As U.S. historian Maurice Meisner noted, "China's GDP expanded by 7.5 percent in 1991, by 13 percent in 1992, and by an extraordinary 14 percent in 1993, with industrial production growing at incredibly high per annum rates exceeding 20 percent. The Chinese economy, it was revealed to the astonishment of many, had become the third largest in the world, measured according to the new International Monetary Fund and World Bank standard of "purchasing power parity," almost the size of the Japanese economy and perhaps only a generation's time away from surpassing the American economy in absolute scale. . . . Improving economic conditions in late 1990 muffled the anger of the millions of citizens who had actively participated in the Democracy Movement and the many millions more who had sympathized with them. For those who benefited from the subsequent economic boom, memories of the [Tiananmen] massacre were submerged under government-promoted waves of consumerism."*
> According to the "purchasing power parity" standards, China was the world's second largest economy by 2005, a year in which the growth rate was 9.9 percent. (Using more traditional standards, the Chinese economy was the world's fourth largest, after the United States, Japan and Germany). All told, the Chinese GDP grew at an average annual rate of approximately 9.5 percent since the reform era began. The growth rate in 2006 was 10.7 percent.

---

* Maurice Meisner, *The Deng Xiaoping Era*, New York: Hill and Wang, 1996, p. 472, 473.

Wealth and
Consumerism

Editor's Introduction: The reforms initiated by Deng Xiaoping in the late 1970s, and intensified during the 1990s, brought unprecedented prosperity to millions of Chinese, particularly those living in large cities. They also created a new middle class and an ethic of rampant consumerism that had never before existed on such a grand scale in modern China. The following 1988 article, by *The New York Times* reporter Elisabeth Rosenthal, described the new phenomenon. [48]

TEN YEARS AGO, this group did not even exist. Today its core of independent businessmen has been joined by a growing number of private-sector lawyers, artists and employees of joint-venture companies.

It is first defined by what its members have: cell phones, washing machines, computers and, increasingly, cars and homes. On Saturday nights they go to concerts; in winter they vacation in Thailand. But the rapid accumulation of material things has left its psychological mark as well, infusing this group with a kind of independence and carefree optimism that has not existed in China for decades.

"For many people, the change in the last decade has really been tremendous—so tremendous it's hard to measure," said Conghua Li, an analyst at Deloitte & Touche Consulting Group in Toronto who was born in Beijing. "Every time I go back I'm shocked and surprised, mostly in a good way."

There is no one statistic that defines this group, which broadly includes both company presidents (who seem to have it all) and young professionals who have just bought their first computer (and want it all, someday). They are people who work hard for what they achieve, for the most part without the family ties to the Communist Party leadership that have long defined China's most privileged class.

The Beijing Xidan shopping Center. (From *China*, Beijing: New Star Publishers, 1999.)

The group portrait is best created like a pointillist painting from 1,000 small facts: Ten years ago, 95 percent of passengers on airline flights in China were foreigners; today, 95 percent are Chinese. Ten years ago, extremely few Chinese had stayed in five-star hotels; today about 10 percent of bookings are from Chinese travelers paying their own way. In 1990, there were no cellular phones in China. Now there are almost 17 million.

The middle class is admired by college students who hope to join its ranks, and after years of ambivalence the Communist Party, since its congress last fall, has embraced it for its contributions to China's modernization. . . .

"The social status of people like me has improved a lot in the last few years," said Fang Zeng, 33, a softspoken real estate developer. "And that's a really big change."

Last year, Mr. Fang represented China at an international business conference and was tapped to be a delegate to his local Chinese People's Political Consultative Conference, an advisory body of distinguished non-Communist Party members.

Mr. Fang and his wife, who teaches at Beijing University, each own their own cars. For next year's vacation, they are deliberating between Europe and Australia. They have donated money to establish university scholarships and children's libraries in Beijing, among other causes. And, although they now live in a one bedroom apartment provided by Beijing University, they are contemplating ownership once they have a child.

"I could never have imagined I would be where I am today," said Mr. Fang. "I have so many capabilities and choices. . . ."

Although Chinese entrepreneurs began accumulating money in the late 1980s, it was not until the mid '90s that the accouterments of middle-class life—cell phones, microwaves, a wide range of cars—were readily available for purchase in China. Then the middle class really took off.

> Life has also improved for many in the countryside. In the following section, Mobo C. F. Gao, a native of Gao Village in Jiangxi province, reflects on the dramatic changes that have taken place in the village. [49]

FOR MOST OF the villagers in the 1990s there was a noticeable improvement in the quality of life, reflected in things such as clothing, housing space and other consumer goods. . . .Throughout the 1960s and 70s Gao villagers used very few consumer goods that they could not make themselves. Even a washbasin was made of wooden boards strung together with bamboo strings. In 1962 my father managed to buy an enamel washbasin at the cost of something like 3 *yuan*. He said it was for me to use at high school when I had to board there. No one was allowed to use the basin and it was safely put away for three years until 1965 when I took it to high school. My father, an avowed Buddhist, never spent a cent on buying something for himself except matches and incense. He used these not to burn joss sticks before the Buddha but to light his tobacco. He grew his own tobacco and he smoked heavily. Very often, he would use a wooden stick instead of incense in order to save money. My elder sister's favourite story of how my father scrimped and saved was his refusal to use an umbrella. He would explain that every time an umbrella was used its life got shorter. Usually, Gao villagers could only afford paper umbrellas painted with tung oil, made by a local craftworker. Only the well-to-do could afford a cloth umbrella.

There was very little that Gao Village would buy from the shops, the nearest shop being some 3 kilometres away. They would have to buy matches, salt, soap, kerosene for lamps, joss sticks, some red paper for writing couplets for the Spring Festival, and rationed sugar if they could afford it. But Gao villagers would make their own soya sauce from soya beans. They would make sugar from sugar cane or from sweet potatoes, or even from rice. . . .

THE LANGUAGE OF CONSUMERISM

Commercial terms are widely used in Shanghai's daily vocabulary. It serves as proof of the penetration of commerce into social life. During the 1950s and the 1960s, a sarcastic remark to mock one's poor hearing was "You have a 20 percent discount ear?" Since the late 1970s there has been a popular remark in Shanghai: one's girl/boyfriend is called an auction clinch, a term used in the decisive settlement of an auction. "Have you got an 'auction clinch?'" means "Have you got a girlfriend?" An "account" also means one's girlfriend. This is the most obvious example that commerce "stains" affection.

Source: Yang Dongping, "City Monsoon: Cultural Spirit of Beijing and Shanghai," *Chinese Sociology and Anthropology*, Vol. 29, No. 2 (Winter 1996-1997), p. 49.

In the whole of Qinglin brigade, with 593 households and a population of 3,610, there were only thirty-six watches, twelve bicycles, twenty-five sewing machines and thirty radios by 1978. Nowadays, however, small consumer items such as gloves and socks, or a torchlight, a hat or a scarf are no longer thought a major consideration in the family budget. There were only two bicycles in Gao village in the early 1980s. Now there are forty-two. There are also a couple of colour, and twenty black and white television sets.

Because of the "consumer boom" in the area since the late 1990s, many villagers have set up small stands selling a variety of goods. A typical stand is made of a small shelter with one opening facing the road where the traffic comes and goes. These can be locked up at night and they are just big enough to store all the goods on sale, which are displayed on three sides. There is a counter at the front, usually with a family member sitting behind it who serves customers. They cannot be called street corner shops because there are no streets in the villages. There is only one road running through the villages to the Boyang County Town and all the shops are installed along this road. A kilometre away to the east of Gao Village, there are now half a dozen shops along the road. About 2 kilometres to the west of Gao Village there are another half dozen shops set up along the road.

A number of factors contributed to the consumer boom in Gao Village, but an increase in agricultural income is not one of them. The principal factor is the cash income from young Gao villagers working as migrant workers. To the present day, around 30 per cent of the people in the area have left as migrant workers. If each migrant worker sends an average of 100 *yuan* a month back to Gao Village (which they in fact do . . .), the cash income from ninety-eight Gao Village migrant workers in 1995 would amount to 117,600 *yuan*. This is a huge amount of money for Gao villagers, on top of which the absence of these migrant workers alleviates a substantial burden on village resources.

Another important factor is that some consumer goods are simply much cheaper now than, say, ten years ago, thanks to the industrial boost since the 1980s. An ordinary watch costs around 50 *yuan,* or even less, nowadays, whereas its cost was at least 100 *yuan* before 1978. Today's prices are such that if inflation is taken into account a villager should be able to buy a watch at a cost equivalent to 12 *yuan* fifteen years ago, whereas the actual price at that time was set at 120 *yuan*! This is just one example of how the government fixed the price of industrial goods to the disadvantage of rural residents. This price change applies to other consumer goods as well, such as bicycles, radios, rubber boots, garments and television sets.

> Dramatic changes have also transformed urban social life and have given rise to new forms of recreation and entertainment. These changes were described by Beijing University mathematics student Shan Dandan: [50]

NEW RECREATIONAL PASTIMES AMONG CHINESE

IN THE LAST decade great changes have taken place in Chinese life-styles. A great variety of recreational items are now available, and more and more people are spending their spare time going out in search of fun. Newspapers have even devoted column space to let readers know when and where they can spend an enjoyable evening.

In the 1950s, '60s, and early '70s, most Chinese were busy with the demands of work and family. In their free time they usually visited friends or relations or went to the park or to the movies on rare occasions. Black-and-white television started appearing in ordinary homes in the late 1970s, and after dinner many people would settle in for an evening of TV. There were, however, only two or three channels across China to choose from at the time.

Dancing was the main leisure activity in the 1980s. At middle school and college, students would try only a few tentative steps at ballroom dancing, then known to many Chinese as collective dances. Soon waltzes and tangos became popular on college campuses, giving way in the mid 1980s to disco and tamer forms of rock music, despite disapproval and criticism from older generations. At the same time, many middle-aged and older people indulged in nostalgia and took up waltzing again, a form of dancing very popular in days past, even in China.

Dancing started to lose ground, however, in the 1990s due to an increase in the number of ways that people could spend their spare time. Business is slow now not only in dance halls, but also at the box office. Many major cinemas have replaced their theaters with snack bars and lounges, while new compact disc technology offers movies with far better sound and pictures than most cinemas. Now when a Chinese couple, usually a pair of starry-eyed teenagers, go to the movies, they must pay anywhere from 15 to 30 *yuan*, whereas only a few years ago the price hovered around 50 fen (100 fen per *yuan*) for a single admission.

There are also many private video parlors springing up, showing a variety of Kung Fu films, soppy love stories and gory horror flicks. Since these showings are usually pretty inexpensive, they always attract large audiences. Pop singers from Hong Kong and Taiwan are favorites among young people on the mainland. In the last years waves of new stars have come and gone, with a new face on the charts almost every other day. Since its first appearance in China in 1986, karaoke has seemed unstoppable. More and more people prefer to hold weddings and birthday parties in karaoke halls, as they think singing the latest pop tune creates a lively and cheerful atmosphere. Karaoke also allows many people to indulge in fantasies about the entertainment world.

Many restaurants now turn into karaoke halls in the evening. All the big hotels in China have a karaoke lounge, and many businesses have purchased a karaoke machine to liven up the lunch hour. Karaoke machines have also won an honored place in many ordinary homes, allowing families to compete to see who can sing the best (or worst).

China had no nightlife to speak of in the past. Now large cities are no longer desolate and deserted at night, what with all-night movie theaters, bars, night clubs, and neon decorated dance halls. People who have worked hard all day come here to relax and enjoy themselves.

Parties at home, a traditional Western pastime, are now practiced by fashionable Chinese. Cocktail parties and masquerades are popular among the young. Having a party at your home is a sure sign of "being in the swim," but at the same time it is practical in the sense that it is a healthy means of recreation as well as social intercourse. Some people have opened music salons in their homes. In Shanghai, China's largest city, there are about 200,000 compact disk purchasers. Some of these often get together and compare their CD collections.

Older people nowadays are fond of group-related sports. These activities are fun and healthy at the same time. Many young people in China also like to spend time exercising. Some activities, like bowling, golf, and indoor swimming, can get pretty expensive in China, but more and more people have the money to afford them.

Until recently, Chinese did not realize that shopping is great fun. In the past many department stores were small, and often disappointed people with their low stock of shoddy goods. At that time people started shopping just for the sake of shopping. Now all across China there is a wide selection of shopping centers, such as Lufthansa, and Parkson in Beijing. Passing by these stores, many ordinary Chinese cannot help stepping inside simply to have a look at all the goods on offer, despite the fact that they have no intention of buying anything.

Problems of the City
and the Countryside

Editor's Introduction: The economic reforms that led to prosperity for many Chinese created serious problems for many others. In the cities, as many factories came under private or semi-private control, benefits for workers were reduced and working conditions deteriorated. Many workers, whose jobs had previously been guaranteed by the government, were laid off. In the countryside, the breakup of the communes into family units led to unprecedented wealth for some farming families but increased insecurity and poverty for others. As governmental and communal support diminished, many peasants could not support their families on their allotted plots of land and were forced to migrate to the cities to find employment. Some migrated to supplement family income. (Indeed, by 2006, the gap between urban and rural incomes was 3.3 to 1, "higher than similar measures in the U.S. and one of the world's highest.")* This massive internal shift of population involved millions of people and constituted one of the largest migrations in history.

The following passage is from Chen Li's book, *Rediscovering China.* Li, who was born and raised in Shanghai, left China in 1985 for graduate study in the United States and is now a professor of government at Hamilton College. He lived in China from 1993 to 1995. His account typifies the problems that exist today in many Chinese cities. [51]

MR. ZHU WAS born into a poor peasant family in a small town near the city. In the early 1970s, Zhu's parents started a small business selling fruit and seafood in the black market. The family moved to Wenzhou in the early

---

* Joseph Kahn, "A Sharp Debate Erupts in China Over Ideologies," *The New York Times,* March 12, 2006, p. 6.

1980s. With the initial capital of 20,000 yuan that Zhu's parents provided, Zhu and his two brothers and three sisters established garment factories, first in Wenzhou, then in Quingdao and Tianjin. The registered capital of their family business increased from 560,000 yuan in 1988 to 3,260,000 in 1995. Zhu told us that each of his brothers and sisters has several million yuan in capital.

"But we still have a long way to go to become a big entrepreneurial family in Wenzhou," Mr. Zhu explained.

At this point, private entrepreneurs like Mr. Zhu seem to be only interested in making their fortunes. No one is really concerned about the socioeconomic well-being of the community. The disparity between rich and poor is a serious problem in the region. A survey of 84 private enterprises showed that the average annual income reported by owners was 35.6 times that of their employees. The real income gap was believed to be even greater. Another study of 50 private enterprises found that 46 percent of workers were not satisfied with their incomes or benefits.

During our trip, we visited a number of shoe factories in downtown Wenzhou. Shoemaking has become one of the core industries, along with the garment and electronic industries, during the reform era. A manager of a shoe factory told us that the city had about 6,000 shoe factories and workshops.

We were struck not only by the large number of shoe factories, but also by their terrible working conditions. Shuixin, a small industrial complex located a few minutes away from the Huaqiao Hotel, has hundreds of shoe workshops and stores. A typical shoe workshop in the complex was actually no more than an old, shabby house where several hundred laborers crowded along the assembly line. These worn-down factory houses used to be one-story houses, but owners or managers of the factories added a second story. Tall workers had difficulty walking through the factory house. Usually, they did not have enough lights, not only because they had few windows, but also because the owners wanted to reduce electricity costs.

What struck me the most, however, was the awful smell caused by chemical glues and other materials. Not surprisingly, the workshops we visited had no ventilation installed. Every visitor would feel nauseated, but these workers had to work for long hours in such a heavily polluted work environment.

"How many hours do you work every day?" I asked a teenage girl.

"It depends on whether I can complete my quota in a day," she replied. "But usually I work from 8 in the morning to 2 at night."

"Do you have a work contract with the owner of the factory?" I asked.

"No."

"Do you have any social welfare benefits?" Joe asked.

"Social welfare benefits?" the girl seemed puzzled by the term. "Yes, I get pay every day."

"Do you have any medical insurance?" Joe asked, more specifically.

"I don't understand," the girl replied. She had never heard of the term 'medical insurance.'

I shared concerns about such benefits. China's safety net has become increasingly inadequate in the reform era. Like many other countries that have gone through a transformation in economic structure, the Chinese government hasn't given high priority to welfare issues and is unable to allocate more resources to social programs in employment, income equalization, pricing control, social security, occupational benefits, health services, housing and so on. In fact, the past few years witnessed a large-scale retreat of the state in service provision at the very time when problems such as unemployment, inflation, polarization, and the fast-rising costs of medical treatment become acute. Meanwhile, the private sector is unable to take over social programs.

"Don't talk to foreigners!" a middle-aged woman who looked like a manager appeared and interrupted our conversation. "Please go away!" she said to Joe and me bluntly.

"We want to know whether your workers have any concerns or problems with the working conditions here," I said to her straightforwardly.

"If they have any problems, they can quit their jobs here any time," the woman replied. "My workers should be grateful to be able to work here. Go see the jobless people in the 'labor markets' [*laodongli shichang*], and you will understand what I mean."

I certainly didn't need her to remind me of the "labor markets." This was one of the most memorable, and indeed most miserable, scenes I observed during my journey in China. In virtually every large and medium-sized city that I visited, there were places in which hundreds of young adults, both men and women (most in their twenties) waited for hours and days, hoping to be picked up by anyone who could offer them jobs, including temporary or hourly work.

These "labor markets" were usually located on busy streets, in the plazas of ports, bus terminals, and railway stations, near construction sites, and in front of the factories that hire temporary workers. Each time I saw this scene, my mind would be filled with words such as "exploitation," "oppression," and "dehumanization."

A MIGRANT'S LAMENT

A young woman from Sichuan, who died in a tragic workplace fire at her factory in Shenzhen that resulted in eighty-seven deaths, had copied these words to a song in her diary.

From Sichuan to Canton
Thru' Ou-yang to Shenzhen
Home is long gone
Mom and Dad we had to leave
Your words forever in my heart.
They say Canton streets are made of gold
It's been over three years
I wish my family were near
But my pockets are still bare. . . .
A day feels like a year
It ain't so easy to be away from home
No cash, no salt, no oil, no grain
To live is an agony.

Source: Anita Chan, *China's Workers Under Assault*, Armonk, NY: M.E. Sharpe, 2001, pp. 113-114.

On my taxi ride from downtown to Wenzhou Airport, I saw a labor market in which about 300 jobless migrants gathered. It was already afternoon, and most of them must have been waiting there since the early morning. Their frustration was visible in their facial expressions.

As the taxi passed these people, I suddenly realized—not what the middle-aged manager in the shoe factory meant about the justification for capitalist exploitation—but ironically, why the Chinese people enthusiastically embraced socialism half a century ago.

> Problems of unemployment and migrant labor have been acknowledged by government officials. An aritcle in *Time* magazine (April 2002) reported that: [52]

URBAN JOBLESSNESS, UNHEARD of when the Maoist government provided cradle-to-grave employment, now averages around 8-9%, according to scholars at the Beijing-based Development Research Center (DRC), a government think tank. (The official rate, by contrast, is a rosy 3.6%.) Joblessness is much higher, perhaps 20%, in industrial rust belts that cut great swaths across the north, where outmoded, bankrupt factories are being shut down and communist-era work units eliminated at a breathtaking pace. Reliable numbers aren't available, but some estimate there are at least 19 million Chinese who are out of work; tens of millions more are unaccounted for by Labor Department statisticians. . . . "In the next 10 years, I predict 150 million farmers will move to cities looking for work," said Chen Huai, a senior research fellow at the DRC. That's a mass of unemployed migrants larger than the total U.S. workforce. After years of downplaying its unemployment problems, now even Vice Minister Wang Dongjin from the Ministry of Labor and Social Security describes China's jobs crunch as "grim." The ministry acknowledges it must create 17 million jobs a year just to maintain its current unemployment rate. Hu Angang, a professor at Tsinghua University in Beijing, warns that China is careering toward nothing less than "an unemployment war, with people fighting for jobs that don't exist."

> In the rural areas, poverty remains a problem for tens of millions although there has apparently been a dramatic decrease in extreme poverty. According to United Nations studies, the number of people living on $1 per day or less dropped from 250 million in 1978 to 30 million in 2000.* However, rural poverty increased dramatically between 2000 and 2003 and several experts reported in 2004 that approximately 70 million farmers had lost their land since the mid-1990s.** The background to the phenomenon of growing rural poverty was provided by Dale Wen in *China Copes with Globalization*. [53]

The dissolution of the commune via de facto land privatization meant that many functions such as marketing and health coops previously organized by the community, or commune, could no longer be sustained. Simultaneously, the government decreased expenditure in rural investment so no replacement systems were established.

---

* Dale Wen, *China Copes with Globalization: A mixed review,* San Francisco: The International Forum on Globalization, 2006, p. 2.

** Martin Hart-Landsberg and Paul Barkett, "China and Socialism: Engaging the Issues," *Critical Asian Studies,* Vol. 37, No. 4, 2005, p. 609.

RURAL PROBLEMS

Wang Fucheng (a peasant who served as Communist Party Secretary of Houhua Village in Henan Province from 1954 to 1984):

Security is very important for farmers. Prices change so much today that there is no certainty. In Chairman Mao's time, there was more certainty. In those days, the government stressed agriculture and made a real attempt to help agriculture, there were no fake fertilizers and fake insecticides. So much of it is fake today. Today the government talks a lot about agriculture, but it does nothing to help the farmer. But as much as the farmers complain, they do not want to go back to the old system. They have more money now and more freedom. They do not like the uncertainty, but they do not want to go back. There is hope for the village in the future if the government gives us more help—more loans, more fertilizer. That is what we need.

Wang Dejun (the son of Wang Fucheng):

Hope for the village is conditional. If the central government reduces the burden on farmers and helps us start new enterprises, there is hope. Without that there is not much hope. In the near future I see little significant change. There is no trend toward mechanization of agriculture. There is no capital to start new industries. The only way farmers can improve their lives is to sell their labor cheap to people in cities. There is not much hope in that.

Source: Peter Seybolt, *Throwing the Emperor from His Horse,* Boulder, CO: Westview Press, 1996, p.128.

The early years of rural reform did experience a surge of agriculture outputs and rural income, largely due to the introduction of chemical fertilizers, pesticides, and hybrid seeds. But when the government lifted price controls on agricultural inputs in the mid 1980s, prices radically increased and many peasants could no longer afford these items. Additionally, the tiny family farms (almost all under 1 hectare) were more vulnerable to natural disasters and market fluctuations.

In addition to declining rural public services, income losses were staggering. . . . When China joined WTO in 2001, cheap, highly subsidized agricultural commodities from industrial nations flooded into the country, posing a further challenge to the already ailing rural sector. As a result of decollectivization and participation in the global trade arena, millions from rural regions migrated to cities and manufacturing centers.

> The problem of the huge internal migration, called a "tidal wave"
> by many in China, is discussed by political scientist Cheng Li.
> [54]

DURING THE SPRING Festival, the most important holiday in China, almost all migrants return to their native homes, where they spend about two weeks with their families. Then they go back to their workplaces in cities, usually bringing with them more surplus rural laborers from their home villages. This is what the Chinese call "the tidal wave of migrant workers" *(mingongchao)*. Faced with this tidal wave, the entire railway system in China has almost shut down during the Spring Festival season of 1994. Another 5 million people were transported by buses and ships.

"Twenty-six million people is roughly the population of Canada," a reporter for China's official newspaper, *People's Daily*, said to me. "Imagine all the people of Canada being relocated by train within a few weeks!"

"This is one of the largest migrations in human history," commented a demographer from the Chinese Academy of Social Sciences. "The scale and impact of China's current internal migration are surely as great as other major domestic migrations in the world, such as the nineteenth-century European industrial revolution and the 1849 gold rush in the United States."

An analysis of the direction of migration shows that an overwhelmingly large portion of interprovincial migrants moved from the west and the north of China to its east and south coast. Just as "Westward ho!" became a catchword for American "forty-niners," the idea "Go East" has inspired millions of China's migrant workers. But unlike the American West in 1849, which was a primitive and relatively uninhabited area, China's east coast is the most developed region in China and one of the most populous areas in the world.

Chinese migrant laborers have created their own folk rhymes: *"Yao facai, pao Shanghai"* (If you want to make a fortune, run to Shanghai) and *"Dongxinanbei zhong, dagong dao Pudong"* (East, west, south, north, center, to find a job, go to Pudong). Pudong, a new district of Shanghai and the largest special economic zone in the country, has become a "realm of fantasy" for surplus laborers in rural China. About 4,000 construction projects have been started in Pudong since 1994, and most construction workers are migrants from other provinces.

Make no mistake, China's tidal wave of migrant workers did not start in 1994 but in the early 1980s. Furthermore, surplus laborers in rural China have not only migrated from west to east in the country, but also from north to south. Guangdong, a southern province, for example, had the largest percentage of migrant laborers in the country until 1990. The number of migrant laborers, however, increased sharply in the early 1990s. According to a study of Sichuan, Anhui, Hunan, Hubei, Henan, and Jiangxi, the number of rural laborers who left their farmland was less than 1 million in 1982 but had increased to 24 million by the end of 1993. As of May 1994 the largest tidal wave of internal migration had already taken place. The east coast near Shanghai has become the main region where migrants seek to find jobs.

The Private Economy

Editor's Introduction: The underpinning of much of the change in China has been the growth of a private economy, which had, during the Mao years, been viewed as the enemy of socialism and was therefore suppressed. The remarkable change, which had taken place in the span of less than two decades, was summarized in the January 22, 2004 issue of the *Beijing Review.* The article noted that, "in 2002 the total number of employees in China was 737.4 million. Of this total ... those with private businesses reached 309 million, making up 42 percent. In the meantime, the private economy employs two-thirds of the total employees in the country's secondary and tertiary industries and 70 percent of the urban labor force." It also reported that, "In 2002 the proportion of the private economy in the country's GDP was 48.5 percent, while that of overseas-funded enterprises was 15 percent" and that "in 2002 alone, private investment reached 1.7 trillion yuan ($205.31 billion) ... accounting for 40.3 percent of the total investment nationwide."* However, although the revival of private business and private foreign investment were crucial elements of Deng Xiaoping's goal of creating a "socialist market economy," aspects of the new policy came under attack as problems began to emerge.

The following analysis contains examples of criticisms of the private market that appeared in China during the 1990s. [55]

1. *A social-psychological imbalance created by the increasing gap between the rich and the poor.*

One investigative study dating to 1993 points out: The abrupt accumulation of great wealth and the abnormal patterns of consumption on the part of a

---

* Huang Mengfu, "Private Economy Is Playing Pivotal Role," *Beijing Review,* January 22, 2004, p. 21.

small number of proprietors of privately run enterprises have made "the overwhelming majority of wage earners and salaried workers [in urban society] and laborers in the rural sector and the countryside come to feel that perhaps the gap in income has become too great, and these people have an intense sense of being exploited." Therefore, they "are angry at what is happening, and feel there is no justice in the world." They begin to experience a "psychological imbalance" and feel that "on the one side, you have those people who can afford to 'dine on fine meats,' while, on the other side, there are those resigned to 'cursing out' everyone else." Indeed, some people have even developed the following frame of mind: "If these people, [i.e., the proprietors of privately run enterprises] can be so brazen as to rob society of its wealth, reap great wealth in the form of windfalls in violation of the law, and then engage in all these abnormal and obscene patterns of consumption and good living, why can't I? After all, I am not without a strong arm or a powerful leg myself. They are reaping ill-gotten gains and illegitimate profits by robbing state-owned property and assets; so what if I squeeze them a bit and take some of this wealth from them? What would be wrong with that? It would only be robbing from the rich to give to the poor, and eradicating that which is unfair and rooting out injustice!" [It is also pointed out in the report that]: "if this continues, then there will be more and more people who turn from all this angry clamoring and cursing to take all sorts of direct action to obtain economic interests for themselves and to make up for their psychological imbalance. . . . When such a [vicious] cycle reaches a certain limit, or a certain depth, the whole society will begin to lose its standards and it will lead to unrest and even send shock waves throughout the society."

2. *The intensification of conflict and contradictions between labor and capital ignited by exploitation and oppression. . .*

In recent years, there have been increasingly frequent reports in the newspapers, popular journals, and magazines of cases that reflect how proprietors of privately run enterprises (including privately run enterprises that are nominally labeled as "collective-owned" enterprises and "individual" entrepreneurs, as well as foreign-invested enterprises) cruelly exploit, oppress, and humiliate their hired workers (particularly women workers and child laborers). There are even reports of how proprietors take revenge on and prosecute their workers, even to the point of causing deaths, or force laborers into slave-like servitude. . . .

3.   The phenomenon of "disintegration within the ranks of the Party" ignited by "sugar-coated bullets" . . .

An article pointed out: We "simply cannot afford to take too lightly" the negative impact that transformations in the structure of the ownership system have on the construction of the Party ranks; instead, we need to "pay attention to preventing distintegration in the ranks of the Party." In addition, the article went on to point out that "the following circumstances and situations are particularly worthy of attention." First, "some people in the Party are now desperate to find a 'way out' for themselves." For instance, "some people are plunging into the sea of business entirely out of consideration for purely personal interests, and have made their lives' ambitions to become successful capitalists; other people are taking to speculation on the stock market, and whether they are directly or indirectly involved personally, and whether surreptitiously or openly, they have their minds making fortunes; still others are sending their children or their relatives and friends overseas or to some other part of the country to establish residence, thus setting up for themselves a 'base of operations.' Furthermore, there are people who make use of the power and authority that they have and get involved in business through the means of supporting and propping up their agents in order to make a lot of money, with the intention of 'becoming not only a government official, but a capitalist as well.'

4.   A major emerging trend in which proprietors of privately run enterprises are actively exerting economic, political, and ideological influence on Party and government departments. . .

There are . . . articles and writings reflecting that: In the political arena, certain proprietors of privately run enterprises have proposed a "plan of reform" labeled, "A Process for Relative Privatization with Chinese Characteristics." In this they claim that: "The overall powerful battle-array of privately run enterprises [today] signals the degree of in-depth penetration that privatization has already made [in our society] and the level of its growth and development, and it serves well as a banner for privatization." Some even go as far as to proclaim openly: "A significant reform and renewal of our country's political system will be launched in the wake of the growth of the privately run economic sphere and the development of the ranks of proprietors of privately run enterprises. From here on out, what shall enter into the

The transaction hall of the Shanghai Stock Exchange. (From *China*, Beijing: New Star Publichers, 1999, p. 155.)

ranks of government leadership at all levels in our country will be large numbers of proprietors of privately run enterprises; we can no longer simply turn proprietors of privately run enterprises into mere 'political flowerpots' [for mere decoration] as delegates to the People's Congresses or commissioners in the Political Consultative Conferences."

> Growing income inequality, as a result of the growth of the private economy, has been widely commented upon in China. The following is an excerpt from *China's Descent into a Quagmire*, a long critical analysis of the reform era written by economist He Qinglian. Completed in 1996, the book was turned down by several publishers in China before being published in Hong Kong. It eventually was published in Beijing in 1998. [56]

IN AN ARTICLE written two years ago, this author concluded that . . . enormous amounts of wealth had been accumulated in the hands of a rather small number of people, a fact confirmed by statistical data made available since that time.

All of this is evident from the following:

1. The nation's financial capital is clearly under the control of a small hand-
    ful. In 1995, the Urban Social Economic Investigative Team of the State
    Statistical Bureau issued a report on financial capital in urban and town-
    ship households in China (including bank deposits, bonds, and cash).
    According to Cheng Xuebin who drafted the report, total financial cap-
    ital in urban and township households in China in 1994 was 1.8547
    trillion yuan, with yawning gaps in its distribution. Those categorized as
    wealthy accounted for only 7 percent of all households (with the super-
    rich accounting for only 1 percent). Combined, they possessed 30.2 per-
    cent of all the nation's financial capital. As for households who were
    barely making ends meet or who were below the poverty line, they came
    to 38 percent of the total and owned a mere 11.9 percent of the total
    wealth.

    Yet another report on the distribution of bank deposits of urban and
    township residents that did not include bonds, stocks, and so forth,
    indicated even more imbalance in the distribution of wealth. According
    to this report, the 10 percent lowest-income people possessed a mere 3
    percent of total deposits while the 10 percent of highest-income people
    possessed 40 percent, a figure that is on the increase with the overall gap
    expanding at a rate of 10 percent.

2. Overall income distribution in China over the past several years sup-
    ports this author's notion discussed in the same article. The evidence
    comes from a July 1995 report out of the Social Survey Center of the
    Chinese People's University in its report on the "PPS" [original in
    English—Ed.] sample survey conducted nationwide. According to that
    report, the 20 percent poorest households in China in 1994 only pos-
    sessed 4.27 percent of total income, whereas the 20 percent wealthiest
    households possessed 50.24 percent, a gap in the distribution of wealth
    that surpassed even that of the United States. As data collected in 1990
    from the United States indicated, the 20 percent poorest households
    there possessed 4.6 percent of total income and the 20 percent wealthi-
    est households possessed 44.3 percent. . . .

    The problem was more recently acknowledged by a leading gov-
    ernment official. According to the *People's Daily* of May 10, 2002,
    [57]

CHINA HAS RANKED itself among countries where resident incomes are very unequal. The problem of income distribution has become the most noticeable issue among current social problems in China, said Lu Zhiqiang, deputy director of the Development Research Center of the State Council, in his speech delivered at the 35th Annual Meeting of the Board of Governors of the Asian Development Bank (ADB) on May 9.

Since the launch of the reform and opening up drive, people's incomes have been raised, but the gap between the rich and the poor has widened. The Gini Coefficient of China's resident incomes has increased rapidly from 0.33 in 1980 to the critical point of 0.4 in 1994, and has now exceeded 0.45. [Ed.: Gini coefficients are a measure of income inequality on a numerical scale in which 0=perfect equality and 1 is equivalent to complete monopolization by one unit. Higher Gini numbers therefore indicate a greater polarization of incomes.]

The fact that the income gap expands along with economic growth in the process of industrialization is not a phenomenon unique to China, but Lu Zhiqiang noted that China's problem is more complicated than other countries and regions, this is manifested in the following four aspects:

- Firstly, the income gap is broadening at a very fast pace. In a period of 20 years, China has changed from a country with a very narrow income gap to its entry into the ranks of countries with great unequal incomes, such a speed is very rare in the world.

- Secondly, the polarization of incomes has a clear community character. Income level is closely related with regions, industries, enterprises and institutions. In terms of residents' incomes, such a yawning gap between different regions, urban and rural areas and different trades as in China is rare in the whole world.

- Thirdly, the general public has shown dissatisfaction over the present income distribution method, especially they do not affirm that part of high income gained by high-income earners. About 70 percent of people think that "the great disparity between the rich and the poor" has adversely affected social stability. People are showing great discontent with the irrationally high income gained through the monopoly of industries, and with the illegal gains derived from graft and corruption, and power-for-money transaction. Such phenomena are rarely seen in other countries and regions.

THE NEW "THREE IRONS"

Yet however moderated, the violence of the market cannot be hidden amidst the dismissal of some 50 million workers from their jobs. This is epitomised by the observation that the old three irons—the iron rice bowl, iron armchair and iron wage (representing job and wage security and lifetime employment)— have been replaced by the iron heart, iron face and iron fist.

Source: Gerard Greenfield and Apo Leong, "China's Communist Capitalism," *The Socialist Register*, 1997, p. 3.

■   Fourthly, it is difficult to reverse the trend of the widening income gap. As the widening income gap is not completely caused by the distribution policy, so the problem cannot be resolved only by adjusting the distribution policy. Many other factors, such as disparities in regional and rural and urban economic development, imperfection in economic and legal system construction and limited means and functions concerning re-distribution of incomes, also increased difficulties in reversing the broadening gap.

> Two years later, a Chinese-born and educated correspondent to *The New York Times* noted that: "Envy, insecurity and social dislocation have come with the huge disparity between how the wealthy live and how the vast numbers of poor do. Clear signs of class division have emerged under a government that long claimed to have eliminated economic classes. . . .
>
> 18 percent of Chinese live on less than $1 a day, according to the United Nations. The poor are visible on the edges of any metropolis, where slums of plywood apartments sometimes abut the Western-looking mansions.
>
> The most recent measure by which social scientists judge the inequality of a country's income distribution indicates that China is more unequal, for example, than the United States, Japan, South Korea and India. In fact, inequality levels approach China's own level in the late 1940s, when the Communists, with the help of the poor, toppled the Nationalist government." *

---

* Yilu Zhao, "China's Wealthy Live by a Creeed: Hobbes and Darwin, Meet Marx," *The New York Times*, February 29, 2004, p. WK7.

POPULAR RHYMES

After thirty years of uphill fight
We're back to the old ways overnight.

—Rhyme from the Northeast

In the 1950s we helped one another.
In the 1960s we denounced one another.
In the 1970s we doubted one another.
In the 1980s we swindled one another.

—Rhyme from rural Shanxi

Ten hundred million alive in our fair nation.
Nine hundred million deep in speculation.
One hundred million primed to join the operation.

—Beijing rhyme, 1989

Source: William Hinton, *The Great Reversal*, New York: Monthly Review Press, 1990, pp.14, 24, 27.

Mao Zedong was bad, real bad,
But with a buck you knew what you had.
Deng Xiaoping is fine, real fine,
But a buck is only worth a dime.

—Popular rhyme current in China in late 1988-early 1989.

Source: Suzanne Ogden, et al., eds., *China's Search for Democracy*, Armonk, NY: M.E. Sharpe, 1992, p. 3.

A survey conducted by the Chinese Academy of Social Science and released in 2004 reported that less than 20 percent of the population possessed 80 percent of the wealth. By 2005, inequality had increased so dramatically that the richest 10 percent of the population earned 45 percent of the income while the poorest 10 percent earned only 1.4 percent.

In that same year, the China Relief Fund announced that nearly 30 million Chinese lived in absolute poverty, therefore lacking sufficient food and clothing, and "another 60 million have incomes below 865 yuan (about $100 a year—well below the $1 a day that the World Bank takes as its standard." *

In spite of the criticisms, the private economy continued to expand with the support of the Communist Party and business leaders were honored as leading representatives of the new China. The culmination of the trend of legitimizing capitalism came on July 1, 2001, the eightieth anniversary of the founding of the Communist Party, when Party General Secretary Jiang Zemin invited leaders of the private economy to join the Party. (His proposal was officially accepted by the Communist Party's Central Committee in September, 2001.)

Jiang declared that, "Since China adopted the policy of reform and opening up, the composition of China's social strata has changed to some extent. There are, among others, entrepreneurs and technical personnel employed by scientific enterprises of the non-public sector, managerial and technical staff employed by foreign-funded enterprises, the self-employed, private entrepreneurs, employees in intermediaries and free-lance professionals." He said that as long as people from these groups work "wholeheartedly for the implementation of the Party's line and program" and meet the requirements of membership, they should be admitted into the Party.** Many in China and overseas viewed this change in policy towards business leaders as a watershed development in the history of modern China.

In March 2004, the Chinese government further enhanced the underpinnings of the private economy when the Second Session of the tenth National People's Congress voted to amend the constitution by protecting the right of private property. Specifically, article 13 was revised to state that, "Citizens' lawful private property is inviolable." "The State, in accordance with law, protects the rights of citizens to private property and to its inheritance" and "The State may, in the public interest and in accordance with law, expropriate or requisition private property for its use and shall make compensation for the private property expropriated or requisitioned."***

The private economy has continued to grow, and by 2005, a 70 percent share of GDP was controlled by the private sector.

---

* Elaine Kurtenbach, "China Income Gap Between Rich and Poor Provoking Alarm, Reports Say," *Associated Press*, September 21, 2005.

** "Jiang Zemin's Speech on Party's 80th Anniversary (part V)," *China Daily Online*, July 1, 2001.

*** "Detailed Amendments to the Constitution," *People's Daily*, March 15, 2004, p. 292.

IMPRESSIONS OF
A VETERAN CADRE TOURING
SPECIAL ECONOMIC ZONES

A certain veteran cadre who had always dreamed of visiting the Shenzen and Zhuhai Special Economic Zones was moved to pen the following lines after he recently got his wish:

Behold the bald blue mountains beyond tile city wall,

Behold the fertile fields holding half-built buildings all.

Behold the throngs of beauties crowding the city streets,

Behold the luxury sedans that flow along in fleets.

Behold the banks weighed down by default after default,

Behold the Party secretaries, well-heeled and jolly fat.

Behold the seafood banquets and feasting great and small,

Behold the idle workers queuing helplessly on the mall.

Behold the stock prices, soaring upward, plunging downward,

Behold government policy, one day leftward, next day rightward.

Behold the Communist Party, its state my heart does rend,

Behold Socialism, come nearly to its end.

Source: *The Nineties*, Hong Kong, January 1997, cited in *Inside China Mainland* (Taipei), Vol. XIX, No. 3, March 1997, p. 31.

Cultural Life

Editor's Introduction: Changes in the economy during the era of Deng Xiaoping have been matched by changes in Chinese cultural life. For decades after the 1949 Revolution, China was relatively isolated from Western cultural trends. Few Westerners visited China or did business there and even fewer Chinese left their homeland. Western movies, television shows, music, fashion and consumer goods were practically unknown in China. However, the cultural situation changed dramatically during the 1980s and 1990s. Suddenly China was opened to the world, as Western businessmen, students and tourists flooded into China. Within a short time Western movies, music, fashion, television shows, food, advertising and consumer goods were to be found in all parts of the country. At the same time, thousands of Chinese students and officials came to the West and were exposed to all aspects of Western culture.

These renewed cultural contacts had a profound effect on the Chinese. Many quickly adapted Western ways and viewed Western culture as a form of liberation from the narrow confines of traditional Confucian or modern Maoist cultural forms. Others saw Western cultural influence as a form of imperialism and feared that traditional Chinese culture and identity were being destroyed. As Western influence continued to grow, so did a sense of cultural confusion. One can say that confusionism replaced Confucianism.

The following passages convey a sense of the rapidly changing cultural scene in contemporary China. The first reading describes the interior of a home in the city of Shashi in Hubei Province. The second is an excerpt from a lengthy article warning of the dangers of Western culture. [58]

I

JIN HAS DECORATED the house in a way testifying to how migration mixes a bizarre brew of conflicting values within a family. In the front room,

"THE IMPERIALISTS ARE BACK"

"Over 150 years ago," grumbled the old man in the tea house, "'foreign devils' *[guilao]* exported opium to China. Now they are selling cigarettes to the China market. Some foreign biochemical factories here have not only polluted China's environment, but have even sold banned medicine to the Chinese people."

"After the Liberation in 1949, everyone in Shanghai was familiar with a popular song," the old man started to hum the tune. *"Socialism is wonderful...the imperialists ran off with their tails between their legs."*

"Now," the old man said, "someone has rewritten the words of the song: *Capitalism is wonderful...the imperialists are back with wallets under their arms.*"

Source: Cheng Li, *Rediscovering China, Lanham,* MD: Rowman & Littlefield, 1997, p. 209.

posters and scrolls either made in the village or bought in the city suggest a melange of traditional, Maoist, and modern mores. "Big fortune upon opening the door; good luck when going out," declare couplets written in black on red paper and pasted on the front doors. Directly across from the doors hangs a colorful five-foot scroll from which the wizened and berobed gods of longevity, prosperity, and official prestige beam as they hug frolicking children on a golden horse-drawn cart. On either side are scrolls. One says, "With the blessings of the three gods, this land of intellect produces people of eminence." On the other side, another scroll says, "With the arrival of the five guarantees, the country is in harmony and the people in peace." (Mao mandated that his "people's communes" guarantee childless and infirm senior citizens five benefits: food, clothing, medical care, housing, and free burial.) Beneath the scrolls, in another tribute to Maoism, glare a female Navy pilot wearing a life vest and helmet, a marine with an AK-47 assault rifle and gunbelt, and a woman in a naval dress uniform. Across the bottom of the large, neon-colored plastic poster are the words "The cream rises together." Among the messages of antiquity and dour militarism are the coy, softly seductive images popular in China under reform. In one poster a dewy-eyed young lady cuddles a kitten against her cheek. In another, a smiling girl clinging to a guitar reclines in a hammock. In a third, a shapely lady in a striped bathing suit dallies by the side of a pool.

II
"FOREIGN WINDS" INVADE CHINA

Not long ago, the elderly Singaporean poet Hai Huari visited China together with the Malaysian woman writer Ai Wei and the Singaporean poetess Qin Zhen. As they lingered along Beijing's Chang'an Boulevard, they remarked with astonishment that the huge "Remy Martin" advertisements, the noisy discos, and the long, snaking lines of imported luxury sedans, limned in the winter's night a new and seductive picture of the ancient nation. After their first surprise and delight, however, these writers—whose roots are in China—were not without misgivings: If such "Westernization" continues, will China still possess her own characteristics?

"THE WOLF IS REALLY HERE"

Chinese culture, with its five-thousand-year history, has been known the world over for its profound roots and unprecedented power of penetration. Since the Opium War, however, Western culture has come again and again to knock at the country's gates, and after each Chinese military defeat a crowd of "foreign demons" came onstage. From "hello" to "John Lee," and from revolvers to Pierre Cardin, Western culture swaggered into our house. Whether in battling against foreign guns or in boycotting foreign goods and foreign dross, the Chinese people have repeatedly displayed magnificent exploits of heroism and tenacity.

The reforms and openness since the end of the 1970s and the early 1980s have caused the land of China to brim with vitality and color. But close on the heels of the ranks of towering highrises has come the negative culture of the West. It has exploited practically every means of access—from foreign cars to foreign residences, from foreign food to foreign garments. The astuteness of the Westerners lies in their making people accept their concepts and their way of life in subtle and insidious ways. The Chinese people do not reject everything foreign, and adapting foreign things to Chinese needs has always been one of our tenets. But the inpouring of the dross together with the essence is not to be recommended. It would be an exaggeration to say that foreign winds and foreign rains are blotting out sky and earth, but ordinary Chinese people of insight indeed sense that the wolf has indeed arrived.

THE GRIM REALITY OF THE SIEGE

Foreign culture has arrived with a fanfare, disturbing the rhythm of thought of the Chinese people. Foreign goods and foreign culture have made China

OLD OPERA LANDMARK
BOWS OUT ON LOW NOTE

The 87-year-old Jixiang Theatre, which has long been a landmark for Peking Opera lovers, was officially closed in Beijing yesterday.

No Peking Opera, an art form rich in symbolism and tradition, will be heard again in the theatre, which is due to be demolished.

The two-story theatre, which stands amid high-priced hotels and stores on Wangfujing, Beijing's largest commercial street, will make way for a Hong Kong-funded shopping complex.

Yesterday morning, a group of nostalgic and disappointed fans stood before its box office, and appeared reluctant to surrender the theatre's illustrious cultural past to the wheels of economic progress.

Theatre workers denied rumours that a decline in Peking Opera's popularity triggered the closure. They said the theatre remained profitable to the end and that an average of 300 plays were staged each year.

Observers said that the ongoing modernization of the Chinese capital has inevitably clashed with traditional customs and structures, and that this conflict reflects a worldwide trend of the old giving way to the new. Peking Opera dates back 200 years and combines acrobatics, song and dance.

It often draws on traditional Chinese stories, or legends, incorporates quite abstract stage language and is regarded as one of the most expressive symbols of the country's culture.

However, audiences have been falling as young people are lured from their cultural roots by the glitter of television and cinema.

A petition signed by dozens of noted artists pleading for the Jixiang Theatre to be saved failed to stop the juggernaut of modernization.

Source: *China Daily*, October 6, 1993.

"modern" but have also caused our great and proud country, with its thousands of years of civilized history, to sense the sorrow of gradually losing its ego. . . .

Foreign restaurants such as McDonald's, Kentucky Fried Chicken, California Beef Noodles, and Pizza Hut have in recent years sprung up like bamboo shoots after a spring rain. Vieing with these restaurants, foreign cigarettes and wines have also trooped in: "State Express," "Hilton," "Camel," "Marlboro," "Gold Award XO," "Martell," "Remy Martin"—and stashed behind this string of foreign brand names are substantial profits. These foreign foods and foreign drinks have made away not only with the Chinese people's money but also with the patriotism of a good number of people.

The chief reason for the inordinate success of these foreign foods and drinks is that they have a market. And this market is the broad masses of consumers. But these well-intentioned consumers do not realize that behind the "satisfaction" of their simple pleasures lies the danger of foreign food and beverage industries taking over the Chinese market. . . . Eating, drinking, and pleasure-seeking are boon companions. In a certain sense, pleasure-seeking is an upgrading of eating and drinking.

With the "renaissance" of social dancing in the last few years and the explosion of disco dancing, the abrupt rise of game machines, and the popularity of bowling, billiards, and golf, a wind of Westernized entertainment has swept our country. And with it a number of professions particular to the West have emerged: the "three accompany girl," the at-your-call male companion, the masseuse, the beautician, and so forth. . . .

In October 1995 I surveyed thirteen movie houses in Beijing and found that the proportion of Chinese-made films was less than 20 percent and that their attendance rate was pitifully low. Meanwhile, the so-called ten major imported films were sweeping the city and attendance rates remained high after repeated screenings. . . .

Foreign ads are the pointmen of foreign culture. "Open a bottle of Remy Martin and all good things are yours." "Toshiba, Toshiba, the Eastern Orchid [Chinese name for Toshiba—Trans.] of the New Era"—these posters and advertising slogans, so fascinating to Chinese eyes and ears, saturate television, radio, and billboards as well as posters sponsoring soirees and social evenings. More than just spiriting away "foreign returns," such foreign advertising propagates a sort of "foreign spirit." The U.S. Coca-Cola company once spent tens of millions of dollars in a small and out-of-the-way African country to put up a huge billboard, which the company's president claimed would stand forever, since it "symbolizes the conquest of this region by the Coca-Cola company."

The shock waves of cosmetics came even earlier. Many fashion-conscious young ladies think it humiliating to use Chinese-made cosmetics. A film actress I am acquainted with is vociferously promoting a Chinese-made cosmetic, but when I asked her if she really uses these cosmetics, she burst out laughing and replied: "People pay me money to root for them. But nobody uses these Chinese made goods!"

In some people's eyes, foreign clothes symbolize money and position. Some fat cats deck themselves from head to toe with foreign garments, foreign hats, foreign shoes, and foreign glasses; the only thing missing is a walking stick. And some foreign brand-name garment makers have lost no opportunity feverishly to develop their business on the Chinese mainland. Exclusive "Pierre Cardin" stores have blossomed forth everywhere. "Apple Texwood" and "Puma," not to be outdone, are setting up camp wherever possible. Huge billboards advertising high-class imported goods have become the new rare-shows in a good many cities.

Foreign culture has also borne down with full fury on the news and publishing business. Through pirated copies that defy all rounding-up efforts, foreign dross that primarily propagates violence and sex are continuously flooding China's book and publications' market. When I visited the Jintai Road Wholesale Books and Publications Market—the largest in Beijing—not long ago, I found that translated works made up a considerable proportion of the publications offered. Apart from a few world-famous literary works, the great majority of them highlighted sex. It can well be said that these Western best-sellers that advocate so-called sexual freedom have played an inflammatory role in the poisoning of [China's] social atmosphere.

FOREIGN EDUCATION CAUSES ANXIETY

Education of children is directly related to the kind of tomorrow we will be harvesting. Foreign cultures, with cartoon films as their precursors, are ingratiating themselves with Chinese children. The first to enter China ten or more years ago was Japanese culture. The animated film *Automan* (Atomu) lingered a good many years, and the film *Smart Yi Xiu* has affected the childhood of virtually an entire generation.

The American cartoons that followed on their heels cut an even wider swathe. The towering figure of the "Transformer" has filled Chinese youngsters with awe.

No sooner are animated films shown, than foreign toys rain down. Various children's toys based on the film and TV images of "Automan," the "Transformer," and "Iron-Arm Atomu"—and named after the latter—

immediately come on the market. Chinese parents, who regard their children as gods, are constrained to open their purses and buy these toys to satisfy their children's insatiable desires.

The aristocratic schools that emerged in the mid-1980s are typical of the Westernized model of education. . . .

Whether it is foreign movies and TV films, foreign toys, or foreign education—all create a concept of Western values in our children, values that hinder the normal development of children and young people, weaken their national self-respect and their patriotic sentiments, and may even affect the nation's future. . . .

China's excellent traditional culture is besieged by Western culture. This is a troubling situation. The unhealthy pigments [sic] of Western culture, in particular, are polluting the organism of Chinese culture. But this, after all, is but a brief birth pain during the reconfiguration of society. This is because the merging of Chinese and foreign cultures consists of a spiraling pattern of separation, merger, and separation again in a higher sense.

"Foreign cultures should not be accused, one and all, of being bad cultures. The fact is that advances in each era took inspiration and impetus from outside cultures. The New Cultural Movement at the beginning of this century, for instance, is in large measure related to the influence of Russian revolutionary culture. In fact, the effect of foreign cultures on Chinese culture has been one of a reciprocal complementing of strong qualities." Such are the impassioned statements of Liu Fuchun of the Chinese Academy of Social Sciences.

But the well-known commentator Tu Tu sees things differently. He looks at the surging tide of foreign culture with apprehension: "Complacency is often the harbinger of disaster. We should be able to claim that our country's ancient culture is a powerful one, but we cannot claim that it is invulnerable. In fact, the massive incursions by foreign cultures have compelled our own culture to withdraw to a very bleak position. This is an abnormal phenomenon, and, in a certain sense, a man-made phenomenon. This phenomenon, if allowed to develop, will definitely not bring any good results. Are there not some countries in the world that started out with deep-seated cultures that gradually disintegrated under the disruptive action of colonial cultures, and that to this day are unable to rediscover their own culture?"

I maintain that the most pressing task today is to exercise guidance and management over foreign cultures.

Confusionism:
Images of Western Influence
and Cultural Confusion

Editor's Introduction: By the 1990s, Western culture had achieved immense popularity in China. Accomplishments of the West had assumed almost mythic proportion in Chinese popular culture. Almost everything Western became desirable and prestigious. Many television drama and variety shows, as well as commercials, copied U.S. models. Images of American and European icons were ubiquitous on advertising billboards and in books and magazines. They also adorned calendars and decks of cards. Many of these images were associated with wealth and power.

In addition, the English language became increasingly popular. Numerous private English language schools were established and growing numbers of English courses were offered in public schools and colleges. Not only was the knowledge of English seen as a requirement for economic advancement, but association with English endowed one with a certain status and prestige. Even though the overwhelming majority of Chinese knew no English or other foreign languages, examples of English writing (and not quite English writing using letters from the Latin alphabet) appeared on billboards, greeting cards, menus, candy wrappers, games and tee shirts. The result seemed to be, for better or worse, a replacement, on the popular level, of images of Chinese culture and history with those of the U.S. and Europe. Cultural confusion was apparent.

The images in this section were all collected (or photographed) in China during the mid-1990s.

The legendary Garden of Eden now in the heart of Beijing

北 京 紫 玉 山 莊
PURPLE JADE VILLAS

Purple Jade Villas – just a 10-minute drive from Tiananmen Square – is one of Beijing's most desirable addresses for investors and residents alike.

Within the vast estate area of 66.7 hectares, only 300 luxury villas of 170 to 500 square metres each are being built – with over 80% of the area remaining wooded. Carefully built and decorated by famous architects and designers, Purple Jade Villas represents your best choice in Beijing real estate.

The Purple Jade Villas Property Exhibition
Dates: June 9-12, 1994
Venue: No. 1, Purple Jade Road East
Chao Yang District
Beijing

Advertisement from the *China Daily*, June 19-25, 1994.

娃娃天地 wá wa tiān dì 1

圣诞老人 Shèng Dàn Lǎo Rén

三 毛
Sān Máo
〈漫 画《三毛流浪
记》主人公〉

14 娃娃天地 wá wa tiān dì

白雪公主
Bái Xuě Gōng Zhǔ
〈格林童话《白雪公主》
主人公〉

Illustrations from a children's book, *Personages*, published in Shanghai (1992).

View from the entrance of "Europe City" theme park in the city of Wuxi.

Shanghai street scene.

Tee shirts worn in Shanghai.

Item purchased in a Shanghai photography shop.

Shanghai street scene.

Items for sale at a street stall in Shanghai.

Shanghai street scene.

Street advertisement in Hangzhou.

Board game, "Strong Hand," purchased in Shanghai.

Office in Xian.

Deck of cards purchased in Shanghai. (Note that the highest cards depict the currencies of the U.S. and the U.K. while the lowest cards depict the currencies of Thailand and Japan.

Top and bottom:
Images from a 1993 calendar
produced in Tianjin.

Probably the last public image of Mao in Shanghai, a fading portrait on an exterior wall of a small apartment house photographed in the Fall of 1993.

Education

Editor's Introduction: As a result of the growth of the market econo-my, serious problems have arisen in the area of education. Dropout rates of students in primary and middle schools have soared. Government spending on education per student is among the lowest in the world and student fees and expenses have risen sharply since the beginning of the reform era. (A policy change in 2005, however, exempted the poorest students from paying fees.)

The following article, by a faculty member at the Northwest Normal University, analyzes the reasons for the high dropout rates in the rural areas. Most of the reasons are related to the reform policies. [59]

THE INCIDENCE OF dropouts is becoming increasingly serious among rural middle- and primary-school students in recent years. Although schools have exhausted all means and adopted all sorts of measures, and government departments have exercised strict supervision, the incidence of dropouts has not been entirely terminated in rural middle and primary schools.

Subsequent to in-depth investigations, studies, and analyses, I believe that the main reasons for the discontinuance of studies among rural middle and primary school students are as follows:

1. *Because of the overall increase in school charges and student expenditures, some poverty-stricken peasant households are no longer capable of defraying such fees and expenditures.*

For a variety of reasons, school fees and student expenditures have been very high in recent years. This is manifested mainly in two aspects:

a: School charges: (1) Schools have increased various fees within the limits permitted by policy in order to make up their shortfalls in education funds, and are charging additional fees for lodging, stoves, and heating; and (2) schools are indiscriminately charging fees under all kinds of pretexts, such

BASIC BUDGET
FOR A PRIMARY SCHOOL CHILD IN SHANGHAI

January - June 1996
(in *renminbi* at 8.3 *renminbi* to one U.S. dollar)

One semester of school fees	150-200 rmb
School lunch (70 rmb x 6 months)	420 rmb
One book bag	75 rmb
One pair gym shoes	7 rmb
Three school uniforms	210 rmb
One pair leather school shoes	100 rmb
One winter coat	300 rmb
Basic meals at home plus one bottle of milk per day (230 rmb x 6 months)	1,380 rmb
Daily pocket money (2 rmb/day x 180 days)	360 rmb
Estimated total	3,052 rmb or 508/month

(508 rmb per month was the average monthly wage of a Shanghai resident in 1996.)

Source: Deborah S. Davis, ed., *The Consumer Revolution in Urban China*, Berkeley: University of California Press, 2000, p. 59.

as desk fees, exam-paper fees, reading-room permit fees, homework-correcting fees, supplementary course fees, coaching fees, and so on.

b: Student expenses: (1) fees for textbooks and materials have risen sharply; (2) prices of various types of reference materials and books, review materials, exercise books, and outside-reading materials are constantly increasing; (3) prices of homework notebooks and all kinds of stationery and study implements are rising. A bottle of ink that cost 30 fen a few years ago now sells for 1.2 *yuan*, which represents a fourfold increase; and an exercise book that could be had for less than 30 fen in the past today costs one *yuan*, or more than three times the price. Peasant households have no "money trees" or "treasure chests," nor do they "operate banks." Such school charges and student expenses have indubitably increased the financial burdens on, and counterweights against, peasant households. . . . Although some peasant households are most eager to give their children a successful career, they are helpless in the face of their poverty. "We're too poor to pay for schooling!" they say. So they can only regretfully give up this cherished hope, terminate their children's schooling, and watch as their children lament their loss.

Financial reasons are the direct and most basic cause of dropping out among rural students.

2. *Inappropriate methods of school education and home education cause some "inadequate students" [scholastically—Trans] and "doubly inadequate students" [in both scholastics and deportment—Trans] to dislike going to school and, further, to play truant.*

3. *Since the reform of the educational system in institutions of higher learning and the gradual implementation of the "merged-tracks system," college and university students are gradually going from public funding to semipublic funding or self-funding, and the gradual increase in school fees has destroyed the "college dreams" of many children in agricultural households.*

4. *Following reforms in the state's personnel system, graduates from colleges and specialized middle schools will no longer be guaranteed job allocations; this has given peasants and rural students grave misgivings about their future, students who had had warm hopes for success on college entrance examinations. They look around cautiously, fearing to see "wolves in front and tigers behind" and cannot make up their minds.*

5. *The effects of "valuing males over females" and arranged marriages are the chief reasons for, as well as the social customs behind, the great number of dropouts among female students in rural middle and primary schools.*

6. *Amid the surging tide of the commodity and market economies, where the furor for engaging in business has brought about such phenomena as "people being turned head over heels by the flood of money-worship," where book-learning is seen as being "useless," and where excessive differences exist in social distribution, many parents focus only on immediate benefits, lack long-range vision, and cut short their children's academic life by taking them out of school and sending them "out to sea."*

As a consequence of the upsurge of the market and commodity economies, "money-worship" is causing people to direct all their attention to making money. Many people with a low level of knowledge but who are good at seizing opportunities have suddenly become rich; *da kuan* [tycoons] and *da wan* [movie stars], make big money and are objects of awe and admiration; moreover, abnormal situations of unfair distribution have emerged in society, where "professors serve as secretaries to illiterates," "makers of atom bombs earn less than makers of pickled eggs," "researchers are worse off than producers of soy sauce," "wielders of surgical knives are poorer than wielders of barbers' razors," and "pen pushers make less than street peddlers." This has given rise to the misconception that "farming keeps you in food, but working at jobs gets you money" among the peasantry who already have a low level of knowledge and culture. This has caused some students to leave school and "go to sea" (i.e., go into business) or to look for temporary jobs. The craze for going into business has given impetus to the theory that book learning is useless, and the commodity economy is seducing students whose families have economic difficulties and no hope of advancing to schools of higher education. Many students simply drop out of school to go home, some to take up agriculture and become "kid farmers," others to go into business and become "kid businessmen," and still others to take temporary jobs and become "kid laborers." This is the external reason for dropouts among rural middle and primary school students.

> The high cost of education is also affecting students, at all levels, in urban areas. The following account appeared in the *Beijing Review*. [60]

IT IS HARD to imagine how much a Chinese student, either at middle school or university, must pay nowadays. At the very least, their expenditures cover tuition and incidental expenses, dues for textbooks, extracurricular activities and extra classes, accommodation and board expenses, living expenses including food, clothing, daily necessities and commuting costs, and fees for additional classes for supplementary schooling. Generally speaking, the annual expenses of a middle school student amount to 10,000 yuan, while that for a university student range from 10,000 to 20,000 yuan. The majority of China's wage-earning families are burdened with this expensive education.

Yang Hongxiu, an accountant serving the Beijing Public Security Bureau, has a 15-year-old daughter. Yang and her husband, an army officer, make less than 3,000 yuan a month. The fixed expenditure of Yang's daughter includes tuition and incidental expenses of each school term, textbook dues, dues for extracurricular activities organized by her school such as visits, outings, parties and movies, as well as fees for supplementary education. Not long ago, it cost the couple 800 yuan to buy a trombone for their daughter, who is interested in playing a musical instrument, and 210 yuan to enter her name for a class that charges 60 yuan for each teaching session. These expenditures accounted for almost half of the family's earnings that month.

Chang Xiaoni is a student at the Beijing Dance Institute. Her annual tuition fees total 6,400 yuan and monthly living expenses are about 1,000 yuan. In addition, the combined expenses for textbooks, accommodation and dancewear average about 1,000 yuan each year. "Arts schools are costly," said Chang, who adds that four years of study at the institute will cost her an estimated 80,000 to 90,000 yuan.

Unofficial statistics show that expenses range from 100,000 to 200,000 yuan for a Beijing child to complete three stages of education involving elementary school, middle school and university. This is certainly a heavy burden.

EDUCATIONAL EXPENSES INCREASE CONSTANTLY

Charges by various levels of schools have risen year after year in China.

Beijing's key middle schools raised their tuition fees and incidental expenses starting last fall, up from 160 yuan to 800 yuan. Also, tuition fees for institutions of higher education have gone up.

The annual tuition fee set by some provinces and municipalities are as follows:

Beijing: 4,200 yuan (minimum) for ordinary majors at regular universities, 5,000 yuan for key universities, up to 5,000 yuan for ordinary scientific and technological universities, and up to 5,500 yuan for key scientific and technological universities;

Shanghai: Up to 5,000 yuan for ordinary majors, 30 percent higher for special majors, 7,500 yuan for institutions of higher vocational education, and up to 5,000 yuan for normal universities;

Heilongjiang: 2,500 yuan (minimum) to 4,500 yuan (maximum) for ordinary majors at regular universities, no more than 6,000 yuan for popular special majors;

Jilin: Between 3,500 yuan and 6,200 yuan.

Those figures mentioned above are only tuition fees, part of a student's expenses. Other expenses include textbook dues, accommodation charges, incidental costs, etc. Because the annual expenses of a college student have jumped to as high as 10,000 yuan, it has gone far beyond what ordinary Chinese families can bear.

Statistics released by the National Bureau of Statistics show that the per capita income of China's urban and rural residents respectively reached 5,854 yuan and 2,210 yuan in 1999. In light of the present standard of charges, however, an urban couple's total income in a year is only slightly different from the annual expenses of a college student. And that's couples with double incomes.

According to relevant departments, the savings of ordinary urban families in today's China average about 20,000 yuan. To support a college student will not only use up all of a family's existing savings, but also part of the family's expected earnings.

MONEY WOES A SETBACK

On September 25, 2000, a Xi'an-based newspaper published a letter from a cash-strapped student who hoped to find parents who would adopt him. The letter reads: "I am 18 years old this year. Though both my father and mother are alive, my impoverished family has almost been destroyed after suffering 10-odd years of natural disasters and disease. I was enrolled in a university this summer, but poverty has failed to allow me to enter it because I cannot afford the required tuition. I didn't want to be ruined by poverty, so I told my story to the leadership of a middle school. The school eventually permitted me to retake classes there and delay paying set dues. At present, I am preparing to take part in the college entrance examination again. Nevertheless, an idea has repeatedly hit me—to be adopted only if the adoptive parents can afford my higher education. I promise to be filial to them like to my own parents, since they will have given me a new life."

Statistics show about 11 percent of college students dropped out in 1997, when tuition fees at institutions of higher education were raised.

As the gap widens between the growth rate of tuition fees at institutions of higher education and per capita social income widens, the number of children unable to enter universities is expected to go up.

Youth

Editor's Introduction: During the last twenty years the situation of young people—and the relationship of youth to their parents—have undergone profound changes. One reason for this change is the success of the government's family-planning policies which has resulted in many Chinese children growing up without brothers or sisters and with few cousins. This phenomenon, unique in Chinese history, has led to a generation of, what the Chinese call, "little emperors," children who are spoiled by their doting parents and grandparents. This, combined with the proliferation of consumer goods, foreign products and advertisements on television, has led to young people becoming much more materialistic and money-oriented than their parents, who grew up in more austere times and were influenced by Maoist philosophy. The result has been not merely a generation gap, but a sense of bewilderment on the part of many parents and loneliness on the part of many young children.

The following article describes the "little emperor" phenomenon and puts most of the blame on parents: [61]

THERE IS NO lack of complaint about today's younger generation. Dubbed "little emperors" Chinese youngsters are said to be lazy, extravagant, self-indulgent, overly dependent, self-centred, irresponsible ... and the list could go on.

But it seems unfair that the children shoulder all the blame.

After all, their generation is the product of an era.

I don't deny, however, that Chinese children have fatal flaws.

A Sino-Japanese summer expedition to the inner Mongolian plains in 1992 exposed their shortcomings to the full.

The group included 67 Japanese and 20 Chinese children. They were each asked to carry a 10-kilogram backpack containing daily necessities, walk 20 kilometers, cook eight meals and camp three nights in the open air.

An in-depth report later revealed the fundamental differences between the two groups of children.

The Chinese laughed and joked all the way, their members going off on their own from time to time. The Japanese, on the other hand, hardly spoke, and followed each other very closely.

After cooking their meal, the Japanese children would help each other to the food and eat the bland-tasting nosh with great relish. In contrast, the Chinese waited for their group leader to fill up their bowls and would throw away the food if they didn't like it. Consequently the Chinese kids were constantly complaining of hunger.

When the time came to sum up their experiences, the Japanese children talked frankly and openly about their adventure. But the Chinese rattled off the well-practised formula "as a result of our experience, such and such virtue was gained and such and-such knowledge was acquired."

This was pretty meaningless because it didn't reveal what they really thought about the trip.

In our everyday life, we also hear of children demanding money from their parents to throw lavish birthday parties, expecting their parents to do all their washing, spending little on homework and calling their parents names if their often unreasonable demands are not met—in short, they show no concern for anybody whatsoever.

But can parents and teachers escape all the responsibility for these brats?

It seems to me that the real tragedy of today's Chinese children is that they are growing up in the shadow of the destructive "cultural revolution" (1966-1976) and its preceding political movements.

In between all the chaos of the 1950s, 60s and 70s, traditional education gave way to political rhetoric. Even now, China's time-honoured educational practices have not fully recovered.

And decades of political turmoil have left their mark on the now middle-aged Chinese, many of whom were deprived of normal schooling and spent their youth being 'reeducated" in the countryside.

It is not surprising that waking up from the political nightmare, they feel cheated. Many of them have become egocentric individuals.

When these people become parents and teachers, it's not hard to imagine what their children and students will be like.

On top of this, many Chinese parents and grandparents pamper the youngsters who are their only offspring.

How can we expect our children to be independent if we do everything for them, carefully watching over them for fear that they cannot get things done or that they will hurt themselves?

How can we expect them to be thrifty if our society worships money?

How can we expect them to be honest and upright if their parents and guardians jump at opportunities for free meals and trips, and if even their teachers expect gifts from them?

How can we expect youngsters to be responsible if the adults themselves make shoddy products—even fake medicine and liquor?

After all, children watch, listen and learn from adults as they grow up.

If even grown-ups have difficulty distinguishing the rights and wrongs in this fast-changing society, children will naturally be confused as well.

The generation gap was made clear in a 1997 survey sponsored by the Chinese Academy of Social Sciences. An article describing the survey noted that, [62]

NEARLY 60 MILLION couples throughout the country felt they had failed as parents.

"I have not succeeded in educating my child. If I could live another life, I'd rather not have any children," a mother declared. Such frustration was prevalent in the answers to the questionnaires. Some parents feel they lack means of educating, some find difficulty in communicating with their children, some feel totally lost at what their children should be taught—traditional Chinese morality such as honesty, modesty, forbearance and caring; or the modern ethos of competition? Educational experts read the answers to the questionnaires, analyzed the problems, and advised parents.

About 58.2 percent of parents are worried about TVs negative influence: children's programs are taking up too much homework time; too many foreign cartoons are neither "scientific" nor interesting; too many explicit love scenes and violence; many TV plays are far removed from reality. . . . Parents want to know how to prevent these influences. . . .

About 19.9 percent of the parents, complained about their children being too carefree with money. "Today's children are spoiled. They will accept nothing but name-brand commodities. When celebrating birthdays they like to give luxurious parties and on festivals they expect expensive gifts," some parents said. Many parents agree that their children are ignorant of hardship, thrift, hard work, and public ethics. . . .

With the implementation of one-child policy, a new problem has become obvious: loneliness. Of the children who answered the questionnaire, 14.8 percent said they had no close friend, and 17.6 percent often felt lonely.

Experts pointed out that not having friends does great harm to a child's character. Human beings are community minded. Every person gets to know

VISIONS OF SUGARPLUMS AND BIG CARS

"When I grow up, I want to be a business mogul, live in a villa in the suburbs, wear a suit by Pierre Cardin, and drive a Mercedes-Benz 600 to work in the World Trade Center in Beijing." So a fifth-grader describes his goals for the future, and he is typical of his generation. A four-year research project by Beijing's Institute of Youth Study has found that most of the city's primary school students are after money, material goods, and fame, complete with luxury villas and big cars. Some researchers think this is cause for concern.

From 1992 to 1996, researchers polled almost 10,000 primary-school students in Beijing. The first three choices of careers, mentioned by 60 percent of the sampling, were business manager, entertainment star (movie, TV, or sports), and scientist. Least popular, mentioned by only 6 percent of all the students, were teacher, worker, and farmer—the occupations that most Chinese children will inevitably find.

It would be nice, the researchers say, if the children had chosen to be managers, stars, and scientists in order to benefit their society. But unfortunately, they chose those careers for material goods and social recognition. This is truly worrisome.

Source: *Sing Tao Daily News* (centrist), Hong Kong, July 28, 1997, cited in *World Press Review*, November 1997, p. 7.

himself, and interacts with others to prove himself. If a child has no friends he or she loses a means of learning social values, he or she can neither enjoy the pleasure of communication, nor can he or she develop a healthy personality. Worse, an only child does not know how to cooperate, and sometimes is afraid of cooperating with others, because only children are over-protected at home. They are used to being loved, cared for, and being the center of attention. When in a new group, they are unable to cope. A child may turn to his or her own inner world or become addicted to electronic games. Lonely children are often morose, finicky, touchy and often cowardly.

The sources of generational conflict among Northern Chinese were analyzed by cultural anthropologist Yunxiang Yan in the late

1990s. Born in China and educated at Beijing University and at Harvard University, Yan is currently a professor at UCLA. He wrote that: [63]

A GENERATIONAL GAP was prevalent in everyday life since the late 1980s, leading, in some respects, to serious social tension between village youth and their elders. For men and women who are thirty-five or older, today's village youth are simply headaches to everyone except themselves; the youngsters, however, have their own complaints about the older people who refuse to understand the new generation.

In public life, young villagers tend to be much more argumentative and disobedient, often causing conflicts with older villagers. The most severe criticism of village youths, however, comes from the village cadres. There have been numerous confrontations, some involving violence, between young villagers and cadres. In an extreme case which occurred in Northgate village, a 19-year-old man was caught gambling and fined heavily by the local police department. He then confronted and accused the village head for leaking this to the police. When their dispute became fierce, he pulled out a knife and chased the village head, threatening to kill him. The panic-stricken village head, who finally climbed a tree to escape, was surrounded by the furious young man and many onlookers. When I interviewed the village head in 1991 he recalled the incident with a great deal of bitterness and embarrassment. "What else could I do except retreat?" he explained, "nowadays these kids are very strong physically but they have nothing in their heads. They are afraid of no one, not even the police. Spoiled by their parents, they have become a bunch of hooligans."

Conflicts between the young and the aged are equally common in the domestic sphere. The main complaint from elders, as can be expected, is the unfilial behavior of the young. Filial piety has long been recognized as one of the key concepts in Confucian ethics and one of the major principles structuring Chinese social life. An important component of the notion of filial piety is the unconditional obedience of the young to their parents and to their senior kin. The term "father" conveys a sense of authority, demanding respect and obedience. In this connection, a father-son quarrel in Xiajia village is illuminating for our understanding of how shaky generation superiority has become in the domestic domain. When a father could not silence his son during a family discord, he yelled: "Don't forget I'm still your father!" Without thinking, the son yelled back: "Nowadays it's hard to tell who's whose father!" The dispute ended quickly, as the son soon realized he had said something extremely stupid. Apparently they both had used the word "father" as a metaphor for the ultimate authority at home. This episode quickly became well-known in the community, and many of my informants cited it as an example of the current state of family relations.

Parents of unmarried young adults and teenagers also complain that village youths sometimes have become too liberal in their interactions with peers of the opposite sex. The more open-minded, active youths usually have their own small groups of close friends with whom they spend most of their spare time, watching TV, enjoying pop music, playing basketball or the newly imported game of billiards. The first time I saw young villagers playing billiards was in Luohou village, Hebei province, during my 1989 fieldwork. I was accompanied by two village cadres, but our presence did not attract the attention of the village youths who were concentrating on their game. I was particularly impressed by the fact that there were several girls standing around the billiards table, but no one seemed to notice. I was less surprised after witnessing many similar scenes during my subsequent fieldwork, in all of the three villages. In Northgate village, a middle-aged village musician is known for being especially nice to the peers of his young son and daughter. Regularly eight to ten village youths stay at his house; as a result, his home is nicknamed "the youth club." When an old friend of the musician heard that teenage girls and boys always play together at this unofficial "youth club," he prohibited his youngest son from going there, causing difficulties in the relationship between the two friends.

Another common criticism about the village youths is their materialistic orientation. Older villagers complain that today's young villagers are only interested in enjoying a good life. Almost without exception, the young dislike working in the fields and always try to avoid heavy manual labor.

But they like to hang out on the streets, displaying their new clothes and leather shoes, and spending money on things that formerly were only consumed by urban people, such as expensive shampoo and cassettes (Hong Kong and Taiwan pop singers are as popular among village youth as they are among urban youth). A former village party secretary told me that his cigarettes only cost 0.39 yuan per pack, while his son's cigarettes cost ten times more—3.9 yuan per pack. An old woman said she simply could not understand why her grandson, a young man, spends so much time in front of the mirror, and why he wears good clothing and leather shoes even to herd the cows in the fields. "Even a young girl should not be like that," she concluded. To meet their increasing material needs, a number of youngsters have engaged in petty thefts, stealing food and household items from their neighbors.

As might be expected, the village youths see nothing wrong with their behavior, and when I interviewed them they all complained that their parents, and sometimes their elder siblings, were very domineering and intrusive. They feel particularly annoyed when older people try to lecture them, because there is nothing new in the lectures. They also think the older villagers simply do not know how to live a good life. In their opinion, thrift, hard work in the fields, and devotion to either Confucian ethics or the communist ideology will no longer help them enjoy a good life. As a 20-year-old man elaborated:

> My parents always tell me what I should do, how I should talk with people, and what kind of family I should have in the future. This is all rubbish. They do not realize how pitiful their lives are and how little they know about the world. My father has never gone more than 200 kilometers away from the village, and my mother only visited the county seat twice. They know probably no more than thirty people outside the village, all of whom are our relatives. True, I am young and not strong enough yet; but I have worked in five cities in the past three years, including Beijing, and I am acquainted with several hundred people. Yesterday my mother tried to teach me how to talk properly with a girl, because she is trying to find a wife for me in her parents' village. But she does not know that I had a girlfriend when I worked in Beijing and I know everything about women. Isn't this funny!

This young man makes an interesting point. Due to the quickly improved living conditions, the flow of information, new values, and the opportunities to work in cities, village youths in the 1990s have embraced a whole new world which was never available to their elder siblings and parents. They are obviously more knowledgeable than the aged, more open-minded than their elder siblings, and in some respects, more competitive socially than their elder siblings and parents.

Women

Editor's Introduction: While many women, particularly highly educated urbanites, have benefited in many ways from the reforms over the past twenty years, numerous reports from China indicate that the conditions of most Chinese women have deteriorated during the era of reform.

An extreme example of this deterioration is the widely-reported increase in the kidnapping and selling of women. As a peasant leader from Henan province indicated: [64]

SELLING WOMEN AND little girls is more and more common. Even in the old society [before 1949] the law didn't allow that. Why is it recurring?

Right here in this village, four young girls from Sichuan Province have been sold in the past few years. Individual families have bought them as wives. There is no formal wedding ceremony. The girls just live with a young man and are considered married. Mostly they come from very poor families.

Some unscrupulous people make their living by selling girls. They convince the girls to come with them, or they kidnap the girls, and then they sell them for 1,000-2,000 yuan. That sort of thing should stop, but there is nothing we can do about it now.

However, a less dramatic but more widespread indication of women losing ground is in the area of employment. A trade union official summarized the situation of women in the following manner: [65]

ONE MIGHT SAY that the hallmark of women's liberation used to be getting more women out of the house and into society to participate in construction in all industries and trades where they might display their talents, make suggestions, contribute their efforts, and advance along with their male comrades. Today, however, amid industrial "restructuring," enterprise

MALE/FEMALE INCOME GAP

A [2001] survey on the social status of Chinese women shows the income gap between males and females has widened by 7.4 percent in cities and 19.4 percent in the countryside, compared with 1990.

Women are often employed in low income jobs, though their level of income has risen during the past decade, Wednesday's *China Women's News* reported.

Statistics show the average annual income of working women in Chinese cities stood at 7,409.7 yuan (892.65 U.S. dollars) in 1999, only 70.1 percent of what was paid to males. Over the same period the annual income of women farmers was 2,368.7 yuan (285.3 U.S. dollars), some 59.6 percent of male farmers' income.

The report said women doing the same job as men tend to be paid less. An example it cited was that the average incomes of female executives and senior professionals are only 57.9 percent and 68.3 percent respectively of those of their male colleagues.

The survey, carried out by the All-China Women's Federation and the National Bureau of Statistics, covered 48,192 people from 30 provinces, autonomous regions and municipalities.

Source: *People's Daily Online*, January 24, 2002.

optimization," and "personnel cutbacks to increase efficiency," women employees are appearing in ever larger numbers among the ranks of laid-off employees—in higher proportion to their presence among enterprise employees. It used to be that women's employment was a manifestation of the state policy of equality between men and women, that it ensured women political and economic status.

Today, however, the number of women among the ranks of those being employed anew does not inspire optimism, and women's political status and economic influence have, to varying degrees, been affected by their loss of work positions. At one time, women could enjoy, along with their male comrades, lifelong wage benefits and medical care guarantees simply by going to work as a government employee and by putting forth their best efforts, faithfully discharging their duties, and refraining from breaking laws or violating discipline. Today, with the reconfiguration of state-owned enterprises, as well as a host of reasons that no individual can reverse, women are not receiving the earnings and benefits due them, and their anxieties are constantly increasing. In sum, one might say that women benefited most from the former planned economy. And they are being hit hardest during the transition to a market economy. In the former case, they benefited from the advantages of the state system and from legal and policy guarantees. The latter case resulted from the pitiless nature of the competition that constitutes an essential characteristic of a market economy.

According to Ministry of Labor statistics women constituted 39 percent of the workforce but almost 61 percent of laid-off workers. In addition, 75 percent of laid-off women remain unemployed after one year compared to less than 50 percent of their male counterparts.

Large numbers of women in the countryside are victimized both by rural cultural traditions, which demean women, and by the new economic realities, which make it increasingly unlikely that they will emerge from poverty. In many instances, family life is disrupted as men leave the villages to work in the cities. As a result, the wives who are left behind have increased family burdens. Ms. Xie Lihua, founder of Rural Women Knowing All magazine, and senior editor at China Women's News, has stated that, "In many rural areas they still think women are useless. . . . They do field work, give birth, take care of the husband, the children, the in-laws. So to them if there is a family problem they think the sky has collapsed."* Many rural women see no hope in their predicament and simply give up. The result is that China has the world's highest rate of female suicides.

---

* Elisabeth Rosenthal, "Women's Suicides Reveal Rural China's Bitter Roots," *The New York Times*, January 24, 1999, pp. 1, 12.

New Morality and
Its Psychological Effects

Editor's Introduction: The rapid changes in China have resulted in
the creation of a new morality or world view among the Chinese
people. Several commentators have noted that the economic
reforms of Deng Xiaoping have led to the growth of individualism, competitiveness and greed, which in turn has fostered both
moral decay and psychological disorientation. The social result
has been an increase in alienation, anti-social behavior and psychological stress.

One notable report links the growing disparity in income
between rich and poor to both illegal activity and social immorality. It states that, [66]

THE LARGE DISPARITIES in social income in China and the enormous
number of poverty-stricken people naturally gives rise to major unsettling
factors in society. Today, the continued widening of social income differences
has reached a state in which a huge gap now exists between the rich and the
poor. The traditional Chinese perception that "inequality rather than want
is the cause of trouble" and the social realities of the rapid—and even
extreme—widening of the gap between rich and poor have caused a considerable number of people to lose their psychological equilibrium. Added to
this are the sharp price rises in recent years and the diminished—in some
cases seriously diminished—living standards among members of society.
Against this backdrop, some people risk the perils of engaging in illegal and
criminal activities. The wide gap between rich and poor is a major cause for
increased cases of theft, fraud, and robbery in recent years, and especially for
the constantly increasing numbers of lawbreakers and criminals among the
peasantry, which constitutes a serious threat to social security.

PSYCHOLOGICAL PROBLEMS ON CAMPUSES

Statistics from the National Center for Mental Health of the China Center for Disease Control and Prevention show that, according to conservative estimations, 16 to 25 percent of college students on the Chinese mainland currently have mental problems such as anxiety, phobia, neurasthenia, paranoia and hypochondria.

A leading factor that leads to cases of psychological problems with college students is pressure from fierce academic competition and, accordingly, high expectations from prospective employers, according to Zhang Minqiang, Director of the Advanced Education Institute in Guangzhou-based South China Normal University.

The majority of college students who suffer from mental disorder are from poor villages.

Source: Feng Jianhua, "Psychological Plague on Campuses," *Beijing Review*, June 24, 2004, pp. 28-29.

Regarding the corruption of social morals the report notes that:

MANY PEOPLE IN the high-income stratum of society become wealthy by illegal means, or by means that are legal but incorrect. These include, for the most part, solicitation of kickbacks, abuse of power for personal gain, tax evasion, manufacturing and sale of counterfeit and inferior products, misappropriation of public funds to speculate in real estate, and even outright embezzlement, smuggling, and drug selling. Due to current imperfections in the legal system and insufficient development of market competition, many of the people who obtain high incomes through unlawful and incorrect means are not sanctioned or denounced, but instead are regarded as "success stories." This encourages social tendencies toward "earning money by fair means or foul" and "making a merit of deception," and corrupts social morals.

Severe social problems, therefore, are seen as related to the new morality associated with the ongoing reforms.

However it is not only anti-social behavior that has been linked to the reforms, but indifference to the plight of others. As writer Liu Zi'an has noted: [67]

STANDING ON ONE'S OWN FEET

It took the Chinese just about a decade to experience profound and indeed revolutionary changes in their ways of thinking and acting, or in a word, living. Values, beliefs, tastes, perspectives, attitudes, rhetoric and metaphors, political, moral, social and personal, have all been dramatically transformed, and continue their transformation.

Today the focus of attention for almost the entire population is neither class struggle nor 'serving the people', but money and wealth. Yet behind such evident materialist and individualist zest, a psychologically deeper and politically far more significant revelation to a hitherto dependent citizenry is that everyone now stands, or must be prepared to stand, on his or her own feet.

Source: Lin Chun, "China Today: Money Dissolves the Commune," *New Left Review*, Vol. 201 (September-October 1993), p.35.

THE RAPIDITY AND severity of the decline in Chinese social morality and ethics is intolerable. The moral crisis in China is more widespread and more serious than the similar crisis in the former socialist nations of Eastern Europe. . . .

The pendulum has swung from the extremism of the Maoist age to the extremism of the current period, from moral absolutism to nihilism, from radical collectivism to radical individualism, from the suppression of all desire to its indulgence. . . .

Some foreign observers of China pay attention only to the unprecedented growth in the economy, ignoring the fact that the current degree of social disorder, alienation, and moral degeneration is also without precedent. At no previous time in her history has China ever seen phenomena such as today's general lack of any feeling of social responsibility paired with the absence of any sense that this is a worrisome thing. Never before have so few citizens suffered pangs of conscience upon harming their fellows or the greater society. Never before have so many gazed upon the suffering of others with such utter indifference.

While many have no trouble functioning in such a changed social environment, others are under severe psychological stress.

The number of Chinese seeking psychological help has grown dramatically during the reform era, and many studies link the growth of psychological problems to the social changes brought about by the reforms. An article in the *Beijing Review* reported the following: [68]

AS URBANIZATION AND industrialization accelerate in China, conflicts and pressure brought about by changing moral standards, values, behavior and interpersonal relationships intensify. Reported psychological problems are on the rise. Sources from the Institute of Sociology of the Chinese Academy of Social Sciences say that 140,000-160,000 people commit suicide in China every year, or 400 a day. Mental problems and resulting suicides have become a serious social problem.

Some experts are challenging the threat of this social problem. In July 1991, psychiatrist and professor Zhai Shutao established the Nanjing Crisis Intervention Center in Jiangsu Province, the first such center specializing in psychological aid in China.

Zhai explained that crisis intervention is a kind of therapy conducted through persuasion and helping those facing a psychological predicament, especially the profoundly depressed, often with suicide tendencies, to abandon their attempt at suicide and gain new hope.

The psychiatrists listen attentively to their problems, encourage them to re-build their confidence, persuade them of their great potential and help them to see their innate ability to extricate themselves from their particular psychological predicament. . . .

As the planned economy of more than 40 years in China is being replaced by a market economy, many people accustomed to the former system are increasingly both mentally and physically exhausted. Among those who have visited or called the crisis intervention center, some are factory directors depressed because they have difficulties in making a profit in their enterprises; some are businessmen too busy making money outside to spend time with their families, and family disputes have thus arisen; some are those who feel despondent, finding it hard to adapt to a competitive society, and some are even teenagers who find no family warmth because their parents are too busy earning a living.

The particular situation of teenagers was noted in an article in the *Shanghai Star*. [69]

TEENAGERS IN THE city nowadays are enjoying a better material life, but feeling mental pressures earlier than their parents did.

This phenomenon has drawn the attention of local psychologists and educators, who are striving to tackle it.

A recent sample survey among 1,200 teenagers in the city showed that 28.5 per cent feel pressure from their studies; some 28 per cent said they had trouble in building good relations with their teachers and classmates; 13 per cent were involved in love affairs; and 9.3 per cent said they could not get along with their parents.

As China accelerates the process of modernization, it requires more and more talented people. To meet this need the courses in primary and middle schools have become much more difficult, and schools and parents have set stricter demands on school children.

All these things have imposed heavy psychological burdens on teenagers, according to some local psychologists.

A student in grade three of a junior middle school said: "At present, I seem to live only for studying, eating and sleeping, and this is meaningless."

Sharing his feelings, many other students summed up school life as, "living in a cage."

Some parents estrange their children by refusing to confide in them. In addition, divorce and gambling cause young people to feel repugnance for their parents.

To help young people solve their psychological problems, Shanghai has set up a number of hotlines and special letter boxes as well as psychological consultancy stations especially for teenagers.

Crime and Corruption

Editor's Introduction: Perhaps the most serious and widely discussed problems linked to the reform movement are crime and corruption. These social ills, which had been widespread before 1949 and had apparently been suppressed as a result of the Communist revolution, reemerged during the 1980s and have been a dominant element in Chinese society ever since. Propaganda campaigns, expulsions from the Communist Party, arrests and numerous executions seem to have had practically no effect in stemming the problems.

The seriousness of the crime problem was noted as early as 1989 in an official central government research report. [70]

MANY FACTORS ACCOUNT for the large increase in criminal cases involving property, but all are closely linked to the present social and economic situation in China. In recent years, there has been a vigorous development of the socialist commodity economy. The commodity economy is a powerful lever improving social development, but it is also a major inducement to crime. With the development of a commodity economy, money has functioned as a "battering ram" knocking down traditional values and concepts. As a result, there have been great changes in people's ideology.

The historical tradition of looking down on trade has disappeared. In its place has emerged a new craze for trade and running businesses. What many people now want is simply to make money. At the same time, there has been one wave after another of consumerism which has engulfed the entire country. The huge gap between the high consumption lust and existing economic buying power of the people has resulted in a serious contradiction emerging. Stimulated by the above factors, some people who cannot fulfill their personal desires for material enjoyment through legal and proper means have taken another route, namely, getting money through criminal activity.

There is another aspect to all this: during this period, China has been undergoing a transition from an old to a new system. While the old order of things has gradually begun to lose its predominant role, the new socialist commodity economy has not yet been perfected and the legal system is still imperfect. Therefore, there are many problems and gaps in the management of society.

As a result, certain types of crime, such as gambling and prostitution, have begun to re-emerge. Additionally, and for a variety of reasons, the security organizations in urban and rural areas are proving to be both weak and lax and enterprises are paying far too little attention to security work. The result is that the ability to control and guard against criminals has been weakened. The gradual increase in social and economic prosperity has stimulated criminal activity and also offered the criminal many opportunities. The reasons for the overall increase in criminal cases, then, can be put down to the combined influence of all these factors. We seriously expect that, with the development of the commodity economy, the continued rising trend of property crime will not abate.

> Reports of criminal activity appear frequently in the Chinese press and on Chinese television.
>
> Although much of the criminal activity is centered in the large relatively prosperous urban areas, the countryside is also suffering from high crime rates. The following accounts are by two peasant leaders from Henan Province in central China. [71]

Wang Fucheng:

WITH THE DECLINE of the authority of the Party and government, crime has been a continually increasing problem. I have heard that in Wei County, just north of here in Hebei Province, the military came in and took over the county government because there were so many bandit gangs.

Wang Dejun:

That problem is not confined to Wei County. In Neihuang County there are bandit gangs too—in Tianshi, Songcun, and Chuwang townships there are bandit gangs. Those townships all border Hebei Province. In the border area along Hebei, Shandong, and Henan provinces, there are a lot of bandits because they can move between provinces easily and escape local police forces. These gangs are very dangerous. They have weapons. They stop travelers in trucks, buses, and taxis and rob them. Buses particularly are stopped, and everyone on them is robbed. Those who resist are often killed. It is called "cutting the road" (*duan dao* or *jie 1u*). Your taxi driver from Anyang yesterday said that Neihuang County is a very dangerous place. He said he wouldn't stop to pick up anyone on the way home because it is too risky. He said he would roll up the windows and lock the doors and drive back to Anyang as fast as possible.

On the whole, this area has less crime than surrounding areas because officials in Liucun Township are tough. They punish severely and do not allow a trend to develop. Some property, such as TV sets, is stolen. I keep equipment like loudspeakers and things from the family temple here in our house, or they would be stolen. But, the thieves are individuals, not gang members. Usually the thieves are from outside the village, but they have people in the village helping them.

We did have one incident with a gang recently. One night last winter a gang from Dongzhuang Township came to Houhua and stole thirty or forty goats from thirty or forty households. They came in a truck, grabbed the goats, and ran. We found out that the bandits were from Dongzhuang and called the county police. The bandits were arrested, but people here were very angry when the police asked them to pay to get the goats back. Some paid, but some didn't and just gave up their goats rather than go to additional trouble and expense. We do not know what happened to the bandits. It is not legal for the police to charge for their services, and it is not common here, but corruption is increasing everywhere.

The farmers in Chairman Mao's time had a greater sense of safety and security than they have now. Even though we did not have enough to eat in Mao's time, we still thought Mao was great. Now we have enough to eat, but everyone curses Deng Xiaoping because there is no security and too much corruption. We have little hope for the future of the village because of corruption.

> It is obvious from these accounts that there is a link between the problems of crime and corruption.
>
> Corruption is apparently endemic at all levels of Chinese society and bribery seems to be an established fact of life for millions of Chinese. The following section contains an excerpt from *China's Descent into a Quagmire*, a book by economist He Qinglian, describing the consequences of China's economic boom. [72]

THE GREATEST THREAT to Chinese society . . . consists of a combination of criminal syndicates acting in cahoots with the local power structure.

MUTATION OF SOCIAL CONTROL

According to reports from various sources in recent years, local criminal forces that grew and prospered, to the point of becoming the effective rulers at the local level, include clans, newly formed groups of the *nouveau riche*, and criminal and semicriminal syndicates. Rural villages and small towns located at great distance from the central government are particularly prone to the growth of these forces. As for the characteristics of local power holders, these can be understood through careful analysis of case studies of areas where the activities of these underground, criminal-type groups are especially blatant.

Take the case of Zhongxin township, Lianping county, in the northern mountainous region of Guangdong province. Here is an especially lawless area that people passing through or near have come to call the "ghost gate" *(guimen guan)*. Beginning in the 1990s, serious cases of robbery in Zhongxin prefecture grew like spring rice seedlings, and yet when investigators entered the area, not one person was apprehended and put on trial. A reporter who entered the area quickly discovered that virtually all of the local public security personnel were deeply involved in gambling and other semicriminal activity. In addition, several dozen cadres working outside Lianping county but originally from that area, sent a letter to various authorities at the county and provincial level, describing the blatant involvement of local officials in prostitution and gambling. They also reported that besides the chaotic situation involving public security, the head of Zhongxin prefecture, a certain Zhu, had been captured by a hundred or so hooligans and paraded around atop a truck. Three months after the case, not one of these people was apprehended, while subsequent investigations revealed that a host of individuals from the local public security were operating in cahoots with the gangs. Evidence was destroyed, and prior to any investigation by outside authorities, the local officials warned their criminal sidekicks of the impending actions, which, of course, allowed the suspects plenty of time to flee.

Certain local cadres in some of the villages took advantage of the new power structure in their locales to gain virtual life-and-death power over the peasantry. One of the most notorious of these cases in recent years occurred in Zhuzhuang village, Yongnian county, Hebei province, where a peasant by the name of Zhang Yanqiao was beaten to death by cadres appointed by the township party secretary, Sun Baocun. The second case was the "incident at

Zhengzhou" in Henan province, where a peasant by the name of Chen Zhongshen from Xulou village, Taoying county, complained about the ill behavior of the village commission and reported it to higher authorities. He, too, ended up being done in: the local party leader personally strangled him.

In short, these and other similar incidents indicate the serious mutation and distortion of the formal institutions of social control in many areas of rural Chinese society. In any country, social control exists, but whether it is done for good or evil depends on the nature of its content as shaped by changing circumstances. **What is clear in China's case is that since the 1980s, in many villages and townships, social control has become a mere matter of exploitative power monopolized by a few people operating in cahoots with the social underground. Under such circumstances, the impact of social control is detrimental both to the process of reform and the government.**

"SYMBIOSIS OF UNDERGROUND AND LEGITIMATE SOCIETY"

Factors Obstructing Legalization in China

Several important consequences are apparent from the above descriptions. First, representatives of the social underground are often in positions of local government authority. Compared to the past, village cadres today are no different from the former "big bosses" that prevailed as local despots over pre-1949 village society. In effect, the distant past has been recreated and these villages seem to have gone back in time. The above-mentioned criminal incidents were not particularly complicated, nor were the facts behind the cases mysterious, yet none could be solved by local authorities. Only when someone from the local area had the courage to take the personal risk and appeal to higher authorities—in some cases, all the way to the central government—were these cases resolved. Cases in point are the above Zhuzhuang and Zhengzhou incidents, which were not solved until central organs became directly involved in the investigation.

Then there is the following phenomenon that society should be especially vigilant about and that is **the growing alliance between the social underground—"black society"—and the "white" or legitimate organs of state authority.** Where this has occurred, the local population has been turned into virtual slaves, while the local security situation is very dire. Take Limin township, Yucheng county, Henan province, where from the end of the 1970s to the 1980s, local township enterprises initially prospered, with local industries turning over to the state almost one million yuan in taxes

THE VIRUS OF CORRUPTION

Corruption is the virus that has eroded the healthy body of the party and the state. If we lower our guard and let it run wild, our party will be ruined, the people's power will be lost, and the great cause of socialist modernization will be forced off track. Our party, our cadres, and our people will never allow such consequences.

—Jiang Zemin, Communist Party general secretary,
August 1993

"Down with corruption" is a slogan that has been chanted by demonstrators and daubed on banners in almost every protest movement in modern Chinese history. Dissidents from KMT days to the present have tried to use popular anger against official corruption to goad the general public into revolutionary action. Communist historians identify corruption as one of the main reasons for the collapse of the Qing dynasty and of KMT rule on the mainland. As Jiang Zemin warned in 1991, "If we examine each dynasty in China's history, we see there existed corruption and struggles against it that were linked to the rise and fall and the life and death of a dynasty. . . . Historical experience tells us that if the anticorruption campaign fails, China's society cannot achieve integrity."

Source: James A.R. Miles, *The Legacy of Tiananmen*, Ann Arbor: University of Michigan Press, 1996, p. 147.

annually. By the 1980s, in fact, the town was held up as one of the models for the rest of the country. Yet by the early 1990s, the situation in the town had rapidly deteriorated, with the local economy suffering to such an extent that most factories, schools, and local organizations were shut down. In 1993, the total tax turned over by local enterprises had shrunk to 30,000 yuan, while the local government was in deficit to the tune of 630,000 yuan, resulting in a failure to pay teachers for ten months. The direct reason for all this was that the deputy head of the township, He Changli, acted in cahoots with a large social underground that he himself headed. As early as 1987, He had recruited eleven individuals into his personal gang, and by 1994, it had grown to sixty-nine members, including party officials and heads of public security and other important state economic organizations, such as the local electrical power bureau. Together, they ran seven of the ten local enterprises, brazenly engaging in such acts as rape and robbery to the point that the entire town was in the grip of terror. With higher level leaders either ignoring these blatant acts or becoming accomplices themselves, the place lacked any semblance of civilized security. And so, when He's nephew was arrested for a series of especially notorious acts, he was immediately released. Even when He and his gang were themselves finally apprehended, the local population was still far from relieved; they remained vigilant, waiting to see if any action would actually be taken against such a well-connected crowd. Nor was this case an isolated incident, for according to sources from Yucheng and other townships, when it came to selecting local leaders, similar acts were reported with their populations also living in terror.

That this is a very widespread phenomenon in rural China is evident from the numerous cases in many regions across the country. Take, for instance, Sijihong township, Hunan province, where local discontent boiled over in reaction to widespread cadre corruption. With the people refusing to hand over their grain quotas or pay taxes to the government from 1990 to 1995, the township descended into a state of virtual anarchy.

Of greatest concern is the fact that these local underworld forces are totally unwilling to adhere to or be restrained by laws or any standard of "morality" *(daode)*. **In contemporary China, traditional customs (that is, traditional moral constraints) have ceased to play a role in restraining people's behavior. . . .**

The deepening of the reform in China is no longer just a question of putting laws down on paper and producing reams of documents. The fact is that the laws decreed so far are no more than rhetorical statements that lack any real restraining influence over government officials and enterprise managers. The reason for this is clear. Throughout the social transition, the Chinese people's views and understanding of their existence and adaptability have fundamentally changed. At the same time that their selfish desires are being largely satisfied, the humanistic spirit of the people has deteriorated badly. Just consider the current philosophy of being an official that goes something like this: "To be an official is to be a likable person, know how to ingratiate oneself with people, dare to repress people, and be good at cheating them."

Environmental Issues

Editor's Introduction: As a result of population growth and the rapid economic advances of the reform era, environmental degradation became a significant public issue. Studies have indicated that hundreds of thousands of people die each year due to air and water pollution. The Chinese government, which in previous decades refused to acknowledge environmental problems, admitted that China was one of the world's most polluted countries.

China contains seven of the ten most polluted cities in the world. In addition, the use of chemical fertilizers in combination with other factors have "seriously polluted water systems, contributed to high degrees of soil erosion and salination, harmed wildlife, and compromised the health of Chinese citizens. Estimates reveal that around 40 percent of the country's arable land is degraded. About one-fifth of arable land is contaminated by heavy metals. . . . Water running off from fields, along with municipal and industrial wastewater dumped into the rivers, has rendered around 60 percent of the water in China's seven major river systems unsuitable for human contact according to China's State Environmental Protection Administration."*

Pan Yue, the Deputy Director of the Administration, noted that, "Over the past 20 years in China, there has been a single-minded focus on economic growth with the belief that economic growth can solve all problems. But this has left environmental protection badly behind."** Serious air pollution, for example, has plagued hundreds of Chinese cities. The following report appeared in *China Today* magazine: [73]

---

* Dale Wen, *China Copes with Globalization: A mixed review,* San Francisco: The International Forum on Globalization, 2006, p. 10.
** Jim Yardley, "Rivers Run Black, and Chinese Die of Cancer," *The New York Times,* September 12, 2004, p. 17.

COAL IS CHINA'S main fuel, and the sulfur dioxide it produces is the major cause of acid rain. In some Chinese cities, such as Changsha, Chongqing and Liuzhou, 90 percent of all precipitation is acid rain. Shanxi Province is the largest coal producer in China, and its backward coking methods fill the air with sulfur dioxide and particulates. Taiyuan, the province's capital, lives amidst a shroud of dirty air, and the situation in the city of Linfen in southern Shanxi is even worse—at noon the visibility is only about 100 meters.

Beijing, the national capital, is also suffering from serious air pollution. The Beijing municipal government started to publish a weekly Air Quality Report as of January 1, 1998. The city's air is usually grade three to four, sometimes even five, which is defined as heavy pollution. Many people experience discomfort under such conditions. The main causes of air pollution in Beijing are waste gases from industrial plants and exhaust from cars. An iron and steel plant in the western suburbs is emitting sulfur dioxide, carbon monoxide and particulates every day, but sufficient funds are not available to move this plant away from the city. Beijing residents worry that their city will become the most polluted capital in the world.

The following cartoons indicate the extent of the problem of pollution: [74]

Environmental issues are an increasingly popular topic in Chinese cartoons, indicating a growing public awareness of China's environmental problems. In this underwater world, fish are carrying umbrellas not to keep off rain but to keep off garbage and debris being thrown into the water. "One umbrella each for safety!" is the sales slogan used by the vendor with the megaphone.

This cartoon offers a pointed comment on the role of politics and bureaucracy in degrading the environment. The first frame, the boss of the Leap Forward Lumber Yard, with a load of logs in the truck he is driving, is cheerfully telling a propaganda cadre how well his yard is doing. In the second, the cadre is about to fill in a form, featuring a picture of the boss and the citation "Excellent Yard Boss Dun Renwu (Honest Dutydoer) who has exceeded his quota for timber, year after year." In the third frame, an important political official sitting at a desk and wearing a Mao cap is awarding promotions to both men: the yard boss is now Forestry Bureau Chief and the cadre takes over as boss of the lumber yard. In the final frame, the moment of truth arrives: the new lumberyard chief goes to inspect his domain and discovers that all the trees have been cut down, leaving only a bird perched on a signpost, weeping for its lost home.

One of the most controversial elements of China's environmental policy concerns the Three Gorges Dam project on the Yangtze River. Designed to be the world's largest hydroelectric station, the dam is 370 feet high and contains a reservoir that is 412 miles long. It began to produce some power in 2003 but it will not be fully operational until 2009. Although planned to prevent flooding and to produce vast amounts of electric power, the project was controversial because of its enormous cost (more than $25 billion), the uprooting of more than one million people, the inundation of more than 1,300 villages and irreplaceable archaeological sites, the projected increase in soil erosion and sedimentation, and the vulnerability of the completed project to military attack. Since the project was formally approved in 1992 it has been severely criticized by many scientists and planners in China and overseas. In the following excerpted article, published in China, both sides of the issue are presented. [75]

OPINIONS DIFFER BOTH at home and abroad over whether to construct the Three Gorges project. The main points of view in support of and in opposition to the project will now be summarized.

I. Construction

Pro: The location and environment of the dam site are very favorable. The project will help solve, in an efficient manner, the problems of flood control, electricity generation, and navigation. Therefore, this grand project should be carried out as soon as possible so that the dream of "A Smooth Lake Over the High Gorges" can be realized in our generation. Some have even vowed that they will not rest until they see the completion of the project.

Con: The immediate start-up of the project is not advisable, considering the scale of certain problems, mainly: excessive investment requirements, a long construction period, extensive population relocation, sedimentation that will hinder navigation, increased chances of flooding in the upper reaches and destruction of the natural environment. The priority at present should be given to work on the tributaries in order to meet the energy requirements for the second phase of the national economic plan, which is to double the gross national product by the end of this century. In other words, plans that can bring immediate results should be carried out first, such as flood-control projects in the plains, establishment of hydro-electric power stations on the tributaries, and dredging of the main waterways. Some in the Expert's Group on Flood Control are totally opposed to the Three Gorges project, arguing that a disaster of unprecedented scale would result if the dam became a military target.

II. Flood Control

Pro: The Three Gorges project will play a key role in flood control at the lower and middle reaches of the Yangtze, and no alternatives exist that could have the same or nearly the same result. The dam will have a capacity for storage and flood diversion of 9.5 to 22 billion m³ [cubic meters] for the areas around the middle reaches. If a flood as serious as the one in 1870 occurred, the Jingjiang River dikes might burst, and hundreds of thousands, even millions, of lives might be lost.

Con: All along the Yangtze River, there are sources of floods from both the upper reaches and the lower and middle reaches. The Three Gorges project can only control flooding from the Chuanjiang River in the upper reaches, but is helpless against floods coming from the Xiangjiang, Zishui, Yuanshui, Lishui, Hanjiang, and Ganjiang rivers and many other tributaries in the lower and middle reaches.

If a flood as serious as that which occurred in 1954 is to be avoided, 50 billion m³ of water will need to be diverted at the middle and lower reaches. Yet the dam will only work for the area above Chenglingji, which means there will still be 30 to 40 billion m³ of water left to be controlled. Wuhan is a key city to protect from floods. Yet the Three Gorges dam will neither lower Wuhan's water level, nor divert water from the nearby areas, leaving it helpless in the face of flooding from Jiangxi and Anhui provinces in the lower reaches. Therefore, the flood-control ability of the project is very limited.

IV. Navigation

Pro: When the backwater of the reservoir reaches Chongqing, a series of rapids will be covered, thus making it possible to control the slope of the descent and speed of the water. This will make it possible to sail 10,000-tonne ships rather than the current 3,000-tonne vessels. As a result, the carrying capacity and transportation efficiency will be increased and shipping costs reduced.

In this way, the demand for 50 million tonnes of freight per year in the upper reaches can be met. At the same time, the water level during the low-water season will be increased by reservoir regulation, thus improving navigability from Yichang downstream.

Con: The Three Gorges reservoir will be located below Wanxian County, making it a perpetual backwater area where navigation will certainly be improved. But, in the area near the end of the reservoir, things could be very difficult. When the backwater level is lowered, the natural river channels will be exposed with their huge sediment deposits that could block navigation, When the clean water from the reservoir washes down the river bed, the water level at Yichang may be lowered, in which case the water level in the locks of the Gezhouba dam will also be lowered, thereby hindering navigation. Improving navigation in the Chuanjiang River area can be better achieved by dredging the waterways in stages, which would increase the annual transport capacity from the present five million tonnes to 18 million tonnes by the year 2000 and 30 million tonnes by 2015. All this needs much less investment than installing shiplocks at the Three Gorges. Only when the waterways of both the tributaries and the mainstream are dredged can an overall network of water transportation be established.

V. The Control of Sedimentation

Pro: There is less sediment in the Yangtze than in the Yellow River. In spite of serious soil erosion due first to deforestation and then to wasteland reclamation on the slopes in the upper reaches, there has been little change in the deposition of sediment in the river. During the high-water season, the water level at the dam will be lowered to the level required for flood control. When this season is passed, muddy water will be replaced with clean water.

This method can clear away most of the sediment. After 100 years, the sediment will be washed away and a balance restored in such a way that the capacity of the reservoir can be kept at between 86 and 92 percent.

Of course, according to models of the backwater area at the end of the reservoir, sedimentation may indeed become serious in the main trough at Chongqing. Sand may pile up, blocking the mouth of the Jialing River, and the flood level in Chongqing will greatly increase. But the sedimentation problem can be solved by improving the regulation system in the reservoir, modifying port facilities, and dredging the river.

Con: The Yangtze River ranks fourth behind the Yellow, Brahmaputra, and Ganges rivers in terms of sedimentation. In recent years, especially in 1981 and 1984, the annual water volume was about average, but sediment deposition was 70 percent and 30 percent higher respectively, and the amount of sediment deposited by the river continues to increase. This problem will become more serious unless water and soil conservation measures are strengthened and soil erosion controlled. Since flood control is the major purpose of the dam, its reservoir water level must be raised when necessary and at the same time, the sand flow must be held back. Sedimentation at the end of the reservoir will inevitably increase and ultimately endanger navigation.

So far, there is no satisfactory solution to the sedimentation problem. Moreover, the relatively clean water from the reservoir will cause erosion of the embankments at the area below Yichang, which might endanger the Jingjiang River dikes. After the wash-down sediment is deposited in the river section between Chenglingji and Wuhan, it will harm flood control in the areas around Dongting Lake and Wuhan.

VI. Population Relocation

According to the plan, the normal pool level in the reservoir would be 175 meters, below which, according to the 1985 census, there is a population of 725,500. When national population growth and the resettlement of entire cities, towns, and factories, are taken into account, the number of people involved could reach 1.13 million by 2008. The rising water level caused by sedimentation might bring the figure to 1.3 million.

Pro: If a spirit of self-reliance and hard work is encouraged, plus compensation of Y11.1 billion, the population relocation can be completed in 20 years. After the reservoir starts generating power, revenue retained at the rate of Y0.003 per kWh produced should be used to pay for population relocation and for construction around the reservoir area. The counties and towns in the area concerned have shown their willingness to be relocated. And they are anxious for an early decision, so they can start developing a new economy in a relocated area and achieve prosperity in the near future.

Con: Massive population relocation like this is rare both at home and abroad. Outside China, the biggest resettlement of this kind involved only 100,000 people, and some projects have had to be abandoned because the population involved was too large.

China's largest resettlement project took place during construction of the reservoirs at the Sanmenxia Gorge, the Xin'anjiang River and the mouth of the Danjiang River. Each case involves more than 300,000 people.

The land around the future Three Gorges reservoir is already overworked and its food production is insufficient. To bring more than one million additional people into the area exceeds the environmental capacity of the land. At present, those who have been promised compensation for migration will be happy, and there are even others outside the reservoir area who are eager to be included, just to get "extra" compensation. But things might become quite different when relocation actually takes place. If the compensation falls short of expectations, social and even political problems could arise.

VII. Environmental Protection

Pro: According to the 175-meter normal pool level, the storage capacity of the reservoir is 3.93 billion m^3, with a flood control storage capacity of 22.15 billion m^3. Compared with the volume of water flowing in the Yangtze River (453 billion m^3 annually at Yichang), the storage capacity of the reservoir is relatively small. Shaped like the gorges, the reservoir will not seriously endanger the local climate, water quality, and temperature. The power produced by the reservoir is a clean energy resource, and will reduce the pollution now caused by the burning of coal. The Three Gorges will become a more attractive scenic spot after the reservoir is completed. Historical relics in danger of being submerged can always be moved to other places. In order to maintain the environmental balance and reduce the damage caused by the submergence of land resulting from the reservoir construction, a more satisfactory plan can be worked out to better facilitate the relocation and reestablishment of cities.

Con: The project will seriously endanger the environment and natural resources of the gorges; for example, the land submerged by the dam and reservoir construction cannot be recovered. Following the 175-meter proposal, the project will submerge up to 357,000 mu of arable land and 74,000 mu of orange groves, which make up the richest land in the area. In the 19 counties involved, hilly areas constitute 96 percent of the land while plains account for only 4 percent. After these relatively flat arable areas are submerged, resettlement will have to be in the hills, where the vegetation will inevitably be destroyed and the soil stripped. Furthermore, a large number of relics below the 180-meter mark will be damaged and the natural beauty of the area ruined.

Along the banks of the reservoir area are 214 hidden landslides, which will become active after being soaked by the reservoir. Being more than 100 meters deep, the reservoir could also cause earthquakes. If landslides and earthquakes induce one another, the entire project will be threatened. If the dam is subject to attack, the biggest flood in the history of the Yangtze River would likely occur. Such a disaster could be catastrophic for the lower reaches.

CARS AND POLLUTION

A recent survey in 20 cities by the Association of Chinese Customers found a third of urban families plan to buy a car within five years. Another study found most people consider knowing how to drive a car to be one of three "basic and necessary skills in modern Chinese society" along with the ability to speak English and use a computer. Such attitudes alarm environmentalists. They warn that if the percentage of the population owning cars in China reaches Western levels, there would be more automobiles [in China] than in the rest of the world combined. Air pollution in many Chinese cities is already several times above World Health Organization standards. It, and cigarette smoking, makes lung disease the leading cause of death in China.

Source: Philip Pan, "Bicycle No Longer King of the Road in China," *Washington Post*, March 12, 2001, p. A1.

> *Editor's note.* By the end of 2005, there were 23.65 million privately owned vehicles in China. In 2006, sales of passenger cars reached 5.18 million while production of the cars reached 5.23 million.

Human Rights

Editor's Introduction: The Chinese government has long been accused by domestic and foreign critics of abusing or violating the human rights of its citizens. These critics charge that Chinese citizens are denied freedoms and rights that are guaranteed to citizens of the United States and other Western democracies. The Chinese government replies by claiming that it has provided its people with the greatest human right, subsistence, and that the U.S. government has a limited and incomplete concept of human rights. The following readings present the Chinese government's views on human rights. The first reading presents the Chinese view in the context of modern Chinese history. The second reading gives a comparison of human rights in China with those in the United States. [76]

I.

HUMAN RIGHTS

*(Excerpt from the Report of China's State Council
of Human Rights in China, 1991)*

I. The Right to Subsistence—
The Foremost Human Right the Chinese People Long Fight for

IT IS A simple truth that, for any country or nation, the right to subsistence is the most important of all human rights, without which the other rights are out of the question. The Universal Declaration of Human Rights affirms that everyone has the right to life, liberty, and personal security. In old China, aggression by imperialism and oppression by feudalism and bureaucrat-capitalism deprived the people of all guarantee for their lives, and an innumerable number of them perished in war and famine. To solve their human rights problems, the first thing for the Chinese people to do is, for historical reasons, to secure the right to subsistence.

Without national independence, there would be no guarantee for the people's lives. When imperialist aggression became the major threat to their lives, the Chinese people had to win national independence before they could gain the right to subsistence. After the Opium War of 1840, China, hitherto a big feudal kingdom, was gradually turned into a semicolonial, semifeudal country. During the 110 years from 1840 to 1949, the British, French, Japanese, U.S., and Russian imperialist powers waged hundreds of wars on varying scales against China, causing immeasurable losses to the lives and property of the Chinese people.

■ The imperialists massacred Chinese people in untold numbers during their aggressive wars. In 1900, the troops of the eight allied powers— Germany, Japan, Britain, Russia, France, the United States, Italy, and Austria—killed, burned and looted, razing Tanggu, a town of 50,000 residents, to utter ruins, reducing Tianjin's population from 1 million to 100,000, killing countless people when they entered Beijing, where more than 1,700 were slaughtered at Zhuangwangfu alone. During Japan's full-scale invasion of China, which began in 1937, more than 21 million people were killed or wounded and 10 million people mutilated to death. In the six weeks beginning from 13 December 1937, the Japanese invaders killed 300,000 people in Nanjing.

■ The imperialists sold, maltreated, and caused the death of numerous Chinese laborers, plunging countless people in old China into an abyss of misery. According to incomplete statistics, more than 12 million indentured Chinese laborers were sold to various parts of the world from the mid-nineteenth century through the 1920s. Coaxed and abducted, these laborers were thrown into lock-ups, known as "pigsties," where they were branded with the names of their would-be destinations. Between 1852 and 1858 40,000 people were put in such "pigsties" in Shantou alone, and more than 8,000 of them were done to death there. Equally horrifying was the death toll of ill-treated laborers in factories and mines run by imperialists across China. During the Japanese occupation, no less than 2 million laborers perished from maltreatment and exhaustion in Northeast China. Once the laborers died, their remains were thrown into mountain gullies or pits dug into bare hillsides. So far more than 80 such massive pits have been found, with over 700,000 skeletons in them.

■ Under the imperialists' colonial rule, the Chinese people had their fill of humiliation and there was no personal dignity to speak of. The foreign aggressors enjoyed "extraterritoriality" in those days. . . .

■ Forcing more than 1,100 unequal treaties on China, the imperialists plundered Chinese wealth on a large scale. Statistics show that, by way of these unequal treaties, the foreign aggressors made away with more than 100 billion taels of silver as war indemnities and other payments in the past century. Through the Sino-British Treaty of Nanjing, the Sino-Japanese Treaty of Shimonoseki, the International Protocol of 1901 and five other such treaties alone, 1.953 billion taels of silver in indemnity were extorted, sixteen times the 1901 revenue of the Qing government. The Treaty of Shimonoseki alone earned Japan 230 million taels of silver in extortion money, about four and a half times its annual national revenue. The losses resulting from the destruction and looting by the invaders in wars against China were even more incalculable. During Japan's full-scale war of aggression against China (1937-45), 930 Chinese cities were occupied, causing $62 billion in direct losses and $500 billion in indirect losses. With their state sovereignty impaired and their social wealth plundered or destroyed, the Chinese people were deprived of the basic conditions for survival.

In face of the crumbling state sovereignty and the calamities wrought upon their lives, for over a century the Chinese people fought the foreign aggressors in an indomitable struggle for national salvation and independence. The Taiping Heavenly Kingdom Movement, the Boxers Movement, and the Revolution of 1911, which overthrew the Qing dynasty, broke out during this period. These revolutionary movements dealt heavy blows to imperialist influences in China, but they failed to deliver the nation from semi-colonialism.

A fundamental change took place only after the Chinese people, under the leadership of the Chinese Communist Party, overthrew the Kuomintang reactionary rule and founded the People's Republic of China. After its birth in 1921, the Chinese Communist Party set the clear-cut goal in its political program to "overthrow the oppression by international imperialism and achieve the complete independence of the Chinese nation" and to "overthrow the warlords and unite China into a real democratic republic;" it led the people in an arduous struggle culminating in victory in the national democratic revolution. . . .

The Chinese people have won the basic guarantee for their life and security.

National independence has protected the Chinese people from being trodden under the heels of foreign invaders. However, the problem of the people's right to subsistence can be truly solved only when their basic means of livelihood are guaranteed.

To eat their fill and dress warmly were the fundamental demand of the Chinese people who had long suffered cold and hunger. Far from meeting this demand, successive regimes in old China brought even more disasters to the people. In those days, landlords and rich peasants who accounted for 10 percent of the rural population held 70 percent of the land, while the poor peasants and farm laborers who accounted for 70 percent of the rural population owned only 10 percent of the land. The bureaucrat-comprador bourgeoisie who accounted for only a small fraction of the population monopolized 80 percent of the industrial capital and controlled the economic lifelines of the country. The Chinese people were repeatedly exploited by land rent, taxes, usury, and industrial and commercial capital. . . .

Ever since the founding of the People's Republic of China in 1949, the Chinese Communist Party and the Chinese government have always placed the task of helping the people get enough to wear and eat on the top of the agenda. For the first three years of the People's Republic, the Chinese people, led by their government, concentrated their efforts on healing the wounds of war and quickly restored the national economy to the record level in history. On this basis, China lost no time to complete the socialist transformation of agriculture, handicraft industry, and capitalist industry and commerce, thus uprooting the system of exploitation, instituting the system of socialism and, for the first time in history, turning the people into masters of the means of production and beneficiaries of social wealth.

*   *   *

II.
A COMPARISON OF HUMAN RIGHTS IN CHINA WITH THOSE IN THE UNITED STATES

Some US politicians have tried their utmost for many years to confuse world opinion regarding the issue of human rights in China. While presenting the United States as a "world human rights model," they wantonly censure China for its human rights situation. The 1995 Human Rights Report recently released by the US Department of State once again spread rumors about China while distorting and attacking China's human rights situation. But the report did not contain a single word about serious human rights problems in the United States. In order to correctly understand and fairly assess the state of human rights in China and the United States, it is useful to make a thorough comparison of the practice of human rights in the two countries.

China and the United States are about the same size in geographical area, but China's population is 4.6 times that of the United States. China's per-capita acreage of farmland is just one-10th of that of the United States, and China's per-capita share of other resources is much lower than that of the United States. Furthermore, China is a developing country with low income, whereas the United States is the world's most highly developed nation.

A comprehensive 1994 estimate made by the World Bank indicated that the per-capita wealth of China's citizens is less than 1.6 percent of that of their American counterparts. In terms of natural resources, economic development and other conditions indispensable to promoting human rights, China lags far behind the United States.

Given the differences in the social systems of the two countries, and the divergent attitudes taken and efforts made by the two governments toward protecting human rights, the human rights situation in China is clearly different from that in the United States.

CONSTITUTIONAL RIGHTS

First, the human rights specified in the US Constitution, that is, the constitutional rights of American citizens, are incomplete and do not include economic, social and cultural rights.

Human rights, as specified by the Constitution's Bill of Rights and other amendments, do not go beyond the scope of civil and political rights.

Various economic, social and cultural rights announced in the World Human Rights Declaration and the International Convention on Economic, Social and Cultural Rights are not recognized by the U.S. Constitution except for the rights to join trade unions or choose a job and a few other rights.

The US Constitution provides no right for Americans to have their basic needs satisfied or their right to avoid starvation or to be free from want.

Second, the US Constitution does not provide full right to equality. Neither the 1787 US Constitution nor the 1789 Bill of Rights contains provisions concerning the right to equality.

To date, the US Constitution has not contained principled provisions concerning equality among various ethnic groups, equality between men and women and equality of civil rights.

Third, protection of human rights as listed in the US Constitution is very limited.

The Constitution merely lists a number of individual rights, but it neither requires nor authorizes the US Congress or the federal government to take measures to promote and protect those rights. . . .

In contrast, China's Constitution contains comprehensive provisions on citizens' basic human rights and the protection of such rights.

Chapter Two of China's current Constitution contains not only general stipulations on civil and political rights, but also full provisions on economic, social, and cultural rights as well. It not only explicitly stipulates that all citizens are equal before the law, but also specifies that all ethnic groups are equal, that men and women are equal, and that all citizens enjoy equal rights in all aspects of social life.

The chapter not only lists various rights of Chinese citizens, but also specifies the responsibilities of the state, society, collectives and individuals in advancing and protecting such rights.

Compared with the United States, the Constitutional rights of Chinese citizens are much more extensive and specific, and the Chinese government assumes much greater duty in advancing and protecting human rights.

Health

Editor's Introduction: As a result of the reform policies, government spending on health care plummeted and China's universal health care system was eliminated. Profit-oriented clinics and hospitals replaced free ones and "barefoot doctors" disappeared. Although specialized medicines and modern medical technology became available and nationwide health indicators improved, doctors were legally allowed to charge their patients market rates for their services and medical expenses soared. The changes were felt both in urban and rural areas. The result was that many in China could no longer afford health care. In addition, deadly diseases which had been eradicated during the Maoist years, such as tuberculosis and schistosomiasis, returned to plague the country. Conditions deteriorated to such an extent that in 2005 the Development Research Center, a leading governmental advisory body, reported that the new market-oriented health system was a "failure."*

Medical care in rural China was described in the following article which originally appeared in *The Far Eastern Economic Review*. [77]

THE FASTEST ROAD to poverty in China today is a visit to the doctor—especially in the countryside. Ask Yang Zhengshan, a 65-year-old wheat farmer with a wispy beard and a lattice of broken veins across his weathered cheeks, who lives in the Ningxia Hui Autonomous Region in the remote northwest. Lying in bed last year, he suddenly found he couldn't sit up. "Half my body was paralyzed. I couldn't move at all," he says, fingering a straw hat he wears to protect himself from the sun.

---

* David Lague, "Health Care Falls Short, Chinese Tell Leaders," *International Herald Tribune*, August 20-21, 2002, p. 1,6; and "Gaps Within Trouble China's Health Sector," *People's Daily Online*, August 9, 2005. http://english1.people.com.cn/200508/09.

On a village doctor's advice, he was rushed from Huoxing village to a hospital in the region's capital Yinchuan, an hour away by truck. Over the next three weeks there, doctors took four X-rays and a magnetic resonance image, or MRI, and diagnosed him as having had a stroke. They prescribed a raft of medicines, and administered injections and massages.

Yang recovered. But his bills came to $1,350, a fortune in this part of China, where people in rural areas earn an average of just $220 a year. The hospital required a hefty cash deposit when Yang checked in, and payment of his outstanding charges every three to five days. And the money all came out of his pocket, because like 90% of the 900 million people in China who live in the countryside, Yang has no medical insurance.

What saved him from ruin was having a lot of sons, he says. All four scraped together the money for the hospital. "One paid 2,000 renminbi ($240). Another paid 3,000. My sons are good children," says Yang. But his sons' savings were completely wiped out and follow-up medications still cost him $30 a month.

It could have been a lot worse. For every tale of a family scraping by, Yang's neighbours cite a case of medical costs pushing families into poverty.

In the village next to Yang's, neighbours talk of Ma Yuqiang and his wife who last ran up medical bills of $850—$370 for his kidney stones and $480 for her hysterectomy. They had to borrow money from relatives and friends to pay the bills. In a place where families are expected to spend hundreds of dollars on weddings for their sons despite their modest means, the Ma family had no money to bring a wife for their son into their family. Instead, in exchange for the woman's family helping to pay their debts, their son married into her family and took his earnings with him. Without his income, neighbors agree, the Mas have little chance of enjoying a comfortable old age.

With health insurance coverage shrinking while medical costs rise far faster than incomes, China faces a humanitarian disaster that threatens to undo one of the country's proudest achievements of the last 20 years: the lifting of an estimated 210 million people out of absolute poverty. Harvard University health economist William Hsiao says his research with Chinese colleagues in several hundred Chinese counties shows that for every 10 Chinese pulled out of poverty, 12 fall into poverty because of the burden of medical expenses. Health officials and outside experts now routinely identify high medical costs combined with an absence of insurance as rural China's No. 1 "poverty generator."

The danger is most acute for China's farmers, because they have lower incomes than their city brethren and almost no insurance coverage. Ministry of Health figures show that by 1999, only one in 10 people in rural areas had

any health insurance—25% down from the number four years before. Even
in the cities, only 42% of residents had any insurance in 1999, a 22% drop
from four years earlier. Yet in the 1990s, according to Ministry of Health statistics, the cost of an average hospital admission leapt 511% while the average cost of a visit to the doctor soared 625%—rates two to three times that
of income growth.

It wasn't always this way. From the 1950s to the 1970s, under Mao
Zedong, China's rural health infrastructure won accolades from the rest of
the world. Mao set up village health stations, township health centres and
county hospitals. At the village level, agricultural collectives paid the salaries
of so-called "barefoot doctors" and put money into collective welfare funds
for drugs and treatment. Patients paid modest premiums and a nominal fee
for consultations and medicines. Local governments also contributed.

The system wasn't perfect. Rao Keqin, who directs the Ministry of
Health's Centre for Health Statistics and Information, notes that a lack of
transparency in commune accounts meant health funds were often mis-
used, and relatives of local leaders often got better treatment than ordinary
farmers. Because barefoot doctors had limited training, they only provided basic medical care. But they did administer vaccinations, prescribe simple drugs and give injections of antibiotics when needed. "It was low-cost
medicine," says Rao." "Everyone could afford it. It met people's needs,
because people's needs then were modest." Infant-mortality rates dropped
and life expectancy soared.

After 1979, however, Deng Xiapong dismantled the agricultural collectives in the name of reform. Because he did not make any new provisions for
funding rural health care, the health infrastructure collapsed. A paper Rao
co-authored last year with a Harvard School of Public Health professor, Liu
Yuanli, shows that within six years of Deng taking power, rural residents covered by the Rural Cooperative Medical Systems of the Mao era fell from
90% to just 9.6%.

Barefoot doctors were left to support themselves with what they could
earn from prescriptions and services such as injections and intravenous drips.
In turn, farmers had to shoulder the cost of every doctor visit and hospital
admission. . . .

Meanwhile medical costs keep climbing. Part of the reason, Rao says, is
the different medical care patients now seek. Because of longer life expectancy, "instead of dealing with epidemics, doctors now are increasingly treating
diabetes and tumours," Rao says. But as important a part of the equation is
the profit motive in medical institutions from the village to the biggest cities.
Harvard's Hsiao says that in many places "village doctors have basically

THE DECLINE OF HEALTH SERVICES

According to the Ministry of Labor and Social Security, only 15 percent of Chinese people enjoy medical security services, and the other 85 percent either fall outside medical insurance schemes or have no reliable medical security services. China ranks 188th in the global ranking of fairness in the distribution of public health resources and 144th in the world in terms of its general level of public health. . . .

Masses are suffering from and anxious about the lagging behind of medical and public health undertakings. Since the early 1990s, medical expenses have kept rising, increasing by almost 10-fold over the past 10 years. Many people complain that they cannot afford to see doctors. In the past, a farmer could afford an operation in a hospital only by selling a pig, but now they cannot afford the same operation by selling 10 or even 20 pigs. Beginning from the late 1990s, those who used to enjoy free medical service have to pay a fee for medical treatment. Moreover, they could not get reimbursement for many medicines. That is why ordinary people complain under such circumstances.

Source: Ba Denian, "A Sound Health System Needed," *Beijing Review*, February 5, 2004, p. 20. (Dr. Ba is the former president of the Chinese Academy of Medical Sciences.)

become drug peddlers, selling the most expensive drugs and the most profitable ones" because they have to finance themselves. They also make money from intravenous drips, Hsiao says, "which they don't know how to give."

At higher levels, doctors not only prescribe unnecessary drugs, but also routinely order unnecessary tests. Yang's care is a case in point. In the West, his weakness on one side of his body would have been enough on its own to diagnose a stroke. If a doctor chose a test, it would usually be a CT scan, rather than an even more expensive MRI. Yang also would probably have been hospitalized for just two days, and then moved to a nursing home for rehabilitation and therapy. And instead of $30 a month in follow-up drugs, he would be taking cheap aspirin.

In Ningxia, Dou Wenmin, deputy director of the region's Health Bureau, says that in the absence of funding for rural health insurance, he and his colleagues do what they can to keep profit-seeking doctors in the countryside in check. In six Ningxia counties that are part of a United Nations Children's Fund project, the Health Bureau has banned village doctors from giving intravenous therapy. They've also required doctors to cut back the drugs on their shelves to 80, and to forego expensive antibiotics in favour of cheaper ones. Doctors get $7 a month each to make up for the income lost by the changes, enough to satisfy them in the four poorest counties, officials say, but not for doctors in the two better off counties.

The Health Bureau is also trying to crack down on doctors who knowingly prescribe drugs—often fakes—produced by unlicensed manufacturers, which they buy cheaply and sell to patients at full price. Ding Zhanming, a former barefoot doctor with a clinic in Huoxing, says inspectors drop by unannounced several times a month to match official receipts to his stocks of 150 kinds of drugs. To prevent doctors reusing single-use needles, used needles should be turned in and checked off against the number bought.

The following account of health care problems in urban areas appeared in the *Beijing Review*. [78]

BEIJING RESIDENTS SEEM to have easy access to medical service, as there are hospitals of various sizes in all corners of the city. But many patients are unwilling to go to the hospital. Instead, they simply get medicine from their work units' clinics or buy medicine from nearby drug stores. Many only go to the hospital when their illnesses are too serious to be dealt with by themselves. Their reluctance to go to the hospital usually stems from previous unpleasant experiences in seeking medical attention.

UNBEARABLE COSTS

Miss Shen went to see a doctor about her lung infection. The doctor diagnosed that she had contracted pulmonary heart disease and suggested she be hospitalized. She paid a 10,000-yuan deposit while going through admission formalities. One week later, she received a bill indicating that she had already used up 6,000 yuan. That sum is equivalent to six months' salary for an average wage-earner. When she was discharged a fortnight later, the hospital's bill came to more than 13,000 yuan. Shen said she insisted on leaving the hospital even though she had not fully recovered because she could not afford the high cost.

According to one of her family members, Shen was only given antibiotic drops and some ordinary medicines such as nitroglycerin. A lot of money had been wasted. For instance, one day Shen was constipated. The doctor gave her two packages of medicine that could be used for two weeks. In fact, two pills were enough, the family member said. Shen occasionally had arterial blood tests several times a day, and each test cost nearly 100 yuan. Shen's family members asked the doctor if the tests could wait until a few days after Shen had taken a new medicine and if unnecessary tests could be avoided as Shen had to pay the cost on her own. The doctor ignored their suggestion.

A senior patient in Shen's ward shared Shen's view about high medical costs. Once she was hospitalized for an operation to remove her gall bladder. Because of her heart problem, she did not have the operation and was discharged from the hospital a week later. Her hospitalization fees, however, cost more than 6,000 yuan.

Many outpatients had the same experience. Going to see a doctor for a cold could result in receiving a prescription costing several hundred yuan.

The relevant authorities have surveyed the costs of seeking medical treatment for a common cold. Some 32.6 percent of the patients answered that it was between 100 and 150 yuan, 26.1 percent between 150 and 200 yuan, and 13.5 percent between 200 and 300 yuan.

Medical costs have remained a focal point of public concern, and patients have consistently complained about the high price of medicine. A questionnaire issued jointly by the China Consumers' Association and the Beijing Consumers' Association indicates that 80 percent of the patients in Beijing are dissatisfied with medical costs, with 92.3 percent complaining about the high price and 71.5 percent about the lack of transparency in hospital charges.

> Another aspect of health is the problem of overwork and stress, called chronic fatigue syndrome, victimizing many white-collar workers. Under heavy pressure to succeed in their careers and to make money, many upwardly mobile Chinese work overtime, forego vacations, and are often fatigued, and fail to get regular health treatments. As a result, many are dying prematurely. An investigation in the Spring of 2005 indicates that 82 percent of the 1,218 informants would work over 15 hours a day for good pay. The report also indicated that, "75.1 percent of Chinese young and middle-aged people are aware that people die of chronic fatigue syndrome, yet only 18 percent would make any change in their lifestyle to avoid it. 'What's the use of good health if we do not have money?' Zhang Liang [a 30-year old project manager at a communications company] argues, and many of his peers agree with him."*

---

* Lu Rucai, "Wealth and Health," *China Today,* Vol. 54, No. 7, July 2005, p. 38.

Population

Editor's Introduction: China has the world's largest population, estimated at 1.3 billion people in the year 2005. Almost one of every five people in the world is Chinese. That staggering fact affects almost every decision made in China. Plans for agriculture, industry, education, health, housing and employment are all influenced by population size and population estimates for the future.

China had a huge and fast-growing population of approximately 540 million at the time of the 1949 revolution, but the new Communist government did not see rising population as a problem. In fact, population growth was encouraged. This policy coincided with the traditional Chinese view that large families were desirable. Because many children died before reaching maturity, many were wanted. Sons were needed to work on the land, to provide old-age security for their parents, to carry on ancestral rites, and to perpetuate the family name. Daughters were not considered as important as sons because they married into other families when they were of age, but even so, they could bring power and prestige to the family and clan through marriage. For economic, social and religious reasons, then, Chinese parents felt it was their responsibility to have large families.

The seriousness of the population problem was not acknowledged by the government until the early 1970s, when population exceeded 800 million. Family planning clinics, offering a variety of contraceptives, including abortions, were opened throughout the countryside and the government used every publicity technique at its disposal to encourage couples to marry at a later age, thereby reducing the number of their childbearing years. However, by the early 1980s, when these policies had failed to stop the population rise, the government instituted a rigid family-planning system limiting most couples to one child. (Exceptions included those who belonged to ethnic minorities.) Couples had to get permission from the local government and workplace in order to have a child, and if they had an illegal second child they faced severe financial penalties. Under this system many women were forced to undergo abortions or sterilization.

These extreme measures were defended by Peng Peiyun, minister of the State Family Planning Commission at the time, in a 1991 interview. [79]

"PEOPLE HAVE RIGHTS, the right to reproduction, but they are constrained by law," she said. "Couples all have a duty to practice family planning. This is stipulated in our constitution."

That duty includes obeying the state on when to have children and how many to bear—one per family in the cities and up to two in the countryside—and voluntarily aborting babies conceived outside the quota system.

It is a system whose critics, notably the U.S. anti-abortion lobby, say has produced documented cases of forced abortions into the ninth month of pregnancy, infanticide, and economic coercion.

For the minister, there is no alternative for a country feeding 21 percent of the world's population with 7 percent of its arable land and overexploited water, forest, and mineral resources.

"If you have too many children, they won't have enough to eat, they won't have a good education," she said. "If a person doesn't have the most basic right, the right to life, how can you talk about human rights then?"

Mrs. Peng, a jovial, bespectacled sixty-two-year-old, oversees the sex lives of a fifth of humanity and calls on people to marry late and have "fewer but better babies.". . .

China enforces its well-known one-child policy in the cities, but in the countryside, home to four out of five Chinese, peasants are allowed a second child if the first is a girl, and the rules are even looser in minority areas.

"We couldn't make the policy any more strict. It is a question of implementing it," Mrs. Peng said. "Currently, we are not really implementing it with success."

The minister reacts with emotion to those who accuse China of forcing people to practice family planning: "They do not understand. How could we possibly have carried out family planning only by coercion and commandism?"

But when asked to specify how much force a family planning official may use to convince a woman to abort, Mrs. Peng said it was " very hard to draw the boundary line."

"Simply said, you can't tie her up and make her do it," she said, but officials should create a "general mood" favoring abortion in their communities and bring pressure to bear to "mobilize" the woman.

"If it doesn't work the first time, the woman must be mobilized a few more times. It may take dozens of tries at persuasion for some," the minister said.

"I talk reason with you. I clearly reason with you. If you aren't convinced, then we'll have a few more ideological work sessions."

"If she was not willing to do it originally, she will do it in the end after giving it some thought. This is all right, and it is no good to insist on calling this coercion or commandism," Mrs. Peng said.

Western diplomats describe China's stated national population policy—which is voluntary and stresses education—as "progressive and enlightened."

But they warn that local enforcement may be overly zealous, with local-level family planning workers pressed to meet quotas.

The population control hierarchy matches China's political structure, with central planners issuing birth quotas to each province, provinces issuing quotas to counties, and down the line to individual work units.

Western reports regularly quote Chinese medical workers saying they are forced to perform abortions against women's will and to kill unwanted newborns by suffocation or injection.

Although the extent of the practices is difficult to gauge, discipline of couples who violate the population policy include financially debilitating fines, the withholding of social services, demotion, and other punishment.

> The efforts of the government since the 1980s to slow down its population growth rate have succeeded to a great extent. Today China's population is growing at the rate of 1.07 percent a year, one of the lowest growth rates in the developing world and down from 1.3 percent in 1976. (The 2000 U.S. growth rate was 0.9 percent.) According to a 1999 article in the *Beijing Review.* [80]

A RECENT AUTHORITATIVE survey showed that during 1971-98, China avoided 338 million births due to family planning. Supported by the National Social Science Fund, the questionnaire survey was conducted in December 1998 in urban and rural areas of 18 counties and six cities in seven provinces. Analysis showed the following results:

■   Influenced by the combined factors of family planning and socio-economic development, Chinese women's average number of births dropped from 5.44 in 1971 to 1.84 in 1998. The Chinese proportion of the world's total population shrank from one-fourth to one-fifth. Without family planning, today's Chinese population would have exceeded 1.5 billion, and the UN World Day of Six Billion People would have occurred four years ago. . . .

■   During 1979-98, as a result of family planning, the per-capita GDP was up from 417.7 yuan to 6,490.1 yuan, and residents' consumption level rose from 227 yuan to 3,094 yuan. Without the implementation of family planning, the per-capita GDP and residents' consumption level of the period would have risen from 363 yuan to 4,099.5 yuan and from 197.3 yuan to 1,954.4 yuan respectively.

> Since the late 1990s the government has somewhat liberalized its rigid policies and eliminated many of its draconian and coercive policies. In many areas women no longer have to get permission to have their first child and others are legally allowed to have a second child for a fee. Nevertheless the birth rates have declined as a consequence of increasing urbanization, increasing choice for women and increasing expenses involved in childrearing.
>
> However, a serious unintended result of the population control policy is the growing imbalance between female and male births. This phenomenon was described in an article that appeared in a Beijing magazine in 1996. [81]

AS EARLY AS 1992, according to detailed analyses conducted in several provinces and regions, males account for 51.45% of the population of 1.2 billion, with females accounting for just 48.55%, so that there are 36.21 million more males than females. Random Surveys further reveal that in the 25-49 age group, there are 15 times more single men than women, accounting for 7.78% of all males in the age group. In other words, 7.26% of young men in China cannot find wives. Combined with single men over the age of 50, authoritative departments relate that the bachelor population had already reached 1.3 million by 1992.

Further statistics reveal that in 1991, 23 million babies were born in China, among which there were 13.3 million boys and 9.7 million girls, or a full 3.6 million more boys than girls. Given such backward concepts as "the most unfilial behavior is failure to carry on the family," and "more sons mean more happiness," many people—especially in the countryside—are anxious to have a son, so that the first thought some people have when they see they have had a girl is to think of how to abandon her, or even drown her in a chamber pot.

With technological advancement, many hospitals are now equipped with scientific devices such as ultrasound used to examine pregnant women and the position of the fetus. However, these instruments, which can also be employed to detect the sex of the infant, have become the leading factor contributing to the infanticide of baby girls. Not only do they aid parents in murdering their baby girls, but they are used by hospitals to make a profit off the practice.

"Half of man is woman," indeed. Life without love cannot become life. A family without a woman is not a family. With the increase in the number of mateless men, some people have built an industry around kidnapping and selling women, while some women have turned to cheating men out of money. In recent years in a certain southern County, nearly 10,000 men were cheated into phony marriages for money, at an average of Rmb 1,000 each or a total of 10 million. In one particular village, 25 older men were victimized by phony marriages, some as many as three times.

> The disparity in births has continued to grow. The normal ratio of boys to girls is approximately 104:100 to 106:100. However, a recent article in the *Beijing Review* reported that the gender imbalance has risen dramatically since the 1980s. [82]

ACCORDING TO PENG Peiyun, President of the China Population Association (CPA), the gender imbalance has risen since the 1980s, and is now a problem that requires immediate attention. The ratio of birth by gender was 107.4:100 in 1980. After 10 years of continuous increase, the result of the fourth national census showed that the ratio rushed to 111.3:100. In 2000, statistics from the fifth national census showed the proportion had grown to be 119.9:100.

In 2000, the gender ratio for the first, second, third and fourth babies in families, respectively, were 107.1:100, 151.9:100, 160.3:100 and 161.4:100. The imbalance was not restricted to a few regions, but was present in almost all parts of the country. The census in 2000 announced that the ratio in 24 provinces, autonomous regions and municipalities exceeded 110:100. And in eight of these provinces, the ratio was beyond 120:100. The ratio in Hainan and Guangdong provinces even reached 135.6:100 and 130.3:100, respectively. Population in the above-mentioned 24 provinces, autonomous regions and municipalities covered 90 percent of the national total. In 1990, there were 12.73 million more boys than girls in the age range of 0-14, while 10 years later, the figure went up to be 18.07 million.

Religion

Editor's Introduction: During the era of Deng Xiaoping, restrictions on religion were eased, temples were reopened or rebuilt, and millions of Chinese openly practiced some form of traditional worship. Many observances and traditions that were widespread before the 1949 Revolution were revived. As a peasant leader from Henan Province said in 1990, "the Communist Party does not believe in gods, so it doesn't approve of the [newly constructed] Auspicious Grandfather Temple, but it doesn't interfere because it is too weak to do anything about it. When Chairman Mao was in control that was not the case." The Party Chairman of the same village elaborated: [83]

WE NOW HAVE big funeral ceremonies again. We don't consider them superstition, either. When people in the village die, all are buried. None is cremated as the Party advocates. There is a public graveyard in the salt area that was established in the 1970s. Everyone is supposed to be buried there, but people prefer to bury their dead in their own farm fields. As Party secretary, I do not try to change that because it is popular in the whole district. In fact, I too will bury our family dead in the fields.

The corpse is ordinarily buried on the fifth day after death. On the third day guests from other places come to the village. Each brings a piece of white cloth showing that they are a relative. Then the younger generation has a procession in the streets: They carry sticks with white paper coiled around them and walk to the Earth Temple, where they and the close relatives kowtow to the Earth God. There are two Earth Temples, one in the east of the village and one in the west. This whole process is known as "pressing paper" (*ya zhi*)—I don't know why. At noon, the man in charge of the funeral announces that the burial will be on the fifth day and all relatives should come.

On the fourth day the sacrifices begin. The married daughters and granddaughters come first and offer food, placing it on a table before the coffin.

They offer 100 steamed buns, 100 jin of meat, 20 bottles of liquor, 10 car-
tons of cigarettes, and 200 to 500 yuan. The in-law families also come and
bring food. The amount depends on how well-to-do they are. Ten of those
families make large sacrifices. When they leave, they take half of the sacrifice
with them and then bring it back the next day. During this process on the
fourth day, thirteen or fourteen people play various musical instruments in
front of the gate of the deceased, and two sit in front of the coffin, playing.
The younger generation kowtow continuously, one hundred times or more,
in front of the coffin. Then they go into the street, blowing instruments and
singing operas. This lasts until one or two o'clock in the morning.

On the fifth day, the younger generation go out to meet the guests.
When all arrive, they eat a banquet made from the food that was sacrificed.
The eldest son then breaks a bowl on the ground that had been used for
burning paper money for the dead. I don't know why he breaks the bowl,
but it has been a custom for as long as anyone can remember. There follows
a parade to the burial ground, with twenty-four people carrying the coffin
through the streets. The coffin bearers have cloths in their mouths soaked
with alcohol to mask the smell of the corpse. Relatives and others carry rings
of flowers and paper statues. At the burial ground, a hole has been dug. The
direction of the hole has been determined by a Yin-Yang master. The coffin
is placed in the hole, and a large pile of paper money is burned. The wife of
the oldest son throws a handful of soil on each of the four corners of the coffin. That begins the burial. It is completed with spades used by the twenty-
four people who carried the coffin.

Twenty-eight days after the death, the relatives come again to offer sacrifices. One year and then three years later they do the same thing. They
burn paper money and bring steamed buns, eggs, meat and liquor. After the
last ceremony they sometimes invite opera troupes to perform. That com-
pletes the ceremonies.

> The situation is similar in Jiangxi Province. The following selec-
> tion describes the return to the village of traditional religious
> practices, particularly those related to ancestor worship: [84]

THE VILLAGERS DO not seem to practise Buddhism for spiritual suste-
nance, but for practical benefits, such as good fortune, luck, or to cure a sick
person. Indeed, for the villagers, the word *pusa* which is translated as "bod-
hisattva" or "Buddha," means a statue of any kind. A statue of Mao is a *pusa*,
as would be a statue of Jesus Christ. The villagers might pray to any statue
for practical purposes. Some *pusa* are simply popular figures from Chinese

history, such as Guan Yunchang (a general) and Zhu Geliang, a prime minister from the period of the Three Kingdoms (AD 220-65). This practice of syncretism is perhaps one reason why the Chinese government's suppression of religious practices is not so hurtful to rural people of Han ethnic communities. The fact that the dozen or so bodhisattvas in *tao hua an* were burned did not bother Gao villagers because they had their own *pusa* to turn to, which was *Wang Taigong*, literally the "great grandfather Wang." Even during the height of the Cultural Revolution, nothing was done to harm *Wang Taigong*, a statue which was passed on from one household to another for prayers. . . .

Another prevalent religious practice in the area is ancestor worship, a practice which again has never been uprooted and which has returned with stronger force since the 1980s. Ancestor worship is practised in two main ways. One is to burn money, joss sticks on *Qingming* Festival at ancestors' graves and again on the New Year's Day of the Lunar Calendar. Those families which can afford it will also set fireworks in front of their ancestors' graves as a way of worshipping, The longer the fireworks last and the louder the sound, the more sincere and genuine the feeling shown is supposed to be. Another practice of ancestor worship is to offer food to the dead. During the Spring Festival, every household gets together to have three banquets, one on each day from the 28th to the 30th of the Twelfth Month of the Lunar Calendar. Immediately before each banquet, all the food is placed in front of the altar for the ancestors to consume first. While joss sticks are burned, all the family members will do obeisance by bowing three times with hands clasped. On New Year's Day, usually in the morning, all male members of Gao Village gather together to perform the ceremony of clan worship, which mainly consists of doing obeisance in the above manner. During the Great Leap Forward and the Cultural Revolution clan worship was stopped, but family worship of ancestors continued, and the villagers were only obliged to do it more discreetly during the most radical periods.

The general theme of change and continuity in village life is exemplified by the location and maintenance of graves. For the villagers, the bigger the grave and the better the maintenance the more sincere and genuine their filial piety. The usual practice is to place the dead in a coffin which is placed in a hole dug in the ground. Then earth is piled on to it so that a dome is formed. The bigger and higher the dome the better the family feels about it. Digging up the grave of someone's ancestor is one of the worst moral crimes that can be committed. However, in the past forty years or so many graves have been leveled and removed and grave domes have become smaller and smaller. This has happened gradually, mainly for practical reasons based on the necessity of survival. As the population grew in Gao Village, every inch of land had to be made use of on the village's definitive territory. Some graves were leveled for growing crops while others were removed for irrigation construction. All this was done gradually, without external interference.

Without the political climate, there might have been resistance by the villagers, but the destruction of graves was not for the sake of politics. Like many things which have happened in rural China, this change can be interpreted as the destruction of religion by the Communist regime. However, it can equally be interpreted as a result of interacting forces, some of which are not political but rather developmental and economic.

The practice of burying the dead in a coffin made of timber continues to this day. Cremation has never been practised in this area. There has never been a crematorium and the villagers would be horrified even to contemplate the idea. They consider the preservation of the whole body as representing the continuation of life. Therefore, it is the duty of the offspring to preserve the dead body of the old in the family as long as possible. This practice is the result of centuries of indoctrination in Confucianist ideas of filial piety. For the same reason, a child has no authority of any kind in the hierarchy. Hence the practice is that the dead body of a child is never considered worth preserving, and the coffin for a child is usually made only of some wooden boards.

For the elderly, however, the better and thicker the timber and the heavier the coffin, the more filial the offspring and hence the more honoured and respected the family is in the eyes of the villagers. The best coffin is considered to be one made of Chinese fir trunks. The trunks must remain whole and be as wide as possible. Small pieces of timber paneled together are not considered to make a proper coffin. The villagers make comparisons and talk and gossip about how much has been spent on a coffin in such and such a family.

There is therefore enormous pressure on the family to find the best coffins it can afford for the elderly. Sometimes, a coffin made of huge Chinese fir trunks enclosing the corpse and some lime used to preserve the body requires twenty-four strong men to be carried to the grave. The cost of coffins is one of the three most burdensome expenditures in a family, the other two being marriage costs for a son and the building of a house. Indeed, for most couples their lifetime ambition is to fulfill the three obligations of building a house for the offspring, getting children married and having their parents properly buried. Enormous sacrifices will be made to achieve these three ambitions.

As wood is becoming more scarce and timber more precious, the cost of a coffin is rising. Even during the 1960s a good coffin would cost more than 300 *yuan*, an enormous amount by village standards, and this did not even include the cost of transportation. Because there was no such wood in the area, the villagers would push a wheelbarrow to transport the coffin from more than 60 kilometres away. The transportation of each coffin would require two strong men, each pushing a wheelbarrow on which there were two pieces of the coffin. The journey would usually take three to four days. As more and more forests have disappeared nearby, places where coffins can be purchased are further and further away. Since the 1980s, a good quality coffin can cost several thousand *yuan* and one has to travel as far as 200 kilometres to buy it. Nowadays, those families who can afford it hire a truck. But there are still those who cannot afford it, and therefore have to transport coffins by wheelbarrow! The burden of tradition is heavy and certainly not as pleasant as the romanticized scholarly view of China sometimes suggests.

PART VI

CHINA AND THE WORLD

Introduction

For many years after the establishment of the People's Republic, China's relations with the rest of the world were severely restricted. Practically its only friends were the Soviet Union and other Communist countries. The United States vowed both to contain and isolate China, viewing it as a pawn in the Soviet Union's alleged desire to dominate and transform the world. China's confrontation with United Nations forces in the Korean War, in the early 1950s, served to confirm suspicions of Chinese aggressiveness.

From the Chinese perspective, the Korean War, and the French military effort to regain control in Indo-China (Vietnam, Laos and Cambodia) on China's southern border confirmed its suspicion that Western imperialists were still trying to dominate Asia, as they had before World War II.

In the late 1950s and early 1960s when its relations with the Soviet Union deteriorated, China became even more isolated. Unwilling to accept satellite status under Soviet domination, like the Eastern European countries, China turned to a policy of self-reliance. Its commercial and political relations with other countries practically halted, especially during the Cultural Revolution when China recalled all but one of its ambassadors. Not until the early 1970s did China begin to reestablish foreign contacts.

China's isolation, then, was imposed both from the outside and from inside. To understand the situation in depth, one must look at history. Traditionally, the Chinese wanted very little to do with foreigners. They considered them barbarians from whom they had little to gain materially or culturally. Foreign diplomats were accepted by the Chinese emperor only if they acknowledged their inferiority and begged to be educated.

In the nineteenth century, Europeans and Americans wanted both diplomatic equality and trade, and were willing to fight to get them. Having defeated the Chinese in the Opium War in 1840, Westerners began to despise the Chinese for their weakness.

"Never the Twain Shall Meet"

Editor's Introduction: In the readings which follow, the arrogance of the traditional Chinese attitude toward foreigners, illustrated in the letter from the Qianlong (Ch'ien Lung) Emperor to King George of England in 1793, is matched by the arrogance of Westerners once they had become dominant in China, illustrated in excerpts from speeches by U.S. Senator Albert Beveridge, President Theodore Roosevelt, and Kaiser Wilhelm II of Germany whose troops were about to lead a punitive expedition against the Chinese in 1900. These selections were all written in the late nineteenth and early twentieth centuries. [85]

EDICT FROM THE CH'IEN-LUNG EMPEROR TO KING GEORGE III OF ENGLAND

[September 1793, on the Occasion of Lord Macartney's Mission to China]

YOU, O KING, live beyond the confines of many seas, nevertheless, impelled by your humble desire to partake of the benefits of our civilization, you have dispatched a mission respectfully bearing your memorial. Your Envoy has crossed the seas and paid his respects at my Court on the anniversary of my birthday. To show your devotion, you have also sent offerings of your country's produce.

I have perused your memorial: the earnest terms in which it is couched reveal a respectful humility on your part, which is highly praiseworthy. In consideration of the fact that your Ambassador and his deputy have come a long way with your memorial and tribute, I have shown them high favour and have allowed them to be introduced into my presence. To manifest my indulgence, I have entertained them at a banquet and made them numerous gifts. I have also caused presents to be forwarded to the Naval Commander and six hundred of his officers and men, although they did not come to Peking, so that they too may share in my all-embracing kindness.

As to your entreaty to send one of your nationals to be accredited to my Celestial Court and to be in control of your country's trade with China, this request is contrary to all usage of my dynasty and cannot possibly be entertained. It is true that Europeans, in the service of the dynasty, have been permitted to live at Peking, but they are compelled to adopt Chinese dress, they are strictly confined to their own precincts and are never permitted to return home. You are presumably familiar with our dynastic regulations. Your proposed Envoy to my Court could not be placed in a position similar to that of European officials in Peking who are forbidden to leave China, nor could he, on the other hand, be allowed liberty of movement and the privilege of corresponding with his own country; so that you would gain nothing by his residence in our midst.

Moreover, Our Celestial dynasty possesses vast territories, and tribute missions from the dependencies are provided for by the Department for Tributary States, which ministers to their wants and exercises strict control over their movements. It would be quite impossible to leave them to their own devices. Supposing that your Envoy should come to our Court, his language and national dress differ from that of our people, and there would be no place in which he might reside. It may be suggested that he might imitate the Europeans permanently resident in Peking and adopt the dress and customs of China, but, it has never been our dynasty's wish to force people to do things unseemly and inconvenient. Besides, supposing I sent an Ambassador to reside in your country, how could you possibly make for him the requisite arrangements? Europe consists of many other nations besides your own: if each and all demanded to be represented at our Court, how could we possibly consent? The thing is utterly impracticable. How can our dynasty alter its whole procedure and regulations, established for more than a century, in order to meet your individual views? If it be said that your object is to exercise control over your country's trade, your nationals have had full liberty to trade at Canton for many a year, and have received the greatest consideration at our hands. Missions have been sent by Portugal and Italy, proffering similar requests. The Throne appreciated their sincerity and loaded them with favours, besides authorising measures to facilitate their trade with China. You are no doubt aware that, when my Canton merchant, Wu Chao-p'ing, was in debt to the foreign ships, I made the Viceroy advance the monies due, out of the provincial treasury, and ordered him to punish the culprit severely. Why then should foreign nations advance this utterly unreasonable request to be represented at my Court? Peking is nearly 10,000 *li* from Canton, and at such a distance what possible control could any British representative exercise?

If you assert that your reverence for Our Celestial dynasty fills you with a desire to acquire our civilisation, our ceremonies and code of laws differ so completely from your own that, even if your Envoy were able to acquire the rudiments of our civilisation, you could not possibly transplant our manners and customs to your alien soil. Therefore, however adept the Envoy might become, nothing would be gained thereby.

Swaying the wide world, I have but one aim in view, namely, to maintain a perfect governance and to fulfill the duties of the State; strange and costly objects do not interest me. If I have commanded that the tribute offerings sent by you, O King, are to be accepted, this was solely in consideration for the spirit which prompted you to dispatch them from afar. Our dynasty's majestic virtue has penetrated unto every country under Heaven, and Kings of all nations have offered their costly tribute by land and sea. As your Ambassador can see for himself, we possess all things. I set no value on objects strange or ingenious, and have no use for your country's manufactures. This then is my answer to your request to appoint a representative at my Court, a request contrary to our dynastic usage, which would only result in inconvenience to yourself. I have expounded my wishes in detail and have commanded your tribute Envoys to leave in peace on their homeward journey. It behooves you, O King, to respect my sentiments and to display even greater devotion and loyalty in the future, so that, by perpetual submission to our Throne, you may secure peace and prosperity for your country hereafter. Besides making gifts (of which I enclose a list) to each member of your Mission, I confer upon you, O King, valuable presents in excess of the number usually bestowed on such occasions, including silks and curios—a list of which is likewise enclosed. Do you reverently receive them and take note of my tender goodwill towards you! A special mandate.

Albert Beveridge (1898)

" . . . He (Ulysses S. Grant) never forgot that we are a conquering race and that we must obey our blood and occupy new markets, and if necessary, new lands. He beheld as a part of the Almighty's infinite plan, the disappearance of debased civilizations and decaying races before the higher civilization of the nobler and more virile types of man.

"Fate puts the American people upon their decision between a Chinese policy of isolation, poverty, and decay, or an American policy of progress, prosperity, and power.

"And in freeing Peoples, perishing and oppressed, our country's blessing will also come; for profits follow righteousness."

Theodore Roosevelt (1900)

" . . .We cannot, if we would, play the part of China, and be content to rot by inches in ignoble ease within our borders, taking no interest in what goes beyond them; sunk in a scrambling commercialism; heedless of the higher life, the life of aspiration, of toil and risk; busying ourselves only with the wants of our bodies for the day; until suddenly we should find, beyond a shadow of question, what China has already found, that in this world the nation that has trained itself to a career of unwarlike and isolated ease is bound in the end to go down before other nations which have not lost the manly and adventurous qualities."

Kaiser Wilhelm II (1900)

" . . . By nature the Chinaman is a cowardly cur, but he is tricky and double-faced. Small detached troops must be particularly cautious. The Chinaman likes to fall upon an enemy from an ambush, or during night-time, or with vast superiority in numbers. Recently the enemy has fought bravely, a fact which has not yet been sufficiently explained. Perhaps these were his best troops, drilled by German and other officers.

"The Chinese have disregarded the law of nations. They have shown scorn for the sacredness of an envoy, for the duties of hospitality, in a manner unparalleled in the history. And this the more reprehensible because these crimes have been committed by a nation which boasts of its ancient culture . . . . You are to fight against a cunning, courageous, well-armed, and cruel foe. When you are upon him, know this: spare nobody, make no prisoners. Use your weapons in a manner to make every Chinaman for a thousand years to come forego the wish to as much as look askance at a German. . . ."

The Village and
the Outside World

Editor's Introduction: Large parts of rural China are still largely isolated from the outside world. While Shanghai, Beijing, Guangdong and other large cities have long been open to foreign contact and have more recently been inundated with Western ideas, products and images, many villages, particularly in Western and Central China, are still relatively isolated from foreign influences. In the following section, scholar Mobo C.F. Gao describes how residents of his native village in Jiangxi Province view the world outside China: [86]

EVER SINCE CHINA'S defeat in the Opium Wars the Chinese have had complex feelings and attitudes towards "foreigners". This is also true of Gao villagers. They know very little of what a foreign country is like and their overwhelming impression of a foreign country or a foreigner is of their wealth and material superiority. They believe that foreign goods have a magic quality. They have one word for everything foreign, which is *yang* (literally meaning "ocean", therefore from overseas). The Chinese used to and Gao villagers still call matches *yang huo* ("foreign fire"), petrol *yang you* ("foreign oil"), motor boats *yang chuan* ("foreign boats"), guns *yang qiang* ("foreign guns"), soap *yang zao* ("foreign soap"), and synthetic fabric *yang bu* ("foreign cloth"). All these goods seem better than their traditional equivalents. The Chinese invented gunpowder, but their guns could not even kill a rabbit. A petrol lamp is much brighter than an oil lamp, and *yang bu* looks shiny and is much easier to wash. They therefore have this built-in notion that "foreign" means "wealth."

The villagers do not know anything about Africa or South America. Their overall impression of the world outside China is the "white" person. They have heard about *yang fang* ("foreign houses") built by foreigners in Shanghai and cities like Qingdao, which are colourful, with two or more storeys and gardens. It is like fairy tales to the villagers because their own houses are grey, functional and have mud floors. Occasionally they would hear that an overseas Chinese from Hong Kong or the United States has come back with a lot of money.

Even the government propaganda give the villagers this impression. In the film *The Red Detachment of Woman Soldiers,* very popular during the late 1960s, a Communist Red Army officer dressed himself up as a rich overseas Chinese from Hong Kong in order to get into a landlord's fortified house to organise a revolutionary uprising. This Communist officer looked very rich and glamorous as an overseas Chinese and even the landlord respected him. . . .

The villagers know so little about "foreigners" that they did not know what to ask me about when I first returned from abroad. A common question was what people eat in Britain. They commented that those foreigners must smell when I told them that they ate lamb and mutton. To them eating raw vegetables and drinking cold milk is uncivilised. They cannot understand why these foreigners do not eat fish heads, or a pig's head, feet or heart. When I gave them some chocolate to taste, none of them liked it. It was too bitter, they said.

The villagers, after they had acquired electricity and television sets, came to know what foreigners looked like. But the images seemed alien. They cannot understand how a black person can be so black. They think that the "whites" are generally too big, too hairy, their eyes too deep-set and their noses too long. In 1994 Cao Junrong, a local government official with whom I was friendly when I was a "barefoot teacher" in the 1970s, asked me what I thought of *waiguoren* ("the foreigners"). After I mumbled something I asked him the same question. This man, who had six years' education and had served in the army for three years and therefore had traveled quite a bit in China, said that these foreigners looked so ugly and yet they would often kiss openly on television. How, he exclaimed, could anyone kiss a woman like that?

During one trip to Gao Village I took along two Australian colleagues of mine. It was an unforgettable event in the village, one that they would keep on talking about for years to come. Everyone, man or woman, old or young, rushed out to look at the two foreigners. It was the first time in their lives that they saw two real "foreigners" in person. One of my colleagues has quite a prominent beer belly, like a happy Buddha. The village kids followed him wherever he went and kept on saying that he was pregnant. On another trip I took a student, a beautiful twenty-year-old woman with blue eyes and blonde hair. When I introduced her to a group of villagers, Gao Renyun, the man who…is now eighty years old, said to me that he did not realise that was a young woman. He thought it was an elderly man with white hair!

While the urban residents in China are fascinated by things foreign, from motorcars to cosmetics, Gao villagers do not seem affected by the trend. When I offered my brother a watch as a gift, he chose a Chinese watch instead of a foreign one. In 1994 when I offered to buy him a colour television my brother again asked me to buy a Chinese made one. He said a Chinese one was better because if something went wrong he could at least find someone to repair it. The villagers have to be practical because they are so poor. A single shopping spree by a young lady in Shanghai could be the equivalent of a poor villager's hard savings of many years.

To the establishment Chinese intelligentsia, and to some extent urban residents, rural people like Gao villagers are just ignorant and stupid. They would say these villagers do not know anything about the outside world and stubbornly hold to their own way of life. In some sense this is true. However, if we are willing to be sympathetic we may see it in a different light. The villagers' values in life and attitudes towards the outside world reveal a sense of dignity, and even a degree of pride. They are very sure of themselves and proud of their way of life. Their life has indeed been an enclosed one and they were not given a chance to be otherwise until very recently.

It is not that the villagers want to be indifferent to the outside world. Rather, they do not see the point in being otherwise. They are always treated as beasts of burden. Who cares what they think? For most of Chinese history, the Chinese elite just wanted to exploit as much as possible the labour of the villagers. Rural conditions became a worry for the elite only when there was a famine which might lead to a peasant uprising. It is true that some of Mao's policies, such as the Great Leap Forward, brought disaster to the villagers, but Mao did take the initiative to change the patterns of their life. He wanted the villagers to get organised and he wanted them to run industry as well as agriculture in order to narrow the differences between the urban and the rural. . . .

Gao villagers' indifference towards the outside world has been conditioned by their economic circumstances and their way of life. Education has some effect on their world outlook, but the effect is very limited. The main reason is that, despite great progress made in Mao's era, most of them have had only a very basic level of education. For these villagers, most of what they learned at school becomes irrelevant as soon as they leave. For those whose economic circumstances have changed as a result of their education

Gao village life has become irrelevant because they. . .have left the village. They are not Gao villagers any more.

Since the late 1980s, however, two developments have emerged which can potentially change the villagers' outlook. One is the villagers' access to television and the other is migrant work. However, change in the villagers' mentality as a result of these two developments has yet to manifest itself. A genuine change of mentality, for better or for worse, takes a long time to take effect.

China and the United States

Editor's Introduction: In 1972, President Nixon visited China, and for the first time since 1949 the hostility that had marked relations between the United States and the People's Republic of China began to abate. The American people began to take a closer look at China and to see some admirable things. The Chinese press became less abusive in its remarks about the United States and even declared that there were things that the Chinese could learn from America.

The differences between the two countries were by no means resolved. They will continue to influence international relations for the indefinite future. But for the first time in more than two decades, the two nations were willing to discuss their differences openly, face to face.

What happened to change this hostile situation and make the Nixon visit and better relations between the two countries possible?

First of all, the United States began to pull its ground troops out of Indochina so that China no longer feared an invasion from the south. The United States, for its part, recognized that the Chinese were not out to conquer the world.

Second, the United States was willing to state that the future of the island of Taiwan (Formosa) was exclusively a Chinese affair. Taiwan is the island off the China coast to which Chiang K'ai-shek fled after his government was defeated by the Communists in 1949. Chiang's continuing presence there was made possible only by U.S. military forces and supplies. And long after the defeat of Chiang's government on the China mainland, the United States and a number of other governments continued to recognize it as the only legitimate government of China. America's promise to withdraw its troops was a major step toward improved relations.

A third and probably the most important reason for improved U.S.-China relations was the rapidly deteriorating relationship between China and the U.S.S.R. America's fear of a Chinese-Russian

China's gift of giant panda bears to the United States in 1972 symbolized a new, friendlier relationship.

alliance in 1949 was one of the major factors shaping our policy toward China. It has now become clear that China and the U.S.S.R. feared each other more than either feared the United States. When in the early 1970s China perceived the danger of a war with Russia, she had reason to try to improve relations with the United States to prevent a two-front war.

For these and other reasons, Chinese and American statements about each other became rather moderate. The basis for improved relations was set forth in the joint communiqué that was issued in Shanghai at the conclusion of President Nixon's visit to China in February 1972. [87]

PRESIDENT RICHARD NIXON of the United States of America visited the People's Republic of China at the invitation of Premier Chou En-lai (Zhou Enlai) of the People's Republic of China from February 21 to February 28, 1972. Accompanying the President were Mrs. Nixon, U.S. Secretary of State William Rogers, Assistant to the President Dr. Henry Kissinger, and other American officials.

President Nixon met with Chairman Mao Tse-tung (Mao Zedong) of the Communist Party of China on February 21. The two leaders had a serious and frank exchange of views on Sino-U.S. relations and world affairs. . . .

The leaders of the People's Republic of China and the United States of America found it beneficial to have this opportunity, after so many years without contact, to present candidly to one another their views on a variety of issues. They reviewed the international situation in which important changes and great upheavals are taking place and expounded their respective positions and attitudes.

The Chinese side stated: Wherever there is oppression, there is resistance. Countries want independence, nations want liberation, and the people want revolution—this has become the irresistible trend of history. All nations, big or small, should be equal; big nations should not bully the small and strong nations should not bully the weak. China will never be a superpower and it opposes hegemony and power politics of any kind. The Chinese side stated that it firmly supports the struggles of all the oppressed people and nations for freedom and liberation and that the people of all countries have the right to choose their social systems according to their own wishes and the right to safeguard the independence, sovereignty, and territorial integrity of their own countries and oppose foreign aggression, interference, control, and subversion. All foreign troops should be withdrawn to their own countries. . . .

The U.S. side stated: Peace in Asia and peace in the world requires efforts both to reduce immediate tensions and to eliminate the basic causes of conflict. The United States will work for a just and secure peace: just, because it fulfills the aspirations of peoples and nations for freedom and progress; secure, because it removes the danger of foreign aggression. The United States supports individual freedom and social progress for all the peoples of the world, free of outside pressure or intervention. The United States believes that the effort to reduce tensions is served by improving communication between countries that have different ideologies, so as to lessen the risks of confrontation through accident, miscalculation, or misunderstanding. Countries should treat each other with mutual respect and be willing to compete peacefully, letting performance be the ultimate judge. No country should claim infallibility and each country should be prepared to re-examine its own attitudes for the common good. . . .

There are essential differences between China and the United States in their social systems and foreign policies. However, the two sides agreed that countries, regardless of their social systems, should conduct their relations on

Chairman Mao Zedong and President Nixon meet on the afternoon of February 21, 1972

the principles of respect for the sovereignty and territorial integrity of all states, non-aggression against other states, noninterference in the internal affairs of other states, equality and mutual benefit, and peaceful coexistence. International disputes should be settled on this basis, without resorting to the use or threat of force. The United States and the People's Republic of China are prepared to apply these principles to their mutual relations.

With these principles of international relations in mind the two sides stated that:

- progress toward the normalization of relations between China and the United States is in the interests of all countries;

- both wish to reduce the danger of international military conflict;

- neither should seek hegemony in the Asia-Pacific region and each is opposed to efforts by any other country or group of countries to establish such hegemony; and

■ neither is prepared to negotiate on behalf of any third party or to enter into agreements or understandings with the other directed at other states.

Both sides are of the view that it would be against the interests of the peoples of the world for any major country to collude with another against other countries, or for major countries to divide up the world into spheres of interest.

The two sides reviewed the long-standing serious disputes between China and the United States. The Chinese side reaffirmed its position: The Taiwan question is the crucial question obstructing the normalization of relations between China and the United States; the Government of the People's Republic of China is the sole legal government of China; Taiwan is a province of China which has long been returned to the motherland; the liberation of Taiwan is China's internal affair in which no other country has the right to interfere; and all U.S. forces and military installations must be withdrawn from Taiwan. The Chinese Government firmly opposes any activities that aim at the creation of "one China, one Taiwan," "one China, two governments," "two Chinas," an "independent Taiwan" or advocate that "the status of Taiwan remains to be determined."

The U.S. side declared: The United States acknowledges that all Chinese on either side of the Taiwan Strait maintain there is but one China and that Taiwan is a part of China. The United States Government does not challenge that position. It reaffirms its interest in a peaceful settlement of the Taiwan question by the Chinese themselves. With this prospect in mind, it affirms the ultimate objective of the withdrawal of all U.S. forces and military installations from Taiwan. In the meantime, it will progressively reduce its forces and military installations on Taiwan as the tension in the area diminishes.

The two sides agreed that it is desirable to broaden the understanding between the two peoples. To this end, they discussed specific areas in such fields as science, technology, culture, sports, and journalism, in which people-to-people contacts and exchanges would be mutually beneficial. Each side undertakes to facilitate the further development of such contacts and exchanges.

Both sides view bilateral trade as another area from which mutual benefit can be derived, and agreed that economic relations based on equality and mutual benefit are in the interest of the peoples of the two countries. They agree to facilitate the progressive development of trade between their two countries.

The two sides agreed that they will stay in contact through various channels, including the sending of a senior U.S. representative to Peking (Beijing) from time to time for concrete consultations to further the normalization of relations between the two countries and continue to exchange views on issues of common interest.

The two sides expressed the hope that the gains achieved during this visit would open up new prospects for the relations between the two countries. They believe that the normalization of relations between the two countries is not only in the interest of the Chinese and American peoples but also contributes to the relaxation of tension in Asia and the world.

President Nixon, Mrs. Nixon, and the American party expressed their appreciation for the gracious hospitality shown them by the Government and people of the People's Republic of China.

> *Editor's Postscript*: Trade and diplomatic relations developed slowly following the Shanghai Communique. Formal diplomatic recognition, with exchange of ambassadors, was not achieved until 1979, under President Carter. But mutual interests in both domestic and foreign affairs contributed to a steady growth in the relationship through the end of the 1980s. Political relations deteriorated after the suppression of the Tiananmen demonstrations in 1989 but generally improved during the 1990s despite periodic flareups. China reacted negatively to U.S. military and diplomatic support of Taiwan, U.S. missile defense plans and growing U.S. military presence in Asia, while the U.S. accused China of human rights abuses and unfair trade practices. Despite underlying suspicions on both sides, trade and U.S. investment increased dramatically, and by 2005 China was America's third-largest trading partner while the U.S. was China's second-largest partner. By that time, U.S. companies had invested over $50 billion in nearly 5,000 projects in China. By 2006, the U.S. trade deficit with China reached $213.5 billion, the greatest imbalance with one country ever recorded. Political relations became closer after the September 11, 2001 terrorist attacks on New York City and Washington, D.C. as China and the U.S. cooperated to fight global terrorism, promote regional security in Asia and control the proliferation of nuclear weapons.

Current Chinese Views
of World Politics

Editor's Introduction: The following articles offer glimpses into Chinese thinking about recent developments in world politics. The first expresses the Chinese view of their own foreign policy. The second discusses U.S. strategy and the war on Iraq. The third describes Chinese military spending. [88]

1. CHINA'S DEVELOPMENT AND SECURITY CONCEPT

By Fu Mengzi, Director of the Institute of American Studies under the China Institutes of Contemporary International Relations

IN THE PAST 26 years of China's reform and opening up, begun in 1979, the country's economy has grown rapidly, contributing significantly to national strength. China's GDP has risen from $147.3 billion in 1979 to $1.65 trillion in 2004, with an annual growth of 9.4 percent. Sustainable development has also boosted China's foreign trade, with the total value of imports and exports growing from $20.6 billion to $1.15 trillion, an annual growth rate exceeding 16 percent, making China the world's third largest trading country, only after the United States and Germany. Meanwhile, China's foreign currency reserves have ballooned from $167 million in 1979 to $609.9 billion last year, next only to Japan. China's increasingly expanding domestic demand and exports are exerting a profound influence on the global market and its role as an engine of regional economic development is being more widely accepted.

China's reform and opening up policy has also made it embrace the world with unprecedented enthusiasm and take advantage of globalization. This is also the process through which China continuously integrates into and participates in, while not denying and excluding, the international economic and political systems. In other words, it is a process by which China denies its rigid economic system and continuously perfects its socialist democracy, participates in international economic competition boldly, and plays an active role in regional and global affairs.

The history of international relations shows that a country will surely seek to further its national interests as a consequence of its economic rise, and so will China in its development process. However, groundless and unrealistic comments on China's development, such as "China Threat," "China Collapse" and "China Weakness," have appeared occasionally, accusing China of squeezing international investments from developing countries, seizing employment opportunities from other countries, exploiting interests from and exerting influence on the Asia-Pacific region, and even challenging the existing international order. Actually, the national interests of a rapidly developing China in the globalization process are connected with those of other countries. That is why "China Opportunity" is increasingly accepted by the world.

China will not challenge or disrupt the existing international order. Undoubtedly, China benefits from globalization since its rise is a process of continuous integration into the international system and participation in regional integration and globalization. This means China is certain to accept, while not challenge, the existing international system. China's rise is a peaceful rise and will not challenge any other country's national interests.

China will not challenge the U.S.-led international political and economic system, though this system also has its injustices and inequalities. China will participate in regional and global political and economic affairs in a constructive manner and make efforts to play a role as a rising power in improving an unjust international order. A permanent member of the UN Security Council, China will assume its full role in dealing with regional and global affairs. Last year, the United States invited China to participate in the G7 finance ministers' meeting, giving China a better channel to communicate with the G7, as well as making China more psychologically and practically prepared to coordinate international economic and financial orders.

At the same time, China's security concept is a kind of comprehensive concept. The history of world economic development shows that 20 to 30 years of development can turn a country of a certain size into an economic power. Japan became a member of the Organization for Economic Cooperation and Development (OECD) in 1968. Germany, South Korea and Singapore are also good examples. But China is not comparable to these countries in terms of per-capita income, which has just exceeded $1,000, owing to a large population. This means China will surely take the path of peaceful development from a long-term view. This also leads to China's important strategic option, a comprehensive security concept.

The content of the concept can be summarized as follows:

■ Security is a comprehensive concept and not limited to one area. A country's development expands its internal and external national interests. Security in one area, such as no outside invasion, does not guarantee the essential security of a country. In other words, a strong military force cannot fully guarantee a country's security. The September 11 events are such examples.

■ Security should be mutual while not one-sided, multilateral while not unilateral, and comparative while not absolute. There is no absolute security. While people in one country maintain absolute security, those in other countries must feel unsafe. This makes security hard to realize.

■ Security should be based on mutual trust. A country's role should be evaluated objectively and one country should not seek confrontation with another country through exaggerating its threats. Cooperative security should be pursued.

■ There are traditional as well as non-traditional aspects of security. During peacetime, it is more important to cope with threats to non-traditional security.

China's security concept in military and at national strategic levels includes the following three prerequisites. The first is to safeguard national sovereignty and territorial integrity. Though no large-scale military invasion occurred after the Cold War, China still has tough tasks to maintain border security. With the development of its economy, China will naturally increase its military expenditure, but China's military strategy is totally defensive.

Second, China is willing to properly solve border disputes with its neighbors on the basis of equal negotiation and mutual trust. The country has completed negotiations, or is negotiating, with Russia, India and Viet Nam on this issue and has made achievements with mutual benefits. China has the will to hold dialogues with countries that have sovereignty disputes with China.

Meanwhile, China should also have the ability to cope with traditional threats. After the Cold War, the international security environment changed greatly, and peace and development have become people's common requirements. However, the reduction of traditional threats does not mean an improvement of the security environment. Terrorism, transnational crime, environmental deterioration and the spread of diseases have become important aspects of national security environments. These challenges are beyond the ability of one country and form the basis of full cooperation among different countries.

China's realistic economic situation indicates the country is still a developing country. This also means China needs long-term and unrelenting efforts to improve the lives of its people and reach its goal of constructing a well off society. China needs to take the road of peaceful development. In this sense, it is vitally important for China to seek a favorable external environment and China's new group of leaders has shown China's diplomatic concept to intensify its diplomatic relations with neighboring countries, world powers and developing countries at the 16th National Congress of the Communist Party of China in 2002. This also ensures China will develop all-round friendly cooperation with countries worldwide, and accept, while not challenge, the international order. Meanwhile, development is also China's internal requirement and the country is still far from the goal.

Economic development will give China more resources to play a constructive role as a world power and give back more to the international community. China is more than willing to do so. After the Indian Ocean tsunamis at the end of last year, China sent timely medical help and humanitarian assistance to the disaster-hit regions. The nationwide donation drive also shows its will to help people. In the process of globalization, China seeks common development and common prosperity.

Meanwhile, prevention of the proliferation of weapons of mass destruction (WMD) meets the interests of China and other countries in the world. China does not support or proliferate WMD and is actively coordinating the six-party talks on the nuclear issues on the Korea Peninsula.

More importantly, China is against hegemonism while not against hegemonic countries. China insists that international relationship should be based on political democracy instead of power diplomacy, and the United Nations should play an active role in important international issues instead of being marginalized. China objects to unilateral actions and intentions. It fights actively against terrorism. In this regard, each country has common interests. China will prevent and fight terrorism together with other countries.

2. US STRATEGY TO BE BLAMED

By Qian Qichen, Vice-Premier (1993–2003)
and Foreign Minister (1988-1998)

The changes of the world's structure in the 20th century were mainly brought about by war. In this century, two world-scale wars, namely, World War I and II, and the Cold War, broke out.

The world has not been clearly reconfigured since the end of the Cold War, which signaled the collapse of a two-polar structure in the world. For some time after the Cold War ended, the United States itself was not entirely sure of where its main threats came from, whether from the still destructible nuclear stockpile left over by the Soviet Union, or China's rapid development, or somewhere else.

For a certain period after the end of the Cold War, the United States focused its main energies on developing new kinds of weapons and building a missile defence shield to overpower its potential strategic rivals. In 1999, the world's sole superpower waged the Kosovo War to consolidate its dominance in Europe and squeeze its strategic scope towards Russia. In 2000, George W. Bush claimed China was a strategic competitor of the United States in one of his presidential campaign speeches.

All the blustering was a clear signal of the US' uncertainty over who was its main foe. The September 11 terrorist attacks in New York and Washington in 2001, however, greatly shocked the United States. Even in the Pearl Harbour Incident of December 7, 1941, mainland US was free from direct attacks from Japan although its Pacific Fleet suffered heavy losses.

The September 11 event shows that the biggest threat to the US homeland is neither sophisticatedly-armed big powers, nor its alleged strategic adversaries, but irregularly based terrorist organizations.

Facing such unprecedented challenges, the US Bush administration substantially adjusted its global strategy, aimed at not dealing with threats from strategic rivals, but from terrorism and the proliferation of weapons of mass destruction.

In the wake of September 11, the "Bush Doctrine" came out, in which the United States created "axes of evil" and "pre-emptive" strategies. It linked counter-terrorism and the prevention of proliferation to the reformation of so-called "rogue states" and "failed states."

Under this doctrine, the United States launched two military actions in Afghanistan and Iraq within two years. It reviewed the structure of the US military forces, and drafted programmes for redeployment of US forces overseas.

Under this doctrine, the United States has tightened its control of the Middle East, Central Asia, Southeast Asia and Northeast Asia, strengthened its response ability to this outstretched "unstable arc," and put forward its "Big Middle East" reform programme.

It all testifies that Washington's anti-terror campaign has already gone beyond the scope of self-defence.

And these latest moves, when seen with the background of the Gulf War and the Kosovo War, have made it obvious that the United States has not changed its Cold War mentality and that the country is still accustomed to applying military means to deal with various threats, visible or invisible.

The philosophy of the "Bush Doctrine" is in essence force. It advocates the United States should rule over the whole world with overwhelming force, military force in particular.

Hardly strange, then, that Bush and his administration still insist on arguing that their decision to go to war in Iraq and US policy on the issue were right.

But the world's situation in response to the war is in effect a negative answer.

In Iraq, the United States did win a war in the military dimension, but it is far from winning peace for itself and the Arab country.

On the contrary, Washington has opened a Pandora's box, intensifying various intermingled conflicts, such as ethnic and religious ones.

The US case in Iraq has caused the Muslim world and Arab countries to believe that the superpower already regards them as targets of its ambitious "democratic reformation" programme. This perception has increasingly aggravated the long-brewing conflicts between the United States and the Muslim world.

Now, Washington's predicament in Iraq has become daily news.

On June 28, the White House hurried to transfer Iraq's power to the country's interim government. But the handover was of more nominal than practical significance. Currently, 150,000 US troops are still deep in the Iraq quagmire, and the death toll steadily increases.

The Iraq War has made the United States even more unpopular in the international community than its war in Viet Nam. Bush did not even dare to meet the public on the streets when he visited Britain, the closest ally of the United States.

From US pre-war military preparations, to postwar reconstruction of the country, the rift between the United States and its traditional European allies has never been so wide.

It is now time to give up the illusion that Europeans and Americans are living in the same world, as some Europeans would like to believe.

The Iraq issue has also presented a heated topic for the US presidential election.

Over the past year, some American think-tanks and politicians have had soul-searching reflections on the issue and given their criticisms.

Many of them believe that the Bush administration did not objectively and clearly assess challenges and difficulties facing the United States when it applied the pre-emptive strategy. In so doing, the administration was only practising the same catastrophic strategy applied by former empires in history.

Both history and practices of "the myth of empires" have demonstrated that the pre-emptive strategy will bring the Bush administration an outcome that it is most unwilling to see, that is, absolute insecurity of the "American Empire" and its demise because of expansion it cannot cope with.

Just as [Harvard political scientist] Joseph S. Nye said, the paradox of the US force theory is that the world's politics have already changed, and even for the world's most powerful country, it is impossible to realize its key goals merely through its own strength, just like that by the ancient Roman Empire.

Neo-unilateralism has seriously underestimated the role a country's soft power and international systems can play, thus denting important means that Washington can apply to practise its new national security strategy.

The Iraq war was an optional war, not a necessary one, and the pre-emptive principle should be removed from the dictionary of the US national security, former US Secretary of State Madeleine Albright also said.

The Iraq War has also destroyed the hard-won global anti-terror coalition.

Mounting hostile sentiments among the Muslim world towards the United States following the war have already helped the al-Qaida terrorist network recruit more followers and suicide martyrs. Instead of dropping, the number of terrorist activities throughout the world is now on the increase.

The US' call for help from the United Nations (UN) for Iraq's postwar reconstruction work once again shows that in the current world, unilateralism is not appropriate in solving international affairs.

The Iraq War provides another negative example of international relations in the new century.

In an increasingly interdependent world, in which the benefits of every country have been closely intertwined, the damages a war can cause will be far more than the benefits it can bring. Any superpower can impossibly force the international community into accepting its own norms merely through displaying its military muscle.

The current US predicament in Iraq serves as another example that when a country's superiority psychology inflates beyond its real capability, a lot of trouble can be caused.

But the troubles and disasters the United States has met do not stem from threats by others, but from its own cocksureness and arrogance.

The 21st century is not the "American Century." That does not mean that the United States does not want the dream. Rather, it is incapable of realizing the goal.

In this century, all big powers should compete in a peaceful way, instead of military means.

3. TRUTH ABOUT MILITARY SPENDING

By Chen Xulong, Chinese Institute of International Studies

Defense budgets are a mirror to a country's strategic intentions and its potential to threaten others. It comes as no surprise therefore that the many China watchers in the West keep a close eye on any movement in China's defense spending. Recent remarks made by senior U.S. and Japanese officials have accused China of upping its spending in this area to alarming proportions.

But as Mao Zedong once said, "Seek truth from facts." A recent internationally accredited report on military matters, including expenditures, flies in the face of accusations leveled against China and puts the country's military spending into perspective.

World military expenditure in 2004 has, for the first time since the end of the Cold War, exceeded the benchmark of $1 trillion. The major determinant of this trend is the increased spending by the United States, which makes up 47 percent of the world total.

These and other revealing facts are detailed in the Stockholm International Peace Research Institute's (SIPRI) latest research report entitled "SIPRI Yearbook 2005: Armaments, Disarmament and International Security" issued on June 7. The latest information on world military expenditure contained in this yearbook by the world-leading institute specializing in research in arms control and disarmament has captured wide attention since its release. The yearbook reports that U.S. military expenditure has increased by 12 percent year-on-year to $455.3 billion, surpassing the combined military expenditure of the following 31 biggest spenders, as well as the combined military expenditure of the entire developing world. China's $35.4 billion pales in comparison. Predictably Japan emerges as Asia's biggest military spender and the fourth largest in the world. Of particular interest is India's military expenditure, which increased by 19 percent in 2004 over the previous year, enjoying the fastest growth among South Asian contries. India has been the world's largest arms importer since 2003.

China's Position

According to SIPRI, China's 2004 military expenditure, 4 percent of the world's total and the fifth largest in the world, converts to $27 per capita, the second lowest among the 15 major spenders. By comparison, U.S. military expenditure in 2004 was 12.86 times greater and its per-capita amount 57 times that of China.

Regionally, China's military expenditure is $7 billion less than its Asian neighbor Japan.

What emerges from the SIPRI statistics refutes accusations from countries like the United States and Japan that China is increasing spending in military hardware. Just days before the release of the report, at the Fourth Asia Security Conference held in Singapore, representatives from the United States and Japan made harsh remarks on China's "high" defense expenditure. U.S. Defense Secretary Donald Rumsfeld claimed, "China has the third largest military budget in the world, and clearly the largest in Asia."

As a matter of fact, China has for a long time maintained moderate defense expenditures, lower than that of some Western countries in absolute terms, as well as lower in its proportion in gross domestic product (GDP) and the government's budget. In the last two decades or so, China's military expenditure's share of GDP has floated below the benchmark of 2 percent, which is lower than the average level of 3 percent of developed countries and the average 2.6 percent of developing countries. Just as Chinese Foreign Ministry Spokesman Kong Quan once pointed out, as opposed to China's huge population, long land border and coastline, its defense expenditure has constantly maintained a relatively low level. Kong said that China's military expenses lag behind major countries in the world in absolute and per-capita terms, amount per soldier, proportion of GDP, and proportion of government expenditure.

Reasons for Increase

Without doubt, along with China's economic development in recent years, the country's military expenditure has also maintained a trend of expansion.

This trend is elaborated upon by the Chinese Government's white paper entitled "China's National Defense in 2004." In accordance with the National Defense Law, the Chinese Government follows the guiding principle of coordinated development of national defense and economy. Based on the economic development and revenue growth, it has continued to increase its defense expenditures moderately, so as to keep up with the changes in the demands of national defense. China's GDP in 2002 and 2003 was 10.5 trillion yuan ($1.3 trillion) and 11.7 trillion yuan ($1.4 trillion) respectively. Its defense expenditure in 2002 and 2003 was 170.8 billion yuan ($20.6 billion) and 190.8 billion yuan ($23 billion) respectively. Its defense budget for 2004 is 211.7 billion yuan ($25.6 billion). In the past two years, the ratios of China's annual defense expenditure to its GDP and to the state expenditure in the same period have remained basically stable.

Furthermore, China has neither intention nor capacity to dramatically increase expenses on armaments. As the increase of China's military expenditure is made possible by the country's economic growth and growing government revenue, the functions of military expenditures have decided that such an increase is necessary and justified. According to China's National Defense in 2004, the increased part of China's defense expenditures has primarily been used for the following purposes.

First, to increase the salaries and allowances of military personnel. It is necessary to raise the salaries and allowances in accordance with socio-economic development and the per-capita income rise of urban and rural residents.

Second, to further improve the social insurance system for servicemen.

Third, to support the structural and organizational reform of the military. China has once again downsized its military by 200,000, and has to increase the expenses on the resettlement of the discharged surplus personnel accordingly.

Fourth, to increase investment in the development of talented personnel. Chinese army has established and refined an incentive mechanism for talented people, improved conditions in military institutions of higher learning, and entrusted non-military colleges and universities with the education of qualified personnel, so as to implement the army's Strategic Project for Talented People.

Fifth, to moderately increase expenses on armaments. This is aimed at facilitating a leap forward in updating weaponry and equipment and stepping up preparations for military confrontations.

Ulterior Motive

It is stated in the annual report by U.S. Department of Defense submitted to the Congress in May that China's military spending had grown rapidly in recent years, reaching $70 billion in 2004, which is almost twice of SIPRI's figure of $35.4 billion. The latter, to many, is more believable than the former, considering that even experts from the RAND Corp., the leading U.S. research institute in military studies and analysis, once pointed out China's military expenses had been overstated by the Pentagon by 71 percent.

In fact, as a country of 1.3 billion people, with booming economy and a heavy defense task, China has maintained a moderate military expenditure and growth rate. What is more, China has adhered to the path of peaceful development, pursuing a national defense policy that is defensive in nature and an independent foreign policy of peace. China will never pose a threat to another peace-loving country.

Regardless, the United States and Japan have continued to make exaggerations and blunt accusations over China's military expenditures and military power, in an attempt to promote the "China threat theory." Many see this as reasoning from a particular mindset along with ulterior motives.

Although it has been a long time since the Cold War ended, the Cold War mindset continues to exert its influence from time to time in countries like the United States and Japan. Those who prescribe to this mindset are obsessed with power politics and have the need to seek absolute security by forming allies and seeking military supremacy. This line of thought translates development of other countries into a challenge to their own advantageous positions. Moreover, adopting an ideology standard and drumming up the "democratic peace theory," they take Western political systems and values as the guarantee for peace, and classify countries with political systems different from their own as those that need defending against and transformation.

There are two ulterior motives behind these overstatements of China's military spending and power.

First, they want to project China as their "imaginary rival" and use it as an excuse to maintain their own strong military power. This becomes an excuse for the United States to continue its military presence in Asia and for Japan to expand armaments in a bid to become a military power.

Second, they intend to make excuses to continue military interference in Taiwan and arms sales to Taiwan.

Third, they are trying to justify their opposition to the EU's wish to lift the arms embargo over China.

Fourth, they intend to make legislatures in both countries ratify more military expenses, in order to stop China's military modernization and maintain their military edges over China.

Admittedly, in a modern world, the military factor influence over international structure and national security is on the rise. Meanwhile, with a quarter-century-long economic advancement and rapid development of comprehensive national strength, China is committed to promoting military modernization in conformity with world trends in this area. From this perspective, it is understandable for foreign powers to pay due attention to any expansion in China's military muscle.

In response to groundless criticism from the United States and Japan, Cui Tiankai, Chinese representative to the Asia Security Conference in Singapore retorted that as a country with military spending much larger than that of China, America's criticism is unjustified. He added that every country is entitled to its own defense focuses, and the size of China's military expenditure is appropriate. While answering questions at a daily news briefing, Chinese Foreign Ministry Spokesman Liu Jianchao noted it warrants no accusation for the Chinese army to update weaponry in order to tackle complicated international situations and defend its sovereignty, security and territorial integrity. He said any word and act aimed at creating and whipping up China's military threat is harmful to regional peace and stability. He also expressed the hope that the United States shall respect facts and contribute more to healthy development of Sino-U.S. relations, increase of mutual trust between countries in the Asia-Pacific region, and peace and stability in this region.

No matter how hard some countries have tried to exaggerate China's military expenses and military power, China is firmly committed to moving down the road of peaceful development.

Epilogue

Editor's Introduction: During the last few years, protests, riots and violent demonstrations have taken place with increasing frequency throughout China. These protests, which threaten to undermine the economic and political stability of the country, are taken very seriously by the government. They are typically responses by poor peasants or workers to land seizures, evictions, industrial pollution, the closing of factories, local political corruption, the perceived abuse of power by Communist Party officials, and the growing gap between rich and poor. To many protesters, the Communist Party that came to power in 1949, "as a champion of peasants and workers seems to have switched sides, backing capitalist businessmen instead of the poor as part of a new get-rich ethic in which bribery plays a big role."* In July 2005, Public Security Minister Zhou Yongkang stated that 3.76 million people had participated in 74,000 "mass incidents" in 2004. The number of incidents rose to 87,000 in 2005. These represented dramatic increases from the 58,000 reported in 2003 and 10,000 reported in 1994.

We can now affirm that classes do exist in socialist countries and that class struggle undoubtedly exists. . . . We must acknowledge that classes will continue to exist for a long time. We must also acknowledge the existence of a struggle of class against class, and admit the possibility of the restoration of reactionary classes. We must raise our vigilance and properly educate our youth as well as the cadres, the masses and the middle- and basic-level cadres. Old cadres must also study these problems and be educated. Otherwise a country like ours can still move towards its opposite. Even to move towards

---

* Edward Cody, "A Chinese City's Rage at the Rich and Powerful," *Washington Post,* August 1, 2005, p. A1.
  http://www.washingtonpost.com/wp-dyn/content/article/2005/07/31/AR2005073101163_pf.html.

its opposite would not matter too much because there would still be the negation of the negation, and afterwards we might move towards our opposite yet again. If our children's generation go in for revisionism and move towards their opposite, so that although they still nominally have socialism it is in fact capitalism, then our grandsons will certainly rise up in revolt and overthrow their fathers, because the masses will not be satisfied. Therefore, from now on we must talk about this every year, every month, every day.*

—*Mao Zedong*

---

* Speech at the Tenth Plenum of the Eighth Central Committee (September 24, 1962) in Stuart Schram, *Chairman Mao Talks to the People: Talks and Letters, 1956-1971*, New York: Pantheon, 1974, pp. 189-190.

Chronology

c. 11th century - 221 B.C.	Zhou Dynasty
551–479 B.C.	Life of Confucius (pinyin=Kongfuzi)
470–391 B.C. ?	Life of Mozi (Mo Tzu)
403–221 B.C.	Warring States Period
221–206 B.C.	Qin Dynasty
206 B. C.–A.D. 220	Han Dynasty
618–907	Tang Dynasty
960–1279	Song Dynasty
1279–1368	Yuan Dynasty
1368–1644	Ming Dynasty
1644–1911	Qing Dynasty [Manchu Dynasty]
1793	British delegation, headed by Lord Macartney, visits China
1839–1842	Opium War
1842	Treaty of Nanjing
1850–1864	Taiping Rebellion
1894–1895	Sino-Japanese War
1899–1901	Boxer Rebellion
1912	Establishment of the Republic of China
1919	May Fourth Movement
1921	Founding of the Chinese Communist Party
1923–1927	Nationalist - Communist collaboration
1927	Nationalist forces of Chiang Kai-shek attack Communists, initiating a civil war lasting until 1936
1931	Japanese invade Manchuria
1934–1935	The Long March
1935	Mao Zedong gains control of the Communist Party
1936	Nationalist - Communist collaboration against the Japanese begins
1937–1945	War with Japan
1945–1949	Civil War between Nationalists and Communists
1949	Establishment of the People's Republic of China
1952	Private businesses nationalized
1954	Beginning of agricultural collectivization
1958–1961	Great Leap Forward
1966	The "Great Proletarian Cultural Revolution" begins
1972	President Richard Nixon visits China
1976	Death of Mao Zedong
1978	Deng Xiaoping becomes paramount leader of China; Economic reforms begin
1979	The U.S. and China establish diplomatic relations
1979	Collective farms begin to be dismantled
1989	Tiananmen Square demonstrations; Jiang Zemin named Communist Party General Secretary
1997	Death of Deng Xiaoping
2001	Business leaders invited to join Communist Party
2002	Hu Jintao named Communist Party General Secretary
2004	Constitution amended to guarantee rights of private property

Sources

1. Yueh Feng and Wang Tien-ch'i, "The Land," *The People of Tai-hang* (Peking: China Youth Publishing House, 1964). Translated in *Chinese Anthropology*, Vol. 4, No. 4 (New York: International Arts and Sciences Press, 1972), pp. 300-306; abridged. Used by permission.

2. Jack Belden, *China Shakes the World* (New York: Monthly Review Press, 1972), pp. 174-188; abridged. Copyright ©1949 by Jack Belden. Reprinted by permission of Monthly Review Press.

3. "Selections from *The Analects*," in W. T. de Bary, et al. (eds.), *Sources of the Chinese Tradition*, Vol. I (New York: Columbia University Press, 1960), pp. 23-33; abridged. Reprinted by permission.

4. Lin Yu-t'ang, *My Country and My People* (New York: John Day, 1935), pp. 172-183; abridged. Copyright ©1935 by Lin Yu-t'ang.

5. Francis Hsu, *Americans and Chinese* (New York: Doubleday Natural History Press, 1972), pp. 226-242; abridged. Third edition, ©1981 by Francis L. K. Hsu. Reprinted by permission of the University of Hawaii Press.

6. Pan Chao, "Lessons for Women," in Nancy Lee Swann, *Pan Chao, Foremost Woman Scholar of China* (New York: Russell and Russell, 1968), pp. 82-90; abridged. Copyright ©1932 by Princeton University Library. Reprinted by permission.

7. *A Daughter of Han, the Autobiography of a Chinese Working Woman*, as told to Ida Pruitt by Ning Lao T'ai-t'ai (Stanford: Stanford University Press, 1967), p. 22. Originally published by Yale University Press, ©1945. Reprinted by permission.

8. Agnes Smedley, *Portraits of Chinese Women in Revolution* (Old Westbury, NY: The Feminist Press, 1976), pp. 5-10; abridged. Reprinted by permission.

9. Hsieh Ping-ying, *Autobiography of a Chinese Girl* (London: George Allen & Unwin Ltd., 1943), pp. 139-144; abridged.

10. Chiang Monlin, *Tides from the West* (Taipei: China Culture Publishing Foundation, 1957), pp. 160-164; abridged.

11. Martin Bernal, *Chinese Socialism to 1907* (Ithaca, NY: Cornell University Press, 1976), p. 11.

12. Wm. Theodore de Bary, et al., eds., *Sources of the Chinese Tradition,* Vol. 1 (New York: Columbia University Press, 1960), pp. 40-41.

13. Lao Tsu, *Tao Te Ching* (New York: Vintage, 1989), pp. 77-78, 80.

14. Lo Kuan-chung, *The Three Kingdoms,* translated and edited by Moss Roberts (New York: Pantheon Books, 1976), p. 5. Reprinted by permission.

15. *The Opium War* (Peking: Foreign Languages Press, 1976), pp. 110-111, 123-124.

16. Franz Michael, *The Taiping Rebellion: History and Documents.* Vol. 2 (Seattle: University of Washington Press, 1971), pp. 313-315; abridged. Reprinted by permission.

17. Chow Tse-tung, *The May Fourth Movement* (Cambridge, MA: Harvard University Press, 1963), p.59. Copyright ©1963 by the President and Fellows of Harvard College. Reprinted by permission; Ssu-Yu Teng and John K. Fairbank, *China's Response to the West* (Cambridge, MA: Harvard University Press, 1954), pp. 240-242, abridged. Copyright ©1954, 1979 by the President and Fellows of Harvard College, copyright renewed 1982 by Ssu-yu Teng and John King Fairbank. Reprinted by permission of the publisher; Geremie Barmé and Linda Jaivin, eds., *New Ghosts, Old Dreams* (New York: Times Books, 1992), p. 199. Copyright ©1992 by Geremie Barmé and Linda Jaivin. Used by permission of Times Books, a division of Random House, Inc.

18. Franz Schurmann and Orville Schell, eds., *Republican China* (New York: Vintage), pp.125-127. Copyright ©1967 by Franz Schurman and Orville Schell. Used by permission of Random House, Inc.

19. Mao Tse-tung, *Selected Works of Mao Tse-tung,* Vol. 1 (Peking: Foreign Languages Press, 1965), pp. 26-28; abridged.

20. Yang Chengwu, "Lightening Attack on the Luting Bridge," in Deirdre and Neale Hunter, *We the Chinese, Voices from China* (New York: Praeger, 1971), pp. 34-41; abridged. Copyright ©1971. Reprinted by permission of Greenwood Publishing Group, Inc., Westport, CT.

21. Mao Tse-tung, *Five Articles by Chairman Mao Tse-tung* (Peking: Foreign Languages Press, 1967), pp. 1-19, abridged.

22. Mao Tse-tung, *On the Correct Handling of Contradictions Among the People* (Peking: Foreign Languages Press, 1958), abridged.

23. Yao Keh-ming, "When the Party Secretary Showed Up," *Chinese Literature,* No. 2 (Peking: Foreign Languages Press, 1973), pp. 36-42.

24. Excerpted from Wang Meng, "A Spate of Visitors," *Chinese Literature,* No. 7 (Peking, July 1980), pp. 9-21.

25. Zhao Shuli, "Meng Hsiang-ying Stands Up," Translated by W. J. F. Jenner, from *Modern Chinese Stories* (London: Oxford University Press, 1970), pp. 121-138, abridged. Reprinted by permission of Oxford University Press.

26. Tang Keng-liang, *The Paupers' Co-op* (Peking: Foreign Languages Press, 1965), abridged.

27. "The Story of the Iron Man," *Chinese Literature,* No. 7, 1972, pp. 62-71, abridged.

28. "'Barefoot Doctors' - Giving Medical Treatment While Taking Part in Farm Work," *Peking Review,* May 1973, pp. 15-21; abridged.

29. From Ken Ling, *The Revenge of Heaven* (G.P. Putnam's Sons, 1972). Copyright ©1972 by Dr. Ivan London and Miriam London. Reprinted by permission.

30. Feng Jicai, *Voices from the Whirlwind* (New York: Pantheon, 1991), pp. 55-61. Copyright ©1991 by Random House, Inc. Copyright ©1990 by Foreign Language Press. Used by permission of Pantheon Books, a division of Random House, Inc.

31. Seaborne Cultural Work Team, Kwangchow, from *Chinese Literature,* No. 4 (Peking: Foreign Languages Press, 1969).

32. Cheng I, "Land and Ocean I Am Grateful to You," *Chinese Youth,* No. 7, 1980. Translated by John Hsu.

33. Zong Huaiwen, comp., *Years of Trial, Turmoil and Triumph—China from 1949 to 1988* (Beijing: Foreign Languages Press, 1989), pp. 127-128, 129, 168-169. Reprinted by permission.

34. Philip C. C. Huang, *The Peasant Family and Rural Development in the Yangzi Delta, 1350-1988* (Stanford: Stanford University Press, 1990), pp. 278-279. Copyright ©1990 by the Board of Trustees of the Leland Stanford Junior University. Reprinted by permission.

35. Robert Weil, *Red Cat, White Cat: China and the Contradictions of "Market Socialism"* (New York: Monthly Review Press, 1996), p. 247. Reprinted by permission.

36. Ibid., pp. 248-249.

37. Mobo C. F. Gao, "Debating the Cultural Revolution: Do We Only Know What We Believe?" *Critical Asian Studies,* Vol. 34, No.3 (2002), pp. 427-428. http://www.bcasnet.org.

38. D. Soled, ed., *China: A Nation in Transition* (Washington D.C.: Congressional Quarterly, 1995), pp. 436-437.

39. "The Fifth Modernization: Democracy (December 1978)," from Wei Jingsheng, *The Courage to Stand Alone,* translated by Kristina M. Jorgeson (New York: Penguin Books, 1997), pp. 207-209. Copyright ©1997 by Wei Jingshen. Used by permission of Viking Penguin, a division of Penguin Group USA Inc.

40. Geremie R. Barmé, *In the Red: On Contemporary Chinese Culture* (New York: Columbia University Press, 1999), pp. 65-66. Reprinted by permission.

41. Wang Fuhua, "Si Wen" (Four Questions), *Renmin fibao manhua zengkan,* March 5, 1983, in Emily Honig and Gail Hershatter, *Personal Voices: Chinese Women in the 1980's* (Stanford: Stanford University Press, 1988), pp. 327-328; Ting Lan, "Nuren bushi yueliang" (Woman is not the moon), *Nuzi shije,* Vol. 6 (June 1985), in ibid., pp.328-329.

42. Geremie Barmé and John Minford, *Seeds of Fire* (New York: Farrar, Straus and Giroux, 1989), pp, 400-402; Andrew F. Jones, *Like a Knife: Ideology and Genre in Contemporary Chinese Pop Music,* Cornell East Asia Series (Ithaca, NY: East Asia Programs, Cornell University, 1992), pp. 138-39. Reprinted by permission.

43. Geremie Barmé and Linda Jaivin, eds., *New Ghosts, Old Dreams* (New York: Times Books, 1992), pp. 149-151, 156-157.

44. Xiao Bingchen and Shi Yunfeng, *Pastoral or Pitfall— A Report about the Problem of Unemployment in China,* in Suzanne Ogden, ed., *China's Search for Democracy* (Armonk, NY: M. E. Sharpe, 1992), pp. 67-68.

45. Han Minzu, ed., *Cries for Democracy* (Princeton, NJ: Princeton University Press, 1990), pp. 135-137. Copyright ©1990 by Princeton University Press, Reprinted by permission of Princeton University Press.

46. Lawrence R. Sullivan, ed., *China Since Tiananmen* (Armonk, NY: M. E. Sharpe, 1995), pp. 7-8.

47. Ibid., pp. 151-154.

48. Elisabeth Rosenthal, "China's Middle Class Savors its New Wealth." *The New York Times,* June 19, 1998, pp. 1, 8. Copyright ©1988 by The New York Times Co. Reprinted with permission.

49. Mobo C. F. Gao, *Gao Village: A Portrait of Rural Life in Modern China* (London: Hurst & Co., 1999), pp. 67-70.

50. Tony Gallagher, *In Their Own Words: Profiles of Today's Chinese Students* (San Francisco: China Books, 1998), pp. 157-160. Reprinted by permission.

51. Cheng Li, *Rediscovering China: Dynamics and Dilemmas of Reform* (Lanham, MD: Rowman and Littlefield, 1997), pp. 71-73. Reprinted by permission.

52. Matthew Forney, "Workers' Wasteland," *Time Asia,* June 17, 2002 http/www.time/com/time/asia/covers/1101020617/cover.html.

53. Dale Wen, *China Copes With Globalization: A mixed review* (San Francisco: The International Forum on Globalization, 2006), p. 7.

54. Cheng Li, *Rediscovering China, op. cit.,* pp. 128-129. Reprinted by permission.

55. Yi Cheng, "Various Materials on the Problem of the Privately Run Economy," *The Chinese Economy,* Vol. 31, No. 1, January-February 1998, pp. 70-94. Reprinted by permission.

56. He Qinglian, "China's Descent into a Quagmire, Part II." *The Chinese Economy,* Vol. 34, No. 2, March-April 2001, pp. 82-83.

57. Li Yan, "China Is Among Countries with Wide Income Gap," *People's Daily Online,* May 10, 2002.

58. James and Ann Tyson, *Chinese Awakenings* (Boulder, CO: Westview Press, 1995), p. 14; Bai Mu, " 'Foreign Winds' Invade China," *Chinese Sociology and Anthropology,* Vol. 31, No. 4, Summer 1999, pp. 58-67. Reprinted by permission.

59. Ma Liang, "A Tentative Analysis of the Reasons for School Dropouts among Rural Middle and Primary School Students," *Chinese Education and Development,* Vol. 30, No. 2, May-June 1997, pp. 53-58.

60. Mu Zi, "The Burden of Education," *Beijing Review,* March 8, 2001, pp. 14-15. Reprinted by permission.

61. Cai Yun, "Parents Responsible for the 'Little Emperors'," *China Daily,* February 24, 1994, p. 20.

62. Xia Hong and Liu Yi, "Parents vs. Children," *China Today,* June 1997, pp. 55-56.

63. Yunxiang Yan, "Rural Youth and Youth Culture in North China," *Culture, Medicine and Psychiatry,* Vol.23, 1999, pp. 78-80.

64. Peter Seybolt, *Throwing the Emperor from His Horse* (Boulder, CO: Westview Press, 1996), p. 96. Copyright ©1996 by Westview Press. Reprinted by permission of Westview Press, a member of Perseus Books, LLC.

65. Wu Xiaoping, "The Market Economy, Gender Equality, and Women's Development from the Viewpoint of Women's Employment." *Chinese Education and Society,* Vol. 33, No. 6, November-December 2000, pp. 44-54. Reprinted by permission.

66. Shen Shuisheng and Yao Yuqun, "On the Problems of Distribution of Social Income in China," *Chinese Economic Studies,* Vol. 29, No. 6, November-December 1996, p. 14.

67. Maurice Meisner, *The Deng Xiaoping Era* (New York: Hill and Wang, 1996), pp. 508-509. Reprinted by permission.

68. Yang Ji, "Help Provided for Psychological Stress." *Beijing Review,* December 11-17, 1995, p. 22. Reprinted by permission.

69. "Teenage Woes Aired," *Shanghai Star,* May 6, 1994.

70. "The Basic Character of Crime in Contemporary China," *Report of the Public Security Research Unit Number Five, 1989,* translated by Michael Dutton. In *The China Quarterly,* March 1997, p. 165. Reprinted by permission of Cambridge University Press.

71. Peter Seybolt, *Throwing the Emperor from His Horse,* op. cit., p. 127. Reprinted by permission.

72. He Qinglian, "China's Descent into a Quagmire, Part II." *The Chinese Economy,* Vol. 34, No. 2, March-April, 2001, pp. 43-46, 72.

73. Ding Mo, "The Menace of Environmental Pollution," *China Today,* Vol. XLVII, No. 8, August 1998, p. 11.

74. Caroline Blunden and Mark Elvin, *Cultural Atlas of China* (Abingdon, Eng.: Andromeda Oxford Ltd., 1998), pp. 44, 45.

75. Dai Qing, ed., *Yangtze! Yangtze!* (London: Earthscan, 1994), pp. 213-214, 216-220. Reprinted by permission.

76. D. Soled, ed. *China: A Nation in Transition* (Washington, D.C.: Congressional Quarterly, 1995), pp. 480-481; Ren Yanshi, "A Comparison of Human Rights in China With Those in the United States," *Beijing Review,* April 1-7, 1996, p. 10. Reprinted by permission.

77. Susan V. Lawrence, "The Sickness Trap," *Far Eastern Economic Review,* June 13, 2002. Reprinted by permission.

78. Li Ronggxia, "Seeking Medical Service: A Headache for Patients," *Beijing Review,* December 11, 2000, pp. 12-13. Reprinted by permission.

79. Bruce Shu, "Population Minister Defends Abortion Policy," *Agence France-Presse,* June 9, 1991 in Lawrence R. Sullivan, ed., *China Since Tiananmen* (Armonk, NY: M. E. Sharpe, 1995), p. 228.

80. Wu Wen, "China's Population Efforts," *Beijing Review,* November 1, 1999, p. 16. Reprinted by permission.

81. Meng Ren, "Confronting Three Populations of 80 Million," *United Front Monthly,* Vol. 8, Beijing, 1996. Excerpted in *Inside China Mainland,* January 1997, pp. 80-81.

82. Da Yu, "A Shortage of Girls," *Beijing Review,* July 8, 2004, p. 28. Reprinted by permission.

83. Peter Seybolt, *Throwing the Emperor from His Horse,* op. cit., pp. 113, 115. Reprinted by permission.

84. Mobo C. F. Gao, *Gao Village: A Portrait of Rural Life in Modern China* (London: Hurst & Co. 1999), pp. 228-230. Reprinted by permission.

85. Dun J. Li, ed., *Modern China: From Mandarin to Commisar* (New York: Charles Scribner and Sons, 1978), pp. 41-45. Copyright ©1978 by Dun J. Li. Reprinted with the permission of Scribner, an imprint of Simon & Schuster Adult Publishing Group.

86. Mobo C. F. Gao, *Gao Village,* op. cit., pp. 248-53. Reprinted by permission.

87. *Joint Communique* (Peking: Foreign Language Press, March 1972).

88. Fu Mengzi, "China's Development and Security Concept," *Beijing Review,* June 9, 2005, pp. 18-19; Reprinted by permission; Qian Qichen, "U.S. Strategy to be Blamed," *China Daily,* November 1, 2004, p. 6; and Chen Xulong, "Truth About Military Spending," *Beijing Review,* July 7, 2005, pp. 10-13. Reprinted by permission.

Index

In this index page numbers followed by *p* indicate a photo can be found in the text, and those followed by *f* indicate a figure.

A

Age of Equality, 66
air pollution, 287–288
Ai Wei, 235
Albright, Madeline, 345
al-Qaida, 345
Analects, 25
ancestor worship, 38*p*, 39–40, 317

B

Ban Zhao (Pan Chao), 41–44
barefoot doctors, 137–141, 138*p*, 303, 305
Bethune, Norman, 90–91, 132
Beveridge, Albert, 327–328
Book of Rites, 43, 63
bourgeoisie, 95–98, 143–153
Buddhism, 37–40, 316–317
Bush, George W., 343–345

C

capitalism
    CCP legitimization of, 223–231
    Deng on, 180–181, 203–206
    sickness of loving (*aizibing*), 200
    within socialism, 351
Carter, Jimmy, 338
Chang Siao-hung, 47–49
Chen Duxiu, 70–71
Cheng Xuebin, 227
Chen Huai, 219
Chen Li, 215–222
Chen Xulong, 346–350

Chen Zhongshen, 283
Chiang K'ai-shek, 11, 14*p*, 84, 88, 333
Chiang Monlin, 54–57
Ch'ien-lung Emperor, 325–326
children. *See* girls
China. *See also* Peoples' Republic of China
    changes, *1840-1949*, overview, 67–68
    chronology of events in, 353
    inventions influence on modern West, 4
    isolationist policy, 4, 323, 325–328
    per-capita income, 340
    wars waged against, 4, 298–299, 323
China's Descent into a Quagmire (He Qinglian), 226–227, 281–282
Chinese Communist Party. *See also* Deng Xiaoping era of reform; government; Mao Zedong era of reform
    beginnings, 70, 83
    cult of Mao repudiated by, 173–174
    ideological struggles, 76–78, 225–226
    legitimization of capitalism, 2001, 231
    power struggle after death of Lin Biao, 159
Chinese Communist Party, criticisms during Deng era
    Democracy Movement, 183–184
    economic growth in suppressing, 206
    liumang mentality, 185
    by social critics, 185–187
    on television, 191–193
    through music, 188–191
    through poetry and writing, 186–187

through student protest, 183–184,
195–201
tolerance for, 177, 179, 184, 198–201
Chinese Communist Party, present-era
corruption in, 351
private enterprise, political influence of,
225–226
protests and demonstrations, increases
in, 351
Chin-pao, story of, 7–10
Chou En-lai, 334
class distinctions. *See also* wealth gap
class harmony vs., CCP ideological
struggle, 76
Deng era, 179, 181
Mao Zedong on struggle against,
351–352
Nationalist government and, 95
the people's dictatorship responsibility to
eliminate, 95–98
in traditional China, 53–54
Cold War, 341, 343, 346
Communism. *See* Chinese Communist
Party
concubines, 47–49
Confucianism, 25, 27–30, 68–72, 95, 318
Confucian official, photo of a, 28*p*
Confucius, teachings of, 27, 29–30, 33–34,
54
consumerism, 207–213, 208*p*
corruption
CCP, present-era, 351
Cultural Revolution, effect on, 105–112
economic growth influence on, 279–286
in health care workers, 305–307
leakage system, 53–57, 55*p*, 105
link to crime, 281–286
reemergence, *1980s*, 279
the social underground and, 283–286
crime
bandit gangs, 280–281
corruption's link to, 281–286
Deng era, 281
economic growth influence on, 279–286
Maoist era, 281
modern youth and, 266, 273–277
reemergence, *1980s*, 279
the social underground and, 283–286

criticism of the government. *See also* self-
criticism
economic growth in suppressing, 206
the people's right to, 99–103, 177
by social critics, 185–187
through music and literature, 186–191
through student protest, 183–184,
195–203
through the media, 191–193
tolerance for, 179, 184, 198–201
as a weapon for change, 90–93,
100–103, 105–112
Cui Jian, music of, 188–191
Cui Tiankai, 350
Cultural Revolution. *See also* land reform;
Mao Zedong era of reform; Revolution of
1949
basis of, 143, 144–148
beginnings, 76, 143, 167
corruption within, 105–112
dates of, 167, 168–169
the official account, 167–171
Red Guards role in the, 143–153
youthful enthusiasm and disillusionment, 159–166
culture, Western influence on Chinese, 200,
233–240, 242–253*p*, 295, 329–332

D
Daoism, 37-40, 64
Democracy Movement, 183–184
Deng Xiaoping
on capitalism, 180, 203–206
on the Cultural Revolution, 180
on foreign investment, 204
ideology of, 76, 143
photo, 204*p*
on socialism, 179–181, 203–206
southern tour speeches, 203–206
Deng Xiaoping era of reform
inital plan for, 179–181
intensification (*1992-*), 203–206
introduction, 177
Maoist policies reversed during, 5, 160,
179, 215, 219–221, 305
the Tiananmen crisis, 195–201
results of
corruption, 197

economic, 206, 207–213, 208*p*,
  215–222, 305
  initial, 183–184
  to land reform, 179, 215, 219–221
  moral and psychological, 273
dictatorships
  Confucianism as, 95
  Nationalist government as, 95
  of the people, 95–98
Ding Zhanming, 307
Doctrine of Social Status, 33
Dou Wenmin, 306

E
economic growth, reform era
  foreign investment in, 180–181, 204
  GDP, 206
  industrial growth, 206
  international relations role in, 342,
    346–350
  military spending and, 346–350
  one-child policy resulting in, 312
  privatization, criticisms of, 223–231
  results of
    consumer boom, 207–213, 208*p*
    crime, 279–286
    environmental issues, 287–294
    income/wealth gap, 215, 223–224,
      226–230, 270, 273–277
    overview, 177
    profit-seeking and corruption, 258,
      279, 306–307
economic inequality, reform era. *See also*
  poverty; wealth gap
  effect on educational attainment,
    255–260
  effect on modern youth, 273–277
  socioeconomic safety net, 217
  urban joblessness, 219, 270
economy
  Maoist era, 126–129, 131, 135–136,
    169–170
  present-day China, 179-181, 203-
    206,223-232, 339–340
education
  Cultural Revolution era, 170
  dropout rates, causes of, 255–260
  of military personnel, 348

present-day rural China, 331
  psychological problems and, 274
  Westernization of, 238–239
England-China foreign relations, 4,
  325–327, 353
English language, popularity of, 241
environmental issues in present-day China,
  287–294, 288*f*, 289*f*
equality. *See also* economic inequality,
  reform era
  the *Book of Rites* on, 63
  Cultural Revolution attempt for,
    113–118, 170–171
  Deng era, 186–187
  Marx on, 155
  Mozi's writings on, 63–65
  New Culture Movement's support for,
    71–72
  Taiping Revolution in support of, 68–69
  U.S. Constitutional guarantee for,
    301–302
  for women, 113–118, 186–187,
    269–271
Evolution of Rites, 63

F
family, present-era. *See also* women; youth,
  modern
  filial piety and the, 265, 316–317, 318
  generational conflict, 263–267,
    276–277
  one-child policy, results of, 261,
    264–265, 309–313
  taking care tradition, 304
  youth in, 261–267
family, traditional China. *See also* women
  ancestor worship, 38*p*, 39–40
  Confucius on, 33–34
  the Cultural Revolution's effect on,
    149–153
  the family ethic, 31–35, 34*p*, 49–51, 89
  filial piety, 38*p*, 39–40, 256
  sinecurism and nepotism in, 34–35
  taking care tradition, 34–35, 105–112
feudalism, 92–93, 185
"The Fifth Modernization–Democracy"
  (Wei Jingsheng), 183–185
five guarantees, 234

five virtues, 29
"The Foolish Old Man Who Removed the Mountains" (Mao Zedong), 91–93, 92*p*
footbinding, 45–46, 46*p*
fortunetelling, 39
Four Cardinal Principles, 180
four modernizations, 184
"Four Questions" (anon), 186
Fu Mengzi, 339–342

G
Gang of Four, 151, 153, 159–160, 165, 166
gentlemen, Confucius on, 29, 53–54
George III, 325–326
Germany, foreign relations with China (1793), 328
girls. *See also* women; youth, modern
    enslavement of, 47–49
    infanticide of, 313
    kidnapping and selling of, 269, 313
government. *See also* Chinese Communist Party
    Confucian writings on, 29–30
    the leakage system, 53–57, 55*p*, 105
Grandmother Ning, 45–46
Grand Unity, the age of, 63–64
Great Britain-China relations, 4, 325–327, 353
Great Harmony, the age of, 63–64
Great Leap Forward, 126–129, 317
Great Proletarian Cultural Revolution. *See* Cultural Revolution
Gulf War, 344

H
Hai Huari, 235
Han Dongping, 170
health and health care
    barefoot doctors, 137–141, 138*p*, 303, 305
    environmental issues affecting, 295
    long working hours and, 308
    Maoist era, 137–141, 305
    medical insurance among the poor, 303–308
    mental health, 274, 276–277
    reform policies eliminating universal

access to, 303
    rising medical costs resulting in poverty, 303–308
    in Rural China, 303–308
    in urban areas, 307–308
He Changli, 284
He Qinglian, 226–227, 281–282
Hsiang T'ou, 30
Hsiao, William, 304
Hsieh Ping-ying, 49–51
Hua Guofeng, 159
Huang, Philip C. C., 169
Hu Angang, 219
human rights
    Constitutional freedoms guaranteed, 90, 97, 99
    Deng on, 184
    five guarantees of Mao, 234
    the right to subsistence, 297–300
    Tiananmen Square protestors, violence against, 198–201
    U.S. policies compared, 300–302
Hunan, peasant movement in, 77–78
Hu Yaobang, 195

I
imperialism, Mao on conquering, 92–93
"Impressions of a Veteran Cadre Touring Special Economic Zones" (anon), 232
income/wealth gap. *See* wealth gap
India, military spending by, 347
industry
    employment of women, 269–271
    environmental issues, 287–294, 288*f*, 289*f*
    Maoist era, 126–129, 131–136, 169–170
    population migration, rural to urban, 215, 219, 221–222
    reform era growth, 206
    urban joblessness, 219, 270–271
    worker exploitation/working conditions, 215–218, 224
"In Memory of Norman Bethune" (Mao Zedong), 90–91
intellectuals, persecution of, 146, 149–153
international relations, historically
    England, 4, 323

imperialist aggression, 298–299, 323
isolationist policy of China, 4, 323,
    325–328
Japan, 70
Soviet Union, 323
Versailles peace treaty and, 70
international relations, present-era. *See also*
    specific countries
    border disputes, 341
    economic development role in, 339–342
    panda bears gift, 334*p*
    world politics, involvement in, 339–342,
        346–350
Iraq-U.S. war with, 344–346
"The Iron Man of Daqing", 131–136, 132*p*
"It's Not That I Can't See" (Cui Jian), 189
"It's Terrible" or "It's Fine" (Mao Zedong),
    79–82

J
Japan-China relations, 70, 298–299, 347,
    349–350
Jiang Qing, 159–160, 168
Jiang Zemin, 5, 231, 284
Jixiang Theatre, 236

K
Kissinger, Henry, 334
Kong Quan, 347
Kosovo-U.S. war with, 343, 344

L
landlord system
    Nationalist government's support of, 95
    peasant life under the, 7–10, 11–13, 15,
        17–21, 79–82, 299
    people's dictatorship responsibility to
        eliminate, 95–98
land reform. *See also* Cultural Revolution
    collective farms, creation of, 121–126
    collective farms, effects of dismantling,
        215, 219–221, 305
    the Cultural Revolution and, 15, 83,
        121–126, 220
    Great Leap Forward and, 126–129
    overturning movement and, 11–13, 15,
        17–21
"The Land System of the Heavenly

Dynasty", 68–69
Laozi, 64–65
leakage system, 53–57, 55*p*, 105
"Lessons for Women" (Ban Zhao), 41–44
Lin Biao, 159, 160, 163
Linxian County: A Recollection of the Past,
    7–10, 11–13, 15, 17–21
Lin Yu-tang, 31–35
Li Peng, 198
Liu Fuchun, 239
Liu Jianchao, 350
Liu Shaoqi [Shao-chi], 127, 143
Liu Yuanli, 305
Liu Zi'an, 274
"Long Life to You, Chairman Mao", 157
the Long March, 83–88, 86*f*
Lu-ting Bridge, battle for the, 84–88, 86*f*
Lu Zhiquiang, 228

M
Maoism as religion, 155–158
Mao Zedong
    about, 75
    assassination attempt, 159, 163
    on class struggle, 351–352
    five guarantees, 234
    ideology of, 54, 76, 143
    Nixon meeting, 335–338, 336*p*
    the official position on, 167–168,
        173–174
    overthrow attempt, 159, 168
    photo/portraits of, 80*p*, 253*p*, 336*p*
    in praise of, 157–158
    repudiation by CCP, 173–174
    on revolutionary violence, 79–82
    on standing up, 4
    values found in writings of, 89
    writings of
        "The Foolish Old Man Who Removed
            the Mountains", 91–93, 92*p*
        "In Memory of Norman Bethune",
            90–91
        "The People's Democratic Dictatorship",
            95–98
        "Preserve the Style of Plain Living and
            Hard Struggle", 93
        "Report on an Investigation of the
            Peasant Movement in Hunan", 77–78

"Serve the People", 90
"Three Constantly Read Articles",
90–93, 94*p*
Mao Zedong era of reform. *See also*
Cultural Revolution; land reform
criticism used as weapon for change, 90,
93, 99–103, 105–112
Deng era policy reversals, 5, 160, 179,
215, 219–221, 305
dictatorship of the people, 95–98
disputes within, 143
five guarantees, 234
freedoms, necessity for restraints on, 99
freedoms guaranteed, 97, 99
ideology, 89–93
success, circumstances of early, 72,
75–76, 83, 88
on taking care tradition, 105–112
task of reconstruction, 75–76
marriage
the Cultural Revolution and changes in,
115–120
in traditional China, 41–44, 49–51,
113–117, 257
Marriage Law, 119–120
Marx, Karl, 155
Marxism, 76, 93, 98, 163, 165, 167, 168,
179, 180
mass criticism, responsibility of the worker
for, 99, 100–103, 105–112
May Fourth Movement, 70, 196–198
media
Cultural Revolution and growth of
unofficial, 171
rights of, Maoist era, 99, 105
Westernization of, 238, 241
Meisner, Maurice, 206
"Meng Hsiang-ying Stands Up", 113–118
mental health, present-day China, 274, 276
middle class, development of, 207–213
"A Migrant's Lament" (anon), 218
migrant workforce, 215, 219, 221–222
Mobo C.F. Gao, 169, 170–171, 209–211,
329–332
morality, the new, 273–277, 285
Mo Tsu (Mozi), 63–64
Mugabe, Robert, 179–181

N
Nationalist government, 75, 83, 95
New Culture Movement, 70–71, 239
"New May Fourth Manifesto" (Wu'er
Kaixi), 196–198
New Youth, 70–71
Nixon, Pat, 334
Nixon, Richard, 333, 334–337, 336*p*
"Nothing to My Name" (Cui Jian), 188
Nye, Joseph S., 345

O
Opium War, consequences of defeat to
China, 67–68, 298
Original Fortune Lee, 17–19
Outlaws of the Marsh, 65
overturning movement, 11–13, 15, 17–21,
25

P
panda bears, 334*p*
Pan Hsiao, 160–166
Pan Yue, 287
"The Paupers' Co-op", 121–126
peasant radicalism
in Hunan, 77–78
novels inspiring, 65–66
overturning movement, 11–13, 15,
17–21, 25, 79
violence associated with, 19–21, 20*f,*
79–82
peasants
1930s, daily life, 7–10, 8*p,* 11–13, 15,
17–21, 32*p*
female slavery, 47–49
the landlord system's treatment of, 7–10,
15, 79–82, 299
land reform benefit to, 11–13, 15,
17–21, 121–129
rich/middle/poor defined, 7
selling girl children due to poverty of,
269
Peng Peiyun, 310, 313
people's communes
collective farms, 121–126, 215,
219–221, 305
five guarantees, 234

"The People's Democratic Dictatorship" (Mao Zedong), 95–98
People's Liberation Army, 153, 159
Peoples' Republic of China
    established, 75, 299
    first three years, 300
Peoples' Republic of China, present-era. *See also* family, present-era; international relations
    global integration, 339–342
    military spending, 346–350
    National Defense Law, 348
    Westernization of, 200, 233–240, 242–253*p*, 295, 329–332
"A Piece of Red Cloth" (Cui Jian), 190–191
population growth
    environmental issues and, 287–294
    gender imbalance within, 312–313
    statistics, 309, 311–312
population migration, rural to urban, 215, 219, 221–222
poverty. *See also* economic inequality, reform era
    collective farms, effects of dismantling, 219–221
    education, influences on, 255–260
    health care costs and rising, 303–308
    selling girl children due to, 269
    statistics, 219, 229–230
    urban joblessness, 219, 270–271
    women in, 271
"Preserve the Style of Plain Living and Hard Struggle" (Mao Zedong), 93

Q
Qian Qichen, 343–346
Qin Zhen, 235

R
Rao Keqin, 305
recreation, changes in, 211–213, 237, 242–253*p*
The Red Detachment of Woman Soldiers (film), 330
Red Guards, 143–153, 159
Rediscovering China (Chen Li), 215–222
religion. *See also specific forms of*
    ancestor worship as, 38*p*, 39–40, 317

the Cultural Revolution and, 317
    Deng Xiaoping era, 315–316
    funeral ceremonies, 315–319
    Maoism as, 155–158
Report of China's State Council on human rights, 297–300
"Report on an Investigation of the Peasant Movement in Hunan" (Mao Zedong), 77–78
revolution, literature as inspiration for, 63–66
Revolution of *1911*, 81
Revolution of *1949*. *See also* Cultural Revolution
    events precipitating
        landlord system, 7–10, 15
        New Culture Movement, 71–72
        overturning movement, 11–13, 15, 17–21, 25
        peasant life, 7–10, 15
        Taiping Revolution, 68–69
River Elegy (television documentary), 191–193
Rogers, William, 334
Roosevelt, Theodore, 328
Rosenthal, Elisabeth, 207–213
Rumsfeld, Donald, 347
rural reform. *See* land reform

S
Selected Works of Mao Tse-Tung (Mao Tse-tung), 3
self-criticism. *See also* criticism of the government
    Green Pines Gardens illustration of, 100–103
    by Mao on steel smelting project, 127
    as a weapon for change, 90, 93
September 11, 2001 terrorist attacks, 338, 343
"Serve the People" (Mao Zedong), 90
Shan Dandan, 211–213
Shen, Miss, 307–308
slavery
    Chinese laborers, 298–299
    female, 47–49
socialist economy, 135–136, 179–181, 203–206

The Spirit of the Great Leap Forward, 128
Spring Festival, 221
standing up concept, 4, 113–118, 275
"A Sticky Problem" (Wang Meng), 105–112
"Stone Wall Village Turns Over", 11–13, 15, 17–21
student protests, influence of, 183–184, 195–203, 206, 338
Sugar-coated bullets, 93
Sun Baocun, 282

T
Taiping Revolution, 57, 63–68
Taiwan, 333, 337, 338, 349
taking care tradition, 105–112, 304
Taoism, 37–40, 64
terrorism, global, 338, 343–345
"Three Constantly Read Articles" of Mao Zedong, 90–93, 94*p*
Three Gorges Dam project, 289–294
Three Irons, 229
The Three Kingdoms, 65–66
Throwing the Emperor from His Horse (Seybolt), 46
Tiananmen Square demonstrations
 1919, 70
 1989, 195–202, 203, 206, 338
 influence on Sino-U.S. relations, 338
Treaty of Nanjing [Nanking], 67, 299
Treaty of Shimonoseki, 298–299
Tung Hua Lu (Annals of the Ching [Qing] Dynasty), 68
Tu Tu, 239

U
Unger, Jonathan, 158
United States
 foreign policy, international relations resulting from, 343–346
 human rights guarantees, 300–302
 Iraq, war with, 344–346
 military buildup, 343, 346–347
 national security policy, 343–345
 September 11, 2001 terrorist attacks, 338, 343–345
 Taiwan, interest in, 334, 337, 338
United States-China relations
 21st century, 338, 343–350

historically, 327–328
 normalization (*1970s-1990s*), 333–338
 September 11, 2001 attacks and, 338
 Tiananmen Square demonstration influence on, 338

V
the Vatican on Maoist doctrine, 156
Versailles Peace Conference, 69–70
Vietnam-U.S. war with, 344
villages
 crime and social control in, 266, 282–285
 foreign influence in, 329–332
 the new youth in, 265–267
 population migration, rural to urban, 215, 219, 221–222
 poverty in, 219
 villagers view of the world outside China, 329–332

W
Wang Chin-hsi, 131–136
Wang Dejun, 220, 280
Wang Dongjin, 219
Wang Fucheng, 46, 220, 280
Wang Meng, 105–112
Wang Yu-keng, 144–148
War Department, U.S., 88
wealth gap. *See also* economic inequality, reform era
 conflict resulting from, 351
 dismantling of communal farms and, 215–222
 influence on social immorality in youth, 273–277
 male-to-female, 270
 the private economy and the, 223–230
Wei Jingsheng, 183–185
Western influence on Chinese culture, 200, 233–240, 242–253*p*, 295, 329–332
Wilhelm II, 328
"Woman is not the Moon" (anon), 187
women. *See also* family; girls
 abortions and the one-child policy, 310–311
 economic inequality, 113–118, 186–187, 269–271
 education of, 257

"Meng Hsiang-ying Stands Up",
113–118
selling of, 269
status, traditional vs. present, 41–51,
42p, 113–120, 116p, 162f, 257,
269–271
suicide rates, 271
Westernization of, 238
worker exploitation/working conditions,
215–218, 224
workers, Maoist era
Constitutional freedoms guaranteed, 90,
99
criticism used as a weapon for change,
90–93, 99–103, 105–112
five guarantees for, 234
"The Iron Man of Daqing", 131–136,
132p
people's communes, 121–126
responsibilities in the people's democratic dictatorship, 95–99
rights guaranteed, 99
Wu'er Kaixi, 196–198

X
Xie Lihua, 271

Y
Yeh Fei, 143–148
youth, modern. *See also* family, present-era;
girls
characteristics of, 261–263
crime and, 266, 273–277
the disillusionment of, 159–166, 162f,
166f
dropout rates, causes of, 255–260
generational conflict, 263–267,
276–277
Japanese youth compared, 261–263
mental health of, 274, 276–277
the new morality of, 273–277
Yunxiang Yan, 264–267

Z
Zhai Shutao, 276
Zhang Minqiang, 274
Zhang Yanqiao, 282
Zhou Enlai, 96p, 183–184
Zhou Yongkang, 351